Narrating Migrations from Africa and the Middle East

Also available from Bloomsbury

The Discursive Construction of Identity and Space among Mobile People,
Roberta Piazza
Constructions of Migrant Integration in British Public Discourse, Sam Bennett
Intercultural Contact, Language Learning and Migration, Barbara Geraghty and
Jean Conacher

Narrating Migrations from Africa and the Middle East

A Spatio-Temporal Approach

Ruth Breeze, Sarali Gintsburg & Mike Baynham

BLOOMSBURY ACADEMIC
LONDON • NEW YORK • OXFORD • NEW DELHI • SYDNEY

BLOOMSBURY ACADEMIC
Bloomsbury Publishing Plc
50 Bedford Square, London, WC1B 3DP, UK
1385 Broadway, New York, NY 10018, USA
29 Earlsfort Terrace, Dublin 2, Ireland

BLOOMSBURY, BLOOMSBURY ACADEMIC and the Diana logo are trademarks of Bloomsbury Publishing Plc

First published in Great Britain 2022
This Paperback edition published 2024

Copyright © Ruth Breeze, Sarali Gintsburg & Mike Baynham, 2022

Ruth Breeze, Sarali Gintsburg & Mike Baynham have asserted their right under the Copyright, Designs and Patents Act, 1988, to be identified as Authors of this work.

Cover image © Getty Images

All rights reserved. No part of this publication may be reproduced or transmitted in any form or by any means, electronic or mechanical, including photocopying, recording, or any information storage or retrieval system, without prior permission in writing from the publishers.

Bloomsbury Publishing Plc does not have any control over, or responsibility for, any third-party websites referred to or in this book. All internet addresses given in this book were correct at the time of going to press. The author and publisher regret any inconvenience caused if addresses have changed or sites have ceased to exist, but can accept no responsibility for any such changes.

A catalogue record for this book is available from the British Library.

A catalog record for this book is available from the Library of Congress.

ISBN:	HB:	978-1-3502-7454-9
	PB:	978-1-3502-8918-5
	ePDF:	978-1-3502-7455-6
	eBook:	978-1-3502-7456-3

Typeset by Integra Software Services Pvt. Ltd.

To find out more about our authors and books visit www.bloomsbury.com and sign up for our newsletters.

Contents

List of Figures   vii
List of Tables   viii

Introduction   Narrating Space and Time in Migration   *Ruth Breeze, Sarali Gintsburg and Mike Baynham*   1

1. Settling Out of Place: Narratives of Housing and Strategies of Ageing by a Ghanaian Migrant in the United States   *Cati Coe*   15
2. 'We will be able to get there – what? – a life!' The Congolese in Kampala Narrating Migration through Time and Space   *Ruslan Zaripov*   29
3. Exile, Time and Gender: Time Negation and Temporal Projection among Refugees from the Horn of Africa   *Fabienne Le Houérou*   51
4. *Und wir sind weggelaufen*: Borders and Walls in Narratives of Forced Displacement– A Study with Middle Eastern Refugees' Visual Narratives in the German as a Second Language (DaZ) Classroom   *Silvia Melo-Pfeifer*   67
5. Children's Narratives about Their Journey from the Middle East to Hungary   *Ildikó Schmidt*   87
6. Families on the Move: Spacetimes in Narratives of Language Socialization within Transnational Multilingual Moroccan Families in Spain   *Adil Moustaoui Srhir*   103
7. Circumscribed Transnational Spaces: Moroccan Immigrant Women in Rural Spain   *Sarali Gintsburg and Ruth Breeze*   121
8. The Route from West Africa to Europe, the Precariousness of Life in Marie NDiaye's *Three Strong Women*   *Odile Heynders*   143
9. Tar or Honey? Space and Time of Moroccan Migration in a Video Sketch Comedy *'al-Kāmīra lakum'*   *Mike Baynham and Sarali Gintsburg*   157
10. Once a Dancer, Always a Dancer: The Story of Ahmad Joudeh   *Jan Jaap de Ruiter*   175

11 Digital Narratives of Syrian Political Dissidence in the Diaspora: Chronotopes of the Syrian Revolution and Transnational Grassroots Activism   *Francesco L. Sinatora*   191

Contributors' Notes   213
Index   216

Figures

2.1	A Ugandan shilling note, bearing inscriptions in English and Swahili	33
2.2	Mahagi – Paidha route used by the majority of Congolese refugees to escape from the DRC to Uganda	37
2.3	Marie uses her lips to show the direction	44
2.4	Marie explains when she arrived in Uganda	45
2.5	Zaynabu shows with her left hand across her body to the right that she returned to the native tribe of her mother	45
3.1	Time negation: street tea sellers. Wadi Halfa, Sudan, 2006. Photo credit: Fabienne Le Houérou	54
3.2	Time and self-consciousness: Afro Beauty Salon, Cairo, 2004. Photo credit: Fabienne Le Houérou	59
3.3	Arbaʿa wa Nuss, a neighbourhood in Cairo which can be considered as a model of rhizome, a horizontal organization of time and space from the documentary film *Quatre et demi* (2012). Photo credit: Fabienne Le Houérou	60
4.1	A wall separating sisters (S6)	74
4.2	The border between Iraq and Turkey (S7)	75
4.3	A protection wall (S1)	76
4.4	A couple in love separated by a wall (S10)	78
4.5	The school diploma as a protection (*Schutz*) (S3)	82
7.1	Skylines of Oujda (left) and Tudela (right)	127
7.2	Old town walls in Tetouan (left) and Granada (right)	128
7.3	An overview of *salon* in two Moroccan homes in the Ribera	129
10.1	Inscription on the shrine of Sidi Mahrez	186
11.1	Layla's post, 21 September 2019. Photo author unknown	200
11.2	Samer's post, 10 April 2019	201
11.3	Samer's post, 18 October 2019	202
11.4	Mural of George Floyd in Idlib, photo by Omar Haj Kadour/AFP	204
11.5	Post on George Floyd's murals in Idlib and Ramallah	204
11.6	Khalid, 11 April 2021. Protest at al-Aqsa	205
11.7	Khalid, 11 May 2021. Homsi from Jerusalem	206
11.8	Layla, 18 May 2021, post urging use of adoptive languages	207
11.9	Layla, 20 May 2021, post in French	207

Tables

2.1	Locatives in Swahili	35
2.2	System of tenses in Swahili	35
2.3	Information on the interviewees	36
4.1	Participants' data	71
4.2	A data set constituted by visual narrative and its verbal explanation (S5)	72
7.1	Moroccan women who participated in the study	125

Every effort has been made to trace copyright holders and to obtain their permission for the use of the copyright material. However, if any have been inadvertently overlooked, the publishers will be pleased, if notified of any omissions, to make the necessary arrangement at the first opportunity.

Introduction

Narrating Space and Time in Migration

Ruth Breeze, Sarali Gintsburg and Mike Baynham

Migration is one of the defining issues of our time. The number of international migrants worldwide has grown enormously over the last half century, motivated by a series of extremely powerful pull and push factors at work on a global level. The scale of this phenomenon is such that today, on a global level, one in every thirty people lives in a country where he/she was not born, with the current number of migrants estimated at 270 million. Substantial numbers of these migrants originated in the Middle East and North Africa region, and also in sub-Saharan Africa, and were motivated, despite danger and hardship, by the promise of a better life elsewhere. Many of them have crossed the Mediterranean or negotiated complex land routes to Turkey and onwards to Europe, while others have remained in countries near their own, hoping to go back or move onwards when their situation improves. In many cases, their migration experiences have been complex, hazardous, sometimes fatal, and even after many years, migrants often have difficulties not only in the practical process of adaptation to their new environment, but in their own inner understandings of who and where they are, and how the different 'places' and 'times' of their life intersect.

The phenomenon of migration has, of course, attracted a huge amount of research interest from sociology, human geography, demography, economics, sociolinguistics, education and many other disciplines. However, many of these approaches address migration from a rather distant, theoretical perspective. Although such research is important to understand the bigger picture of what is happening, it sometimes misses the human face of migration, failing to offer insights into the real experiences of being a migrant that can affect people's lives on the profoundest level. In this volume, our aim is to engage with the voices of the migrants themselves, exploring narratives of many different kinds produced by very varied groups of Middle Eastern and African migrants or refugees from a range of backgrounds. To home in on the experience of migration, we focus specifically on two key themes in these accounts, namely time and space, on the grounds that these are essential to understand the way people experience migration and confer shape and meaning on that experience. Time, though a measurable phenomenon, is also socially constructed: it is experienced differently in different calendars, we know that a different importance is given to time in general in different cultures (Africa, Europe), and time has a different meaning in rural and urban societies. Cultural, often religious factors influence the calendar and timetable, while social organization (work, play, gender) determines how people organize their day. Space, too, is defined socially (who goes where, who inhabits what), both on a macro-political level (countries and borders) and on the micro-level of everyday life (public and private spaces). In what follows, we will set out some basic notions concerning time and space in migration narratives, and explain how these two seemingly different concepts are interlinked in the migration experience. We will then bring out some of the key issues that emerge in the course of the book, showing how the chapters shed light on the same issues in different ways. Finally, we will suggest some ways in which this volume opens doors for future research.

Time and space in narrative

We start from the broad view that narrative is a mode of communication that occurs in a large number of circumstances and pervades different genres (De Fina and Georgakopoulou 2012). In Bruner's words, the narrative mode is a mode of thought, contrasting with the 'logico-scientific mode', which presents events from the point of view of a character and operates through stories that 'create a reality of their own' (Bruner 1986: 43). As such, the narrative mode permeates many other phenomena (including conversations or interviews) and can operate through different symbolic systems (the spoken word, texts, drawings, social media posts). It is scarcely necessary here to say that narrative, broadly understood, can be studied in a vast number of ways. Competing approaches from the humanities and social sciences range from more philosophical approaches, through others that are grounded in literary studies or take a sociolinguistic or interactional perspective, to studies explicitly designed to elicit information (about educational or medical processes) that can be used to design improved professional practices. Our aim in this volume is not to develop new narrative theory, or to obtain data that can be immediately applied to social intervention, but rather to open a number of issues that have surfaced in previous studies of migrants' narratives, but which have not been pursued in depth. These issues are related to the overarching questions of time and space.

The consideration of time in narrative has long been a subject of discussion. For Ricoeur (1984), for example, narrative is linked to philosophical reflections on the role of time and memory in human life: narrative imposes order, constructing rather than reflecting experience and memory. This concept reflects the long-standing Western tradition grounded on Aristotle and Plato, in which a logical, chronological structure forms the cornerstone of our understanding of time. In literary studies, another of the most influential approaches is that based on Bakhtin (1981), who developed his theoretical approach based on European and Russian literature (particularly, the tradition of the novel) with its clear (for us) cultural context and consistent plot development. It is often assumed that oral and written narratives should somehow resemble the literary canons studied by Bakhtin. These reflections have given rise to a large number of studies of different kinds and have influenced sociolinguistic and discourse-based analyses of narrative in contexts similar to ours, but although they are often stimulating and may be perceptive, it is clear that their grounding in Western philosophy may introduce a bias at the very outset that could blind us to other ways of seeing narrative.

From a sociolinguistic and discourse analytic perspective, linguistic studies of narrative were initiated by Labov's classic study of fight narratives (Labov and Waletzky 1967, 1972), out of which Labov proposed a generic structure for oral narrative that has been widely accepted:

- Abstract
- Orientation
- Complicating action
- Evaluation
- Result
- Coda

The orientation in this structure is the time/space location of the complicating action, which is understood as a sequence of events unfolding in time, with temporal/causal relations implied: X does this and Y responds with that. It has been argued more recently that this approach privileges time over space and enshrines what could be called a 'backdrop' version of time-space, seen as the setting for the action, rather in the way that the Aristotelian unities of time and space were interpreted in the poetics of the European Renaissance by scholars such as Castelvetro (Baynham 2003). Labov's fight narratives, the basis for his influential narrative theory, observe rather closely the three unities of time, place and action. Migration narratives with their central focus on displacement in space/time frequently disrupt these unities in ways that might have been predicted from literary theory, such as Bakhtin's (1981) work on the novel.

Indeed it is through the work of Bakhtin (1981) that approaches to the space/time dynamics of migration narrative have developed more recently, through his concept of the chronotope.

> We will give the name chronotope (literally, 'time space') to the intrinsic connectedness of temporal and spatial relationships.
> (Bakhtin 1981: 84)

Bakhtin focused entirely on literary texts, but left open the possibility that the chronotope could be applied to analysis of the social world, an approach developed by Agha (2007) and others such as Blommaert and De Fina (2017), Divita (2019), Koven (2019) and Perrino (2015). As well as the emphasis on time/space, Agha emphasizes a third dimension crucial to the Bakhtinian chronotope, that of personhood (Blommaert and De Fina 2017 similarly emphasize identity). So we can begin to see the space/time of narrative not as a simple backdrop to the action, nor just as the temporalization/spatialization of narrative action, but more in terms of the affordances that enable certain kinds of action to become possible for the narrated/narrating subject, certain forms of what Bakhtin has called 'ideological becoming':

> Our ideological development is just such an intense struggle within us for hegemony among various available verbal and ideological points of view, approaches, directions, values.
>
> (Bakhtin 1981: 346)

It is not hard to see migration processes as an intense ongoing struggle between different points of view (to go? to stay?), so that mobility itself becomes a kind of transformative identity work.

It has been pointed out that work on migration narratives has frequently privileged the male migrant, what Baynham (2005) describes as the heroic myth of the trailblazing male migrant, and underplayed the experience of women (cf. Relano-Pastor and De Fina 2005, or Gintsburg and Breeze, this volume) or indeed children migrating (see chapters by Melo-Pfeifer and Schmidt, this volume). If the notion of the migrating subject has expanded in more recent work on migration narratives, so indeed has the sense of who the protagonist is in the migration story. Juffermans (2018) has brought to the attention of researchers on migration narratives the point that the back story of migration, all that leads up to the decision to migrate, is a vital element in the migration itself. This can include those whose desire to migrate is frustrated and those who stay behind. These 'non-migrants' will themselves become protagonists in the migration story in the chapter by Baynham and Gintsburg (this volume).

It would be logical to assume that literary canons in other, non-European, cultures may also influence the temporal/spatial organization of narratives produced by those who belong to these cultures, somehow unpicking or contradicting the temporal/causal connections of the dominant in European narrative. So what do we know about them? Given the context of this volume, namely migration from the Arabic world and from Africa, it would appear to be important to look at the characteristic features of time in the traditions associated with these cultures.

In Arabic literature there is a long tradition of narrative literary creation in both written and oral form. Some researchers (Hamad and Kabha 2020) suggest that one of the specific characteristics of contemporary Arabic literature is fragmentation of its parts, where, unlike in the Russian and European novel of the nineteenth–twentieth centuries with their temporal/causal logic, the sequence of events often does not follow a strict causal logic and thus appears to Occidental theorists as confusing. This, they argue, is due to the fact that the contemporary Arabic novel was influenced not only by the European school of writing but also by the canons of the *maqama*, a medieval chapter genre, in which separate chapters did not necessarily connect to each other (Dolinina 1984, Pérès 1944) other than through the principle of randomness or chance. One of the main protagonists of the *maqama* was the witty vagabond, and this in turn influenced the European genre of the picaresque, but also left a deep legacy on both written and oral literature in the Arabic sphere.

Like Western understandings, the Arab or, in a broader sense, Islamic understanding of time is also based on Greek philosophy. However, Islamic philosophical thought formed under the influence not only of Aristotle, but also of Plotinus and Democritus.

Therefore, there are important differences to consider: in Islam, every moment of human life is determined by God and written down in the book, so that our life consists of a set of predetermined events that we understand are supposed to take place at a certain time (and at a certain place). The feeling that everything is predetermined has had its impact on, for instance, the Arabic language, where Arab grammarians did not (and still do not) differentiate between past and present verbal forms, but rather between complete and incomplete ones (Böwering 1997), thus privileging aspect over tense. The infinity of the Universe created by God, together with the predetermination of life events, seems to diminish the role of time in lives of Muslims and strongly colours their perceptions of the passing of time.

African narrative, on the other hand, tends to be more didactic, more epic, more linked to the rich oral traditions and mythology of the African peoples. Just as is the case with the African novel, the African oral narrative is suffused with local beliefs and oral traditions. The character's happiness depends on the idea of social acceptance, becoming a member of a socially accepted group, rather than on finding a way to oneself (as is often the case in Western narrative). As Sullivan puts it (2006), in the African novel, the aim of the protagonist's journey is often to enter the heart of the community. The protagonist is running away from the colonial cultural clash, from being nowhere, to having a community and an identity: 'the African hero's question for identity is the quest for her/his society identity' (Sullivan 2006: 184).

Accounts of traditional African cultures suggest that they tend to be focused on the past and present rather than on future, so that time is neither cyclic, nor linear. In African languages, mirroring the development of various European language families (Dahl 2008), the future appears to be less firmly conceptualized than the past and present, and some authors have speculated that this reflects a kind of reverse teleology: the final purpose lies in the past rather than in future (Booth 1975). According to the Kenyan-born philosopher John Mbiti (1931–2019), time moves not forward but backward: Mbiti argued that African time is not abstract, it is tied to events rather than to abstract units (Mbiti 1971). Following this logic, the future is unreal because it contains no events and so it cannot be measured. As a result, a traditional African speaks of the future as completion of events that have already started and need to be completed, so that it is directly related to the past, and to move towards the future or to move through time in general always means to move through the past (Booth 1975: 86). Past then is the only variety of time that matters: what is completed is sacred, tradition and myth come out of the sacred, and Africans rely upon them to understand their present and, if that is possible at all, predict their future. In this vein, Mbiti (1990), seeking to define the concept of time in the Bantu-speaking world, introduced two major terms: (1) *zamani* – past behind past in the Bantu languages; and (2) *sasa* – or something that happens now, or related to current life and events. With colonization, however, Africans became acquainted with the concept of future, so that *zamani*, the sacred past, is being replaced by the future, and only *sasa* remains.[1]

Compared with time, the role of space in narrative has generally received less attention, perhaps because its role is perceived as less essential to the plot (at least in Western tradition where stories are understood as temporally anchored, with a beginning, a middle and an end), or because it appears to be more concrete (and therefore less mysterious). Yet every story can also be seen as a journey (de Certeau 1988: 115). We know very well that our understanding of space is socially constructed, and that space (in general) and spaces (in particular) have different meanings in different cultures and societies. In fact, these aspects are clearly bound up with those discussed above, since location and progression in space are often used as metaphors to understand phenomena related to time.

Space is an essential theme in these narratives, because migration across space disrupts people's personal geography and spatial orientation. Mobility is the story. Transitions from rural to urban environments affect people's understanding of space, as does the sense of safety/danger they may encounter on their journey. Migrants' lives may be conducted in two or more places (e.g. homeland and land of residence) concurrently, or may undergo regular consecutive shifts from one 'existence' to another, or what Ennaji terms as 'two paradoxical social lives', such as when a poor cleaner in Italy transforms into a socially well-positioned citizen in Morocco (Ennaji 2014: 85–6). This kind of 'bilocation' has been accentuated through the advent of social media, which enable people to maintain lives in 'other' places as never before. Importantly, space is also shaped by social constraints of different kinds, and in particular, space may be gendered, particularly in cultures with strong gender differences.

To understand the stories in our volume, we again need to begin from the insight that Arabic and African understandings of space (e.g. in the culture) may be quite different from the current Western one. In the Arabo-Islamic tradition, space and time are seen as a complex and inseparable construct – this is reflected, for instance, on the level of Arabic grammar, where Arab grammarians distinguish a separate subclass of nouns – *ismu-l-makān wa-z-zamān*, or 'noun of time and place'. This category includes precisely nouns that are meant to indicate time and place, where an act, semantically linked to the meaning of the stem, is used to construct it; all nouns of time and place are constructed following the same pattern. In addition, space appears to have more importance than time – already in the Qur'an, the rhetoric is based on contrasting places/spaces and not times (Neuwirth 2006). One should not forget either that in the Arabo-Islamic tradition the organization of space is also different from the Christian one – the world, in both a religious and a secular sense, is oriented towards the Kaaba, the direction to which, called *qibla,* is regularly calculated by practising Muslims to perform their prayers. In its turn, African geography is very different when considered in an autochthonous, tribal perspective from when it is seen on the official (post-)colonial map. But the differences in the conceptualization of space go far deeper than this. Just by way of example, in the Bantu languages, Alexis Kagame (1912–81), a philosopher from Rwanda, defined three kinds of place: physical locality, localization and external space (Kagame 1976). Based on the specific linguistic characteristics of the Bantu languages, Kagame introduced four essences that satisfactorily describe everything that exists in the Universe. Interestingly, he suggested that one of these essences, called *hantu* – place, represents a location of an object in both space and time, that is, the boundaries of time and space coincide.

One major point that emerges from the above discussion is that it is increasingly hard in this context to keep time and space in separate mental categories. In the Arab world, both time and space are predetermined, while in African cultures, the two categories seem to merge on various levels. Previous approaches to this fusion of space and time include sociological approaches (from Durkheim ([1912] 2003) onwards), and literary approaches like the chronotope (Bakhtin 1981) or, as Epstein ([2003] 2007) has more recently argued, the topochrone, or the timescape (Adam 2000), which opens up a way of operationalizing the interrelatedness of space and time in personal experience. In fact, the evidence from an in-depth consideration of the narratives in this volume suggests that – at least in migration contexts, where the 'journey' is inevitably the main theme – space takes precedence over time. In contrast to Bakhtin's analysis, which is firmly grounded in literary evidence through which time provides the logic that underpins the plot, in these migration narratives the 'chronotope' somehow re-emerges as a 'topochrone', so that space (journeys, movements, border crossings, being 'out of place') comes into the foreground. As Epstein ([2003] 2007) suggested, in a very different cultural context, when, for whatever reason, cultures are not forward-driven and future-oriented, time ceases to have the same importance: space, following the Archimedes principle, will 're-place' it as our main means of self-orientation. Here, as we have seen, time may be pre-defined (as in Islam) or past-oriented (as in African cultures), and so its relationship to space is subtly reorganized so that the psycho-physical reality of the 'journey' will feature in most narratives more prominently than the passing of time.

Themes and chapters

In this book, the chapters approach this question of time and space in migrant narratives from a variety of perspectives. Each chapter looks at migration out of Africa and the Arab world, but the circumstances of migration are very different in each case: an elderly lady reflecting on her life transiting between Ghana and the United States and her quest to gain a foothold by owning real estate (Coe); economic migrants living on the margins in rural Spain (Breeze and Gintsburg); refugees fleeing the conflict zones in Ethiopia and the Sudan (Le Houérou); people escaping from the war in Congo to subsist in poverty in nearby Uganda (Zaripov); a professional ballet dancer from Syria trying to build a new life in the Netherlands (de Ruiter); Moroccan families in Europe trying to strengthen their children's ties to their homeland (Moustaoui); child refugees escaping from Syria and Afghanistan to build new lives in Germany and Hungary (Melo-Pfeifer, Schmidt); an African woman sent on a perilous migration trail by her in-laws (Heynders); satirical Moroccan accounts of migration (Baynham and Gintsburg); and political activists narrating the Syrian diaspora by evoking the chronotope of the Arab Spring (Sinatora).

In each case, the migrants' circumstances are found to condition the way they experience space and time in multiple ways. In what follows, we will address some of the main themes that emerge, providing a brief sketch of the findings where relevant. Many themes surface across several of the chapters, so in this overview we will endeavour to relate them to each other in order to prompt some fruitful comparisons, without excluding the possibility that other comparisons might be equally stimulating.

Borders and border crossings have been a leitmotif in the bibliography on migration (De Fina 2003), and the stories in this book are no exception. Several of the chapters centre on frontiers, walls and crossings, with reflections on the issues of safety/danger and freedom/confinement (Melo-Pfeifer, Zaripov, Gintsburg and Breeze, Heynders). On the basis of refugee children's drawings, Melo-Pfeifer uncovers how these young migrants perceive walls as protections or threats, depending on the narrative temporality in which they are placed. Borders, on the other hand, are almost always negatively connoted, associated with hazardous crossings. These border crossings are often relived as a decisive moment of transition and perhaps also transformation (Gintsburg 2019). Reflecting their inner perceptions, these children distinguish sharply between safety 'here' and danger 'there', with walls as sheltering structures that offer physical and emotional protection. However, the older children in her study also perceive that barriers do not vanish once one has crossed national borders, but that less visible mechanisms of exclusion exist that also keep young people from entering the chosen sphere of safety. The study of Congolese migrants by Zaripov uses linguistic and multimodal evidence to bring out the way that traumatic border crossings are still very present to the migrants who experience them. Not only do these narrators shift into present tenses to tell the hardest moments of their tales, but they also tend to put themselves in the narrative 'place', emphasizing the 'here and now' of the story for them. Such tense shifts are a characteristic involvement strategy in oral narrative (cf. Wolfson 1982). On the other hand, migrants' journeys are sometimes so painful to remember that language itself breaks down during the telling: Schmidt's child refugees appear to lose their grip on (their newly acquired) Hungarian at certain moments in the narrative, a phenomenon which reminds us of the powerful relationship between language and affect.

In a rather different approach to frontiers and barriers, the evidence from Moroccan women living in Spanish villages discussed by Gintsburg and Breeze shows how gendered barriers are perceived as generating safety, but also paradoxically lead to a form of isolation. For the narrators in this chapter, traditional dress also creates a specific dilemma for Muslim women, since the hijab is felt both to preserve integrity and to set up barriers dividing them from their neighbours (see also Breeze 2013, 2014 and Hassan 2020). Finally, Heynders devotes attention to the ultimate tragedy, namely death on the border, in her exploration of Khady Demba in Marie NDiaye's novel *Three Strong Women*. Her chapter argues that literature is vital to understand migration because it can take us 'right up to the border', that is, into realms beyond the reach of real-life accounts, in order to push our imagination to a deeper understanding of migrants' experiences through a form of 'individual narrative enfranchisement'.

Themes of 'belonging' and 'not belonging' in space and time are also frequent in migrant stories (De Fina and Georgakopoulou 2012). Here we read of situations whereby migrants belong nowhere (Coe), or where they achieve 'belonging' by creating their own space (Moustaoui, de Ruiter, Breeze and Gintsburg). Thus Coe's Ghanaian lady makes multiple attempts at achieving belonging by acquiring a home in both the United States and Africa, all of which are doomed to failure. As in African novels, where the return to community is the ultimate goal, this story is reliant upon the teller's cultural context. The Ghanaian lady travels across the Atlantic in search of acceptance, she is not looking for her new self, she is looking to become a true member of the community, first in the United States, then in Ghana and then back in the United States again. Her ultimate solution seems to be to accept the transient nature of all human aspirations and agree to 'settle out of place'. On a somewhat more optimistic note, in his study of language socialization among the Moroccan diaspora, Moustaoui investigates family temporalities embedded in different scale levels, which generate new spaces that are both transnational and delocalized, pointing to significant changes occurring in the context of globalization, in which society is reformulated as multi-located social fields (Levitt and Schiller 2004) and in which delocalized spaces connect various scale levels (Blommaert 2007; Dong and Blommaert 2011). The Moroccan families in Spain are conscious of themselves as different, and anxious to maintain their distinctiveness. Moustaoui concludes that nation states are increasingly limited in their capacity to control linguistic and identity diversity on a micro-scale level, in an overwhelming context of globalization, transnationalism and the mobility of resources. In a very different scenario, De Ruiter focuses on one migrant, a Syrian dancer who has fled the conflict zone and finds security, identity and fulfilment in the practice of his art in the Netherlands. This chapter also offers some hope, showing how people can transcend disruption to build new spaces for belonging, trusting in the universal function of creative art.

Another theme that is particularly present in the chapters dealing with trauma is that of time negation or timelessness. Although we have to be wary of reading too much into the details of these migrants' narratives, since these could have been influenced by multiple factors including the setting, the interlocutors or the mode (spoken, written, drawing, video), we can point to some interesting features that could reflect disruption or blurring of temporal continuity. Zaripov finds that for the Congolese migrants in Uganda the future does not exist: their past, which they have not overcome yet, intertwines with their present. The women interviewed by Gintsburg and Breeze seem to inhabit a timeless present, and their rare attempts at imagining the future are vague in the extreme. Time seems to become less significant in these migrants' lives – we see that their narratives contain numerous references to spatial aspects of their lives, while time is outlined only vaguely (although it is, of course, risky to equate how people express time to how they actually experience it). For Sinatora, on the other hand, it is clear that the Syrian activists not only inhabit the chronotope of the Arab Spring, but are actively engaged in trying to evoke, relive and reactivate it for political reasons. In a very real sense, for them, time is the crucial factor governing their experience and aspirations. For them, the future is the past: they fully intend to bring back the 'glorious past' of the Arab Spring and relive the experience of protest and reform. On the other hand, for many of Le Houérou's Ethiopian and Sudanese migrants, the future is the most shadowy of concepts, while the past is well known. We might again suggest that these ideas could be related to the account of African time concepts by Mbiti (1971, 1990) (see above), whereby the past is indeed a point of return, while the future lacks any real entity. However, as has been observed elsewhere (Baynham and De Fina 2016), conventional use of historic present as a storytelling practice, or the tendency to adopt a 'generic' voice when speaking 'in the name of the community', may also influence the tense systems used in the narration.

Literature and literary motifs from different traditions also come into several of these chapters to shed light on the migration phenomenon (Baynham and Gintsburg, Heynders, this volume). In Middle Eastern literature, the story is built based on different literary canons that might be influenced by oral narratives in which space and time take on particular roles.[2] Baynham and Gintsburg analyse the online performance of a Moroccan comedian, whose narrative/sketches are organized in the best traditions of the oral performative genre known as *halqa*, in which different times and spaces are juxtaposed to create ironic effects. When *halqa* goes digital, they argue, space becomes superior over time, so that, again, the notion of topochrone can be useful to describe the spatio-temporal aspect of online performance. Heynders uses a novel written by an African author in the Western tradition to get closer to understanding the tragedy of migration, using the conventions of the novel to take us into a time and space that is not normally accessible to researchers. From a different perspective, the chapter by de Ruiter explores the potential of creative arts as a way of overcoming displacement by the appropriation of a cultural space that transcends borders, in this case, through dance. Literary and oral performance genres take us back to Bakhtin's construal of the topos and chronos in the novel, but it should be noted that quite a few features of the various oral narratives of migration gathered in the course of the sociolinguistic and ethnographic research reported here also reflect aspects of literary and oral performance genres.

As the different chapters in this volume show, the chronotope/topochrone of migration somehow encompasses and is expressed by a wide range of narrative genres, the 'strangeness' of which starts to make sense when the different ways of construing space/time, identity and agency discussed above are considered. It is not that these stories are incoherent and illogical but they operate on different logics. There are occasions when this observation is crucial. Katrijn Maryns (2005, 2006), in her research on the role of narrative in asylum hearings, talks of the dangerous potential for stories to be misinterpreted and disallowed according to institutional norms of factuality, when such logics are ignored. Indeed it is worth quoting what she says about space and time in this context:

> Maybe one of the most articulate expressions of the gap between institutional standards and speaker production lies in the structuring of the narrative in terms of time and space. Whereas the procedural report requires exact time reference and a chronological ordering of the events, temporality and time are very complicated concepts for refugees. Displacement leads to confusion about time. Detention in isolated cells, weeks or even months of hiding in the bush or days of hiding on a ship, blur any perception of time. Reference to places and events, on the other hand, serve as much more useful orientation tools for the asylum seeker ... Asylum seekers' stories are organized around place.
>
> (Maryns 2005: 185)

The research by Maryns reminds us that how a story is received can be a matter of life and death and that a misunderstanding of the logics by which it is organized (i.e. assuming because it seems confused it is unreliable) can have dire consequences.

Regarding the central question raised here of the topochrone/chronotope, several of the chapters develop considerations of concurrent and parallel spaces/times in migrants' lives (Gintsburg and Breeze, Zaripov, Moustaoui), a perception which is also linked to the non-arboreal, non-linear organization of subjective space-time experiences (rhizome) (Le Houérou). Shifting of tenses is frequent in the narratives of the Moroccan women in Gintsburg and Breeze, who seem to inhabit their (distant) Moroccan villages at the same time as they often fail to venture out into their (close) Spanish surroundings. Although it might at first seem that these tenses are being 'mixed' in a loose or unsystematic way, we think it is more appropriate to interpret these phenomena in terms of the agency of the speaker and the deployment of different logics of communication, rather than communication that is somehow a dysfunctional *Mischsprache*. The Congolese narrators analysed by Zaripov sometimes appear to be locked in a traumatic present, unable to put their experiences of dangerous crossings behind them, while Schmidt's child refugees temporarily lose their grip on their new language when confronted with the task of 'telling' the past. Le Houérou describes various aspects of the chronotope, including the way that migrants live in their new surroundings according to homeland calendars defined by religion and tradition, or the inability of traumatized, disenfranchised refugees to engage with the local chronotope. Her chapter also brings in the metaphor of the rhizome, which 'has no beginning or end; it is always in the middle, between things, interbeing, intermezzo', as a key to understanding the dislocation of exile (Deleuze and Guattari [1980] 1987: 25).

These migrants' accounts of the journeys to their host country and their memories (or recreations) of 'home', the spaces they occupy (or not) in their new country, the spaces and times they share with local populations, the different conceptions of space and time across genders and generations, bring out a number of important themes that recur in myriad different manifestations across the world. We hope that the approaches to migrants' and refugees' narratives in this volume will provide stimulating material for discussion in the classroom, and that the various analyses of the representations of space and time will inspire further research. Regarding the specific context of migration from Africa and the Middle East, we believe that the analysis of narrative and narration in these chapters may provide insights into the motivations and experiences of migration from these areas, and shed light on the stories these people tell and, crucially, on the way they tell them and the 'logics' that underpin them (Maryns 2005). In particular, these chapters bring out patterns regarding the blurring of time and space, the disarticulation resulting from displacement and the breakdown of linguistic competence in high-stress situations, which should be borne in mind when interviewing people about their migration experiences. Finally, the wealth of different methodological and theoretical approaches in this volume will make this a useful resource for students and researchers approaching the topic of migration in other parts of the world.

Notes

1   It should of course be recalled here that it is not just in the semantics of Arabic and African languages that the future is a somehow problematic category but also in the analysis of tense systems in languages such as English, as evidenced in the work of generations of linguists such as Palmer ([1979] 1990) and Leech (1971) and more

recently Copley (2002). Indeed some such as Palmer ([1979] 1990) have wondered whether there is such a thing as future tense in English rather than a bundle of modal and epistemic orientations towards the future. See Dahl (2008) for a historical overview of this question.

2 Literature in the Arabic-speaking world has developed along different lines from Western literature, and could be regarded as timeless, in that the same genres have been cultivated and appreciated over the centuries. For instance, *Muʻallaqāt*, or the so-called the Suspended Odes, created by pre-Islamic poets, still enjoy popularity in the Arab world (and are well understood by the modern reader).

References

Adam, B. (2000), 'The Temporal Gaze: The Challenge for Social Theory in the Context of GM Food', *British Journal of Sociology*, 51: 125–42.

Agha, A. (2007), 'Recombinant Selves in Mass Mediated Spacetime', *Language & Communication*, 27 (3): 320–35.

Bakhtin, M. (1981), *The Dialogic Imagination: Four Essays*, Austin: University of Texas Press.

Baynham, M. (2003), 'Narratives in Space and Time: Beyond "Backdrop" Accounts of Narrative Orientation', *Narrative Inquiry*, 13 (2): 347–66.

Baynham, M. (2005), 'Network and Agency in the Migration Stories of Moroccan Women', in M. Baynham and A. De Fina (eds), *Dislocations/Relocations: Narratives of Displacement*, 11–35, Manchester: St Jerome Publishing.

Baynham, M. and A. De Fina (2016), 'Narrative Analysis in Migrant and Transnational Contexts', in M. Martin-Jones and D. Martin (eds), *Researching Multilingualism. Critical and Ethnographic Perspectives*, 31–45, London: Routledge.

Blommaert, J. (2007), 'Sociolinguistic Scales', *Intercultural Pragmatics*, 4 (1): 1–19.

Blommaert, J. and A. De Fina (2017), 'Chronotopic Identities: On the Timespace Organization of Who We Are', in A. De Fina, D. Ikizoglu, and J. Wegner (eds), *Diversity and Super-diversity*, 1–14, Washington, DC: Georgetown University Press.

Booth, N. (1975), 'Time and Change in African Traditional Thought', *Journal of Religion in Africa*, 7 (2): 81–91.

Böwering, G. (1997), 'The Concept of Time in Islam', *Proceedings of the American Philosophical Society*, 141 (1): 55–66.

Breeze, R. (2013), 'British Media Discourse on the Wearing of Religious Symbols', in K. Wachter and H. van Belle (eds), *Verbal and Visual Rhetoric in a Mediatised World*, 197–212, Leiden: Leiden University Press.

Breeze, R. (2014), 'Reporting Public Manifestations of Religious Beliefs: Sikhs, Muslims and Christians in the British Press', in I. Olza, O. Loureda, and M. Casado-Velarde (eds), *Language Use in the Public Sphere*, 271–307, Bern: Peter Lang.

Bruner, J. (1986), *Actual Minds, Possible Worlds*, Cambridge, MA: Harvard University Press.

Copley, B. (2009), *The Semantics of the Future*, London: Routledge.

Dahl, Ö. (2008), 'The Grammar of Future Time Reference in European Languages', in Ö. Dahl (ed.), *Tense and Aspect in the Languages of Europe: Tense and Aspect in the Languages of Europe*, 309–28, Berlin and New York: De Gruyter Mouton.

de Certeau, M. (1988), *The Practice of Everyday Life*, Berkeley: University of California Press.

De Fina, A. (2003), 'Crossing Borders: Time, Space, and Disorientation in Narrative', *Narrative Inquiry*, 13 (2): 367–91.

De Fina, A. and A. Georgakopoulou (2012), *Analyzing Narrative. Discourse and Sociolinguistic Perspectives*, Cambridge: Cambridge University Press.

Deleuze, G. and F. Guattari ([1980] 1987), *A Thousand Plateaus: Capitalism and Schizophrenia*, trans. B. Massumi, Minneapolis, MN: University of Minnesota Press.

Divita, D. (2019), 'Discourses of (be)Longing: Later Life and the Politics of Nostalgia', in R. Piazza (ed.), *Discourses of Identity in Liminal Places and Spaces*, 64–82, London: Routledge.

Dolinina, A. (1984), 'Sudba zhanra makami v sovremennoy arabskoy literature' [The Afterlife of the Genre of Maqama in the Contemporary Arabic Literature], *Rocznik Orientalistyczny*, 43: 57–63.

Dong, J. K. and J. Blommaert (2011), 'Space, Scale and Accents: Constructing Migrant Identity in Beijing', in J. Collins, M. Baynham, and S. Slembrouck (eds), *Globalization and Language in Contact: Scale, Migration, and Communicative Practices*, 42–61, London: Continuum.

Durkheim, E. ([1912] 2003), *Les formes élémentaires de la vie religieuse: le système totémique en Australie*, Paris: Presses Universitaires de France.

Ennaji, M. (2014), *Muslim Moroccan Migrants in Europe: Transnational Migration in its Multiplicity*, London: Palgrave Macmillan.

Epstein, M. ([2003] 2007), *Amerussia. Selected Essays*, Moscow: Serebrianye niti.

Gintsburg, S. (2019), 'Identity, Place, Space, and Rhymes during a Pilgrimage to the Shrine of Moulay Abdessalam, Morocco', *Journal of Religion in Africa*, 48 (3): 204–30.

Hamad, M. and A. Kabha (2020), 'The System of Gaps and Alerting the Reader in Modern Arabic Literature', *IAFOR Journal of Literature & Librarianship*, 9 (1): 60–75.

Hassan, S. (2020), 'The Representation of Afghan Refugees. Corpus-assisted and Qualitative Discourse Studies', PhD diss., University of Navarra.

Juffermans, K. (2018), 'Micro-landsc§apes and the Double Memiotic Horizon of Mobility in the Global South', in A. Peck, C. Stroud, and Q. Williams (eds), *Making Sense of People, Place and Linguistic Landscapes*, 201–22, London: Routledge.

Kagame, A. (1976), *La Philosophie Bantu Comparée*, Paris: Présence africaine.

Koven, M. (2019), 'Narrating Desire for Place: Chronotopes of Desire for the Portuguese Homeland before and after "Return"', in R. Piazza (ed.), *Discourses of Identity in Liminal Places and Spaces*, 42–63, London: Routledge.

Labov, W. (1972), *Language in the Inner City*, Philadelphia: University of Pennsylvania Press.

Labov, W. and J. Waletzky (1967), 'Narrative Analysis: Oral Versions of Personal Experience', in J. Helm (ed.), *Essays on the Verbal and Visual Arts*, 12–44, Seattle: University of Washington Press.

Leech, G. (1971), *Meaning and the English Verb*, Harlow: Pearson Education Limited.

Leech, G. (2004), *Meaning and the English Verb*, 3rd edition, London: Routledge.

Levitt, P. and N. Schiller (2004), 'Conceptualizing Simultaneity: A Transnational Social Field Perspective on Society', *International Migration Review*, 38 (3): 1002–39.

Maryns, K. (2005), 'Displacement in Asylum Seekers' Narratives', in M. Baynham and A. De Fina (eds), *Dislocations/Relocations: Narratives of Displacement*, 174–93, Manchester: St Jerome Publishing.

Maryns, K. (2006), *The Asylum Speaker: Language in the Belgian Asylum Process*, Manchester: St Jerome Publishing.

Mbiti, J. (1971), *New Testament Eschatology in an African Background: A Study of the Encounter between New Testament Theology and African Traditional Concepts*, Oxford: Oxford University Press.
Mbiti, J. (1990), *African Religions and Philosophy*, Oxford: Heinemann.
Neuwirth, A. (2006), 'Spatial Relations', *The Encyclopaedia of the Qur'ān*, 5: 104–8, Leiden: Brill.
Palmer, F. ([1979] 1990), *Modality and the English Modals*, London: Routledge.
Pérès, H. (1944), 'Les origines d'un roman célèbre de la litterature arabe moderne "Hadit Isa Ibn Hisam" de Muhammad Al Muwailihi', Beyrouth, Institut Français de Damas. *Bulletin d 'Études Orientales*, 107–8.
Perrino, S. (2015), 'Chronotopes: Time and Space in Oral Narratives', in A. De Fina and A. Georgakopoulou (eds), *Handbook of Narrative Analysis*, 149–59, Oxford: Blackwell.
Relano-Pastor A. M. and A. De Fina (2005), 'Contesting Social Pace: Narratives of Language Conflict', in M. Baynham and A. De Fina (eds), 36–60, Manchester: St Jerome Publishing.
Ricoeur, P. (1984), *Narrative and Time*, Chicago: University of Chicago Press.
Sullivan, J. (2006), 'Redefining the Novel in Africa. Research in African Literatures', *Research in African Literatures*, 37 (4): 177–88.
Wolfson, N. (1982), *CHP, the Conversational Historical Present in American English Narrative*, Berlin: de Gruyter.

1

Settling Out of Place: Narratives of Housing and Strategies of Ageing by a Ghanaian Migrant in the United States

Cati Coe

All over the world, migrants invest in housing if they can, building elaborate houses in their hometowns or nearby cities in their countries of origin. Although such houses may remain vacant, as people construct their lives in the country of migration and delay the moment of return, they remain symbolic of continued political belonging to the country of origin. Because houses become vehicles for social personhood, they take on profound affective qualities, including the capacity to make and unmake a sense of belonging more broadly. Through place-making through home ownership, a person aims to establish her political belonging, and losing such a property similarly makes her feeling a lack of political belonging. This chapter develops this proposition through the narratives of an ageing long-term elder care worker from Ghana over a period of four years (2016–20), when she lived in both Ghana and the United States. The experience of losing her house in the United States to foreclosure in 2017 – in the wake of physical illness, marital instability and the economic crisis of 2008 – led her to express bitterness about the American Dream and about racism, as a place that stripped her of wealth and did not allow her to retire after a lifetime of work. In contrast, she praised Ghana, where she had built a house over twenty years, as a place that would allow her to grow old. She retired to Ghana, anticipating the foreclosure and plagued by ill-health. Although her health improved due to the increased opportunities for rest, she found that her kin were not willing to care for her, but instead were mainly interested in inheriting her house. Disappointed, she returned to work in the United States, sleeping on a friend's coach to save money and relying on a chosen family of non-kin young women who were also migrants from Ghana. Houses symbolically serve as a visible sign of success, and also can enable other forms of security, both financial and social. The fact that her houses did not constitute a form of financial savings – in the United States – and a secure recruitment route for kin labour – in Ghana – unsettled the care worker's sense of having a place where she belonged. Instead she chose a temporary physical location, a network of adopted kin, and continued work despite poor health. Ultimately, the chapter argues that the material and social conditions of emplacement influence other affective kinds of belonging, including political and social orientations. Her example also shows that being 'in' and 'out' of place can shift across a person's life course in relation to these material and social conditions.

* * *

People tell stories about themselves and their experiences to provide meaning and sense. In representing themselves to themselves and others, they stitch together a sense of self. Often, this narration shapes their everyday actions and plans for the future. However, sometimes, there can be slippage between the narration and what people actually do, particularly when they generate strategies that do not correspond to existing cultural models. In previous work (Coe and Alber 2018), I, along with Erdmute Alber, have called this process age-inscription. Age-inscriptions correspond to more indeterminate and transitional levels of changes in ageing trajectories and life stages than the concept of norms or cultural models. Age-inscription accounts for the ways that transitions, expectations and markers around age and life-course stages are modified in interplay with social change.

Migrants may feel a more profound need for narratives of life review than others. Migrants can feel out of time and place through practices of marginalization by the state and other key actors; suffering prompt recalibrations of possible identities and paths of action (Parish 2008). Migrants also tend to have a transnational perspective which keeps open many different pathways, leading to greater fluidity and flexibility in identifications and material and social investments that are aimed at securing a sense of place in the world.

I illustrate the malleabilities and continuities in identification in the various stories told by an ageing woman from Ghana to me over a period of five years. Sometimes, her narratives lined up directly with her actions, as we might expect. At other times, they did not correspond to the pathways she was pursuing, with the narratives continuing to express the dominant cultural models through which she understood her life, and the course of action representing a new way of ageing, or an age-inscription. I use a theoretical approach drawn from psychological anthropology regarding the self, cultural models and narration, combined with insights from the literatures on transnational migration and on ageing, to elaborate more fully on a concept I developed with Erdmute Alber, on age-inscriptions and their importance in creating social change. This chapter represents a more individualized and psychological approach towards understanding why age-inscriptions emerge in social life and how they are enacted in material and social spaces.

When I met her, Elizabeth had worked as a home care worker in the United States for over forty years. During the period I have known her (2016–21), she returned to Ghana for a year, but then came out of retirement, to continue working in the United States with the goal of finishing a house in Ghana. These journeys back and forth between Ghana and the United States were prompted by her ambition to secure permanent material spaces in the form of houses, which served as powerful symbols of social personhood, well-being and political belonging, and encapsulated concerns about care, financial stability and relations with others over time. The houses served as objects which constituted her as a particular kind of self, and she understood her own self to be at stake in their construction or loss. 'People often grasp part of the cultural world as if parts of self, and then turn around to throw these pieces of themselves back into the world and enter their lives on the often fragile footing these provide' (Parish 2008: 5). Through her stories about her houses, Elizabeth made claims about her belonging and emplacement, as someone worthy of dignity, even as she felt increasingly embittered by life circumstances, as the cultural models which she followed to ensure her well-being through the acquisition and occupation of property failed her.

There can be different strategies for coping with traumatic experiences – complete negation of them through negation of time and place (Le Houérou, this volume), drawing pictures (Melo-Pfeifer, this volume), maintaining silence (Zaripov, this volume). Elizabeth chose to tell stories, through which she aimed to create order out of the chaos and disorder of suffering (Law 1994), and to make meaning out of the cruelty and disappointments of life. Order was generated in part through cultural models of success, like the American Dream or resting under the mango tree, and also through dichotomies pitting the country of migration of the United States against her home country of Ghana. Although all humans experience disorder and cruelty that generate existential questions, migrants may face these experiences more extensively, and they have different frames for understanding these experiences, due to their migration experience (Gibson and Ogbu 1991). They have more options and a wider cultural repertoire. Another country can be idealized or denigrated in contrast to the country in which they are living, prompting new dreams in the midst of disillusionment (Schielke 2012). Through her stories of her life, Elizabeth negotiated her stance towards cultural models of success like 'the American Dream' or relaxing under the mango tree associated with Ghana. She could not fully abandon them in her narratives, even though her actions seem less and less oriented towards those cultural models.

I tell the story of her storytelling in three acts. In the first act, Elizabeth was in the process of losing a house to foreclosure in the United States and idealized Ghana as a place to grow old, in contrast to the United States. In the second act, she had returned to Ghana and continued to think of Ghana as ideal, in contrast to the United States. In the third act, embittered by her experience in Ghana, she continued to explore whether she would grow old in the United States or Ghana. She lived in a temporary physical location, dependent on a network of adopted kin and continued to work part-time despite poor health. Open to various future possibilities, she seemed to have given up on her earlier dreams of stable housing and supportive kin relationships in favour of warmer but more precarious kin-like relations, due to feeling out of place in both Ghana and the United States. In the end, after disillusionment with both Ghana and the United States, rather than claiming belonging to one place or another, she seems to have reached an accommodation with temporary and contingent arrangements, a belonging forged not through national frames or ownership of material space, but through personal relations of interdependency. During these three acts, her sense of betrayal in the United States remained, but her interpretation of Ghana was more malleable. Her actions and her narratives also became more and more misaligned, as she began to develop age-inscriptions, which lacked the narrative possibilities of the cultural models her societies had provided as resources for self-making.

Narratives in migrant selves

Narratives are very important for migrants in numerous ways. Among the Ghanaian migrants I know, narratives circulate widely within communities because migrants find them so useful (Coe 2013, 2019). There are certain kinds of stories told over and over within the Ghanaian diaspora. Migrants draw on the narratives of other migrants' lives and experiences to determine both their goals and strategies of action. They learn about what is possible and what is not. They see what others successfully pursue, and where they fail. The experiences of others, as narrated, make some courses of action more conceivable than others (Swidler 2001), since one must imagine taking the kind of action (like building a house) before one begins. These stories shape the cultural models that migrants use to interpret their experiences. Transnationalism, as well as the migrant community, gives migrants access to a range of cultural models which they can use in shaping their lives and how they might proceed.

Migrants also use narratives to make sense of their lives. Many, although not all, migrants endure a sense of dislocation or unsettledness; some even experience suffering in the process (Gintsburg and Breeze, this volume). Suffering, as a disordering process, spurs self-awareness and pushes people to develop the possibilities of selfhood (Parish 2008: 126). It prompts them to order their lives, through narrative. These narratives can represent an active working out of possible selves or the period when a self has become settled. The stories organize a particular stance towards cultural models, build a bridge between the past and the present, and help generate or cement a new possible self. Stories enable the narrator to locate herself in time and place or represent a tentative stab at doing so.

Older adults are often considered settled, and their cultural worldviews stable, while those of younger people are more turbulent. However, older people are encountering ageing in their own life for the first time and are active cultural brokers of the process of ageing (Cole 2013). As migrant older adults, like Elizabeth, encounter the vicissitudes of ageing, these can prompt a change or realignment in selfhood.

One sign of this unsettledness is age-inscriptions. A product of an individual response in relation to contradictory or failed cultural model, an age-inscription has not become a cultural model or a norm. This is one reason that it is hard to narrate, and it causes a disconnection between the ways that someone might represent his or her own life and what they actually do, because they have not yet found a common language with which to share it.

Stories over time

I met Elizabeth in February 2016 through a project on African elder care workers in the United States (Coe 2019). Elder care work is a niche employment field for many African immigrants, in both the United States and the United Kingdom. Elizabeth was somewhat unusual in having lived so long in the United States, since 1974, whereas most of my research participants had arrived within the last fifteen years. When I met her, Elizabeth walked slowly, and with difficulty, as if she was in pain. Age sixty-six years, she told me that she had high blood pressure and had been a diabetic for two years, which made her feel lethargic, bloated and sleepy. She was using bitter melon as an herbal medicine to help control the diabetes, and she found it very helpful.

Thereafter, I maintained contact with her through phone calls and WhatsApp messages. After losing her house in the United States to foreclosure, Elizabeth returned to Ghana in October 2016, and one of her adopted daughters in the United States reported she was 'very happy' and 'enjoying life much more than in the United States' (notes from phone conversation, 5 December 2016). I was able to visit Elizabeth in her house in Accra in December 2016, where she cooked me a delicious meal under the mango tree in her yard. She returned to the United States in October 2017. In May–June 2019, I made a short film about Elizabeth (Coe 2020b), which gave me the opportunity to listen again to the narratives of her life, and document the changes she had undergone in her thinking. I have written about her situation previously (Coe 2019, 2020a), but this chapter presents an update of her trajectory, demonstrating how I too continue to revise and refine my interpretations in light of her new circumstances.

Elizabeth understood both the book and the film as being 'a voice for home care workers' (notes from phone conversation, 9 September 2018), and participated eagerly because of her sense that they were overlooked and underappreciated. Although some scholars have analysed the malleability of people's discourses through interviews (Swidler 2001), this long-term research means that I can actually document how her narratives about her life change over time, in relation to her experiences, actions and relationships to people and places, unlike single interviews which capture a moment in time.

Act 1: Anticipating foreclosure (February 2016)

On our first meeting, I sat with Elizabeth in her small bedroom in dim light one evening in February 2016. We sat on two plastic chairs, facing her bed. Multiple suitcases were stacked high, almost to the ceiling, in a corner of the room. A computer sat on the desk behind us. In our conversation, about her experiences with elder care, she focused on two betrayals she had experienced during her period of living in the United States.

One centred on work. The most personal was a time when she was working for a nursing home and she hurt her back when lifting a heavy patient. After filing worker's compensation, the administration made a 'plot with my co-worker. They said that a patient – who couldn't talk! – said that I beat him up'. Elizabeth was surprised by the accusation, because the patient was cooperative when she took care of him: 'I didn't understand what had happened initially, or why this accusation was made.' Later she understood this as connected to her worker's compensation claim. She lost her job with the nursing home, and went into home care thereafter. If she was very careful, her back did not hurt her. Having one patient to lift at a time, rather than eight to fifteen in the nursing home, also helped. However, watching her walk with difficulty and pain made me wonder that she could lift anyone at all.

The second betrayal was that she was about to lose the house in which we were sitting. Its imminent foreclosure explained why the house was a bit run-down, particularly in the kitchen. From the outside, the house was a solid brick two-story, four-bedroom house with a driveway, two-car garage and yard in a suburban middle-class African American neighbourhood in Maryland. Elizabeth had calculated she had paid half a million dollars in mortgage payments over the thirteen years since she bought the house for $320,000 in 2004. Zillow, an online source of housing information, estimated the house was worth $240,759 at the time of our interview, or half of what she had spent on the mortgage, including interest payments, because the house had lost its value since the 2008 housing crisis. Elizabeth had made sacrifices for the sake of the house: for instance, for thirteen years, she did not visit Ghana in order to pay the mortgage. She had not been able to make mortgage payments during a period of time when she was sick and could not work. The house was also co-owned by her husband, who did not contribute his share of the payments.

What made both situations feel like betrayals is that the life force she had put forth for the house and her work were not being rewarded. Similar to Ghanaian fishermen who travelled to Italy (Lucht 2012), she felt that the universe had not reciprocated her contributions. These events made her feel like an outsider, and she recounted to me other stories of racism and lack of appreciation for her care in her work. They also 'don't care how many years you have toiled'. 'We [Africans] are treated [here in the US] like we are nothing.' Now, as an older person without much energy, who needed her previously made investments in life-energy to pay off, she felt disappointment at the lack of reciprocity.

The home was an extension of the self, but also represented a secure footing for her future. In the United States, home ownership is intimately tied to the American Dream. Not only is home ownership a sign of adulthood (Hummon 1989), but for most Americans, their home is their major asset and form of wealth. Americans expect houses will appreciate in value and provide a nest egg for retirement and other needs. Because of the centrality of home ownership to stable and middle-class adulthood in the United States, owning a home has been supported by the federal government, particularly for whites, through publicly backed loans (Freddie Mae and Mac). Immigrants adopt this American practice of signalling social class and building wealth through home ownership.

However, for African Americans, home ownership does not seem to pay off as it does for white Americans. Although all houses lost value in 2007–8, leading to the financial crash of 2008, the housing market in general has regained its – but not in African American neighbourhoods. A *Washington Post* analysis of the Atlanta area and an analysis by Black Knight Ridder financial services of the 300 largest metropolitan areas found that housing values were less likely to recover from the housing market crash of 2008 in zip codes where African Americans were the largest group (Badger 2016). In the zip code of Elizabeth's mainly African American middle-class neighbourhood, there were twice as many foreclosures than in the United States as a whole (6.5 foreclosures per 10,000 homes compared to 3.2, reported Zillow). Even upper-middle-class African Americans who bought large homes in suburban neighbourhoods around Atlanta saw their homes decrease in value, such that they ended up paying more on their mortgages than the house was worth (Badger 2016). Like Elizabeth, many African Americans may feel they end up with nothing. Home ownership among the African care workers I knew was sometimes a source of wealth extraction, as it can be for African Americans and as it was for Elizabeth. Houses thus become a mechanism for making a self, and attaining a sense of self-work, but one through which inequalities of race and class are instantiated, putting some kinds of selves at risk of degradation and making some kinds of social persons vulnerable to downward mobility. This becomes especially critical when a person is no longer able to work and needs to depend on previously accumulated social and financial resources. Thus, property ownership is central to the cultural model of success in the United States, and a key symbol in the 'American Dream'. Migrants often adopt this formulation of success, seeing home ownership as central to wealth accumulation and belonging. As Umut Erel (2010) has noted, migrants can adopt new forms of cultural and symbolic capital in the country of migration, generating migrant-specific forms. The belief and promise of housing represents such a situation in Elizabeth's life story.

For Elizabeth, the loss of her house after more than a decade was also a sign of her lack of acceptance in the United States: she could not establish a home there. Elizabeth told me that sometimes she just shuts the door to her room in her patient's home and cries. When people go to Ghana, she told me, they are welcomed as 'sisters and brothers' lost through the slave trade. But when Africans come to the United States, 'we are not accepted'. She sounded a little choked up saying this to me.

Pragmatically, she could not afford to stay in the United States if she stopped working. Reflecting on her betrayals, Elizabeth felt, 'The arrangement is that when you are old, they leave you with nothing. Now that I am retiring, they are attacking your little money.' Because of this 'arrangement' with the rules stacked against her, she thought she would return to Ghana soon. She had built a house in the capital, where she was from. Her son, in his thirties, and his wife and children would stay in the United States; Elizabeth had divorced her husband for infidelity some years before. Social Security would not stretch very far in the United States; it will not cover the mortgage or rent and the utilities. 'There is not enough money. Here you cannot make it. You would be compelled to go and work again. Your health is gone. You have broken your back, your wrist, and your shoulder.' Her words made me think that what was broken was her heart, or at least her sense of hope.

In narratives, and in establishing meaning in their lives, people rely on creating order. As William Sewell (2005) has noted, one way people tend to organize their experiences is through hierarchies, comparisons and dichotomies. One way to do so, which is particularly available for transnational migrants, is through national comparisons. By attacking the unfairness of the United States, she explained what had happened to her and buttressed her sense of self diminished by these losses. Elizabeth idealized Ghana in comparison to the United States, perhaps because she had not visited Ghana since 2002. In her view, the United States was racist and not accepting of African migrants; Ghana was a place of rest and relaxation where her investment of energy would bear fruit. She represented space through national borders, reifying both the United States and Ghana, and placing her future self in the idealized space of Ghana, where she thought she would be warmly accepted and be allowed to flourish.

Act II: Under the mango tree (December 2016)

When Ghanaian migrants talk about the pleasures of home (Ghana), they often talk about 'sitting under the mango tree' associated with a cool breeze in the shade, chatting with friends and relaxation. Through the image of the mango tree, Ghana is associated with rest and sociality; migration with long hours of work and stress about money. This is a cultural model of ageing and leisure, shared by migrants in their conversations. Thus, on a visit to Ghana, I was delighted to find Elizabeth reclining on a bed under an actual mango tree in her garden.

Her house in Ghana was a symbol of success as a migrant. Houses serve not only as performative signals of social class, but also can objectively make and maintain social class, as a source of wealth and income. Their relative permanence, in comparison to ritual celebrations (Feldman-Savelsberg 2020, Pauli 2020), makes them ideal for the stabilization and maintenance of social class. Housing shores up claims to land ownership in Ghana, and land is becoming more important as a sign of class differentiation, as in other parts of Africa (Mercer 2014). Furthermore, a house can be a source of further income and wealth creation, by renting out or even selling the house, as a real estate market is developing in urban areas of Ghana. Housing may be safer than other kinds of investments in periods of rampant inflation or be the site for a business or other economic activity for residents (Smith and Mazzucato 2009).

On the non-economic side, owning a house allows one to be less reliant on others and to provide housing for relatives, thus establishing a middle-class, patron role (Van der Geest 1998). Fifty-one per cent of Ghanaians live rent-free in a kinsperson's house (Ghana Statistical Service et al. 2009). In the urban areas of Accra, Kumasi and Berekum, house owners had more people in their households than non-owners, signalling their ability to attract dependents (Tipple et al. 1999). A house also reduces the house owner's reliance on others, which is a source of humiliation. For example, a retired pastor complained to me about returning to his hometown in Akyem Abuakwa in retirement and having to live in a family house: 'Your nephew or some other member of the family has a house and they have to divide it to give you a place to live. So every day you are a burden on the family; they will scold you so much' (conversation, July 2014). In contrast to the stigmatization of those without their own house, a house owner can expect the service of other residents to provide domestic chores like sweeping the compound, running errands and fetching water. Additional residents provide security because someone is always around. Most importantly, through houses' visibility and ability to attract people, they generate social respect, as a sign that one has made it in life. Although houses in Ghana are important for their ability to create more economic capital, they also convert economic wealth into social relations, and thus to status – what Pierre Bourdieu (1986) would call symbolic capital.

In Accra, Elizabeth lived with her nephew, his wife and their affectionate toddler on whom she doted. She lived on her Social Security payments and was experimenting with making bread for sale, with the help of her nephew, an unemployed chef. During my visit, when she called him to bring her something while she was cooking, he did so promptly.

While we sat together, Elizabeth blamed her travails on the United States and praised Ghana for its opportunities and fairness in contrast: in Ghana, a house could not be taken away from you, she said, although I knew people who had lost land through litigation and multiple sales of the same property. She also compared ageing in Ghana positively to the United States, idealizing Ghana in comparison to the disappointments of the United States: She told me that she thought elder care in Ghana was much better than in the United States: 'Here [in Ghana], people take care of you', referring to her nephew and his wife. She lived on her Social Security payments and was also experimenting with making bread for sale. As for her house in the United States, she informed me that the bank's seizure was imminent. Half a million dollars put into it, and she was getting only $3,000 from its sale. 'American Dream!' she said scornfully. She said that, most unfairly, you end up in the nursing home. In Ghana, in contrast, she was growing old by enjoying the fruits of her many years of work, in the shade of her mango tree. She said in Ghana, on the other hand, you build a house and you can give it to your children and grandchildren. She thought Ghana was much better in regards to housing than the United States.

Thus, she continued to reify Ghana and the United States as completely different, with Ghana offering opportunities for social class mobility in contrast to the United States. However, such an opportunity to live a good life in Ghana was dependent, in part, on her period of migration in the United States. For example, her Social Security payments, which allowed her to live a better life in Ghana than she would in the United States, were based on her many years of working abroad.

Although Elizabeth continued to struggle with her diabetes and other health conditions, it was wonderful to see her happy, relaxing and cooking house. She told me that she was slowly losing weight. The stress in the United States made her eat, and studies have documented the link between the long hours and stress of low-income work in the United States and food habits that lead to weight gain (Chard 2020). Elizabeth was able to take two naps a day in Ghana. Again, she contrasted Ghana with the United States negatively: She said that in the United States, you just worry about bills, but not here in Ghana.

Despite a house's allure for its stability and permanence, houses can be a precarious social and economic investment for lower-income migrants, leading to both status and shame (Nieswand 2011). Houses' use in the performance and economic consolidation of social class depends on the specificities of historical context in particular social fields, such as rising land prices and the real estate market in Accra, and the housing boom, enabled by easy credit and followed by a crash, in the United States.

That the house ensured care for Elizabeth, through the co-residence of her nephew, was also tenuous. Ultimately, she considered him to be dangerous, rather than a source of care. In 2019, after she returned to the United States, she told me that she had feared that her nephew was trying to poison her through witchcraft, so she would pray over the food, so she would not die. The nephew knew that her son was not ready to leave the United States, and so the nephew would be able to live in the house if she died. She told me that this is how people are. She wanted to ask him to leave for a long time, but her stepdaughter told her to pray about it. Similar kinds of conflicts between the generations over houses have been noted in South Africa (Van Dongen 2008).

When Elizabeth returned to the United States, her stepdaughter moved into the house with her children. Elizabeth managed to sell the house in 2018, after some effort, because of the muddy roads leading up to it, to contribute to the $20,000 she needed to complete another house she was building. The house in Ghana was as precarious as the one in the United States, in terms of providing both care as an ageing person and a financial investment.

Act III: Temporary housing and adopted kin (May–June 2019)

I spent three days with Elizabeth for the purpose of making a film in May and June 2019. In the film, she continued to express her disappointment with the American Dream, which centred on the loss of her house. In the four years since I had met her, the sense of bitterness about the United States remained, but the idealization of Ghana was more muted.

> The American Dream fell apart on my end. I walk in that house with money, and walk out with nothing. Yup. If I did not build a house in my country, I am stuck – no money, nowhere to go.

And:

> Your system is not good for old people, I am telling you. It's good for young people.

She had oriented her own life in relation to the cultural model of the American Dream. She continued to consider Ghana to be a better place to grow old, although she no longer expressed confidence that kin would care for her, opening the possibility that she would hire a stranger to provide care instead.

> I thought of all that: I got two beautiful houses, and in Ghana, I can get someone to take care of me, either a family member, or somebody you hire, even the money you pay is not that much, like here. To me, getting old, when you are foreigner [in the United States], is a raw deal. How can you be in your own house, and when you get old, you have to sell the house, in order to get some money to get care in a nursing home? You own the house, but you don't own it. It's unbelievable. When you get a house, you own it. But you're saving money so when the house is sold, you use it.

Although she expressed the ways that Ghana would allow her to retire, in comparison to the United States, in oppositional ways, I learned that she was, in fact, hedging her bets. She was both earning money to save up to complete her second house in Ghana, and she was on the waiting list for a nursing home in the United States.

In the United States, she was not able to work full-time because of her poor health. She was also not able to take some care jobs because of the requirements to lift and turn bedridden patients. She supplemented her home care work with baking meat pies and other pastries. She slept on a friend's coach to save money. She stayed with someone from her church, but this situation was unsatisfactory. She told me that 'that woman is disrespecting her, and so she said nothing in response, because she has no place to go' (fieldnotes from phone conversation, 9 September 2018). She continued to live with this woman and complained that she was not treating her well (fieldnotes from phone conversation, 6 April 2019). When I was collecting the footage for her film, we rode around in her car. The back seat and trunk were full of cans of food and aluminium pans, as if her car served as her pantry. At one point, while she transported her patient, I found myself filming from the back seat, with the empty aluminium pans and full tomato cans knocking against me. I also could not meet with her at her place of residence, but only in her car or other public venues, making the filming quite difficult. I gained a visceral sense of her temporary housing from the shoot.

Elizabeth was also reliant on two young women, also home care workers and migrants from Ghana, whom she considered 'surrogate daughters' (phone conversation, 27 March 2016). They had helped her pack up her foreclosed house, did many physical chores and errands for her, and helped her with her baking, as I was able to film. They would stop by to help her with lifting at a particular job (phone conversation, 6 April 2019). They were obligated to her for reasons I could not discern. Elizabeth did not seem in touch with her own son who lived in the area. She was also in touch with her stepchildren through her divorced husband, in both Ghana and the United States, and wished that they were more reliable. These close relationships with younger people who were not her biological kin were not unusual among women in Ghana, who pursued security and well-being through caring for younger adults, including child fosterage (Coe 2016). However, in relying on an adult version of fosterage so intensely, Elizabeth seems to have adapted a cultural model to her own life circumstances and thus forged an age-inscription, a new practice which could not be easily narrated, or at least explained to me. She secured a social space, adapted from the models she had inherited to her new circumstances.

The fact that her houses did not constitute a form of financial savings – in the United States – and a secure recruitment route for kin labour – in Ghana – unsettled Elizabeth's sense of having a place where she belonged. Instead, she chose a temporary physical location, a network of adopted kin, and continued work despite poor health, as she kept various options for retirement open. Her narratives of Ghana and the United States, in which she continued to orient herself towards Ghana, were not completely aligned with the course of action she was pursuing, which was more flexible and contingent.

Conclusion

Through her stories, Elizabeth was navigating and making sense of the world around her and her place within it. As an ageing person, she was analysing whether her previous financial and social contributions would provide her with care and financial security when she could no longer work. She made sense of her disillusionment in the cultural models in which she had believed: why did the American Dream fail for her, as represented by the loss of her house? Why did her nephew seek to kill her, when she had provided him with housing? Houses were both an extension of her 'self', whose loss and construction profoundly affected her sense of self-worth, and a source of the material wealth and social support that were necessary for her well-being as she aged. They were symbols of the world's fairness. The central question governing her life during these years was whether she could expect a return for the material and social energy she had given out over her years of labour – as a caregiver and as a stepmother and mother.

Her narratives cemented certain versions of realities, in which she remained wedded to her stance in relation to the opposition between Ghana and the United States, while her actions became more flexible. She kept open her options to age in either country, even as she denigrated one context as a bad place to grow old, and another as more welcoming. In response to the fact that neither cultural model was working well in her life, she generated age-inscriptions through her behaviour, even as her stories remain more fixed.

Ultimately, Elizabeth's stories show that the material and social conditions of emplacement influence how she locates herself physically, socially and affectively. These conditions affect her sense of self and how she orients herself in future actions. Her example also shows that being 'in' and 'out' of place can shift across a person's life course in relation to these material and social conditions. Although she had been emplaced in certain periods – and satisfied with her situation and choices – those moments shifted with new events. For the moment, she has decided to depend on contingent kinship and temporary housing, shaping a life betwixt and between possibilities, as she keeps her options open. Thus, after a lifetime of living in the United States, she seems to be a migrant who has settled 'out of place' in her actual practices, if not her stories.

References

Badger, E. (2016), 'The Nation's Housing Recovery Is Leaving Blacks behind', *The Washington Post*, May 2. Available online: https://www.washingtonpost.com/graphics/business/wonk/housing/atlanta/ (accessed 17 November 2021).

Bourdieu, P. (1986), 'The Forms of Capital', in J. Richardson (ed.), *Handbook of Theory and Research for the Sociology of Education*, 241–58, Westport: Greenwood.

Chard, S. (2020), Social Justice, the Worker Compact, and the Emergence of Diabetes over the Life Course. Presentation at the Biennial Anthropology of Aging and Gerontology Conference, online, July.

Coe, C. (2013), *The Scattered Family: Parenting, African Migrants, and Global Inequality*, Chicago: University of Chicago Press.

Coe, C. (2016), 'Orchestrating Care in Time: Ghanaian Migrant Women, Family, and Reciprocity', *American Anthropologist*, 118 (1): 37–48.

Coe, C. (2019), *The New American Servitude: Political Belonging among African Immigrant Home Care Workers*, New York: New York University Press.

Coe, C. (2020a), 'Social Class in Transnational Perspective: Emotional Responses to the Status Paradox among Ghanaian Transnational Migrants', *Africa Today*, 66 (3–4): 161–80.

Coe, C. (2020b), Stories from Home Care, Video, 13:22 min. https://youtu.be/qGSHX-0iiTY.
Coe, C. and E. Alber (2018), 'Age-Inscriptions and Social Change: Introduction', *Anthropology and Aging Quarterly*, 39 (1): 1–17.
Cole, J. (2013), 'On Generations and Aging: "Fresh Contact" of a Different Sort', in C. Lynch and J. Danely (eds), *Transitions and Transformations: Cultural Perspectives on Aging and the Life Course*, 218–30, Oxford: Berghahn.
Erel, U. (2010), 'Migrating Cultural Capital: Bourdieu in Migration Studies', *Sociology*, 44 (4): 642–60.
Feldman-Savelsberg, P. (2020), 'Class Performances: Children's Parties and the Reproduction of Social Class among Diasporic Cameroonians', *Africa Today*, 66 (3–4): 20–43.
Ghana Statistical Service, Ghana Health Service and ICF Macro. (2009), *Ghana Demographic and Health Survey 2008*, Accra: Ghana Statistical Service.
Gibson, M. A. and J. U. Ogbu, eds (1991), *Minority Status and Schooling: A Comparative Study of Immigrant and Involuntary Minorities*, New York: Garland.
Hummon, D. M. (1989), 'House, Home, and Identity in Contemporary American Culture', in S. M. Low and E. Chambers (eds), *Housing, Culture, and Design: A Comparative Perspective*, 207–28, Philadelphia: University of Pennsylvania Press.
Law, J. (1994), *Organizing Modernity*, Oxford: Blackwell.
Lucht, H. (2012), *Darkness before Daybreak: African Migrants Living on the Margins in Southern Italy Today*, Berkeley: University of California Press.
Mercer, C. (2014), 'Middle Class Construction: Domestic Architecture, Aesthetics and Anxieties in Tanzania', *Journal of Modern African Studies*, 52 (2): 227–50.
Nieswand, B. (2011), *Theorizing Transnational Migration: The Status Paradox of Migration*, New York, London: Routledge.
Parish, S. (2008), *Subjectivity and Suffering in American Culture: Possible Selves*, New York: Palgrave Macmillan.
Pauli, J. (2020), 'Class-Switching: Migrants' Multiple Class Identities in Rural and Urban Namibia', *Africa Today*, 66 (3–4): 114–36.
Schielke, S. (2012), 'Engaging the World on the Alexandria Waterfront', in K. Graw and S. Schielke (eds), *The Global Horizon: Expectations of Migration in Africa and the Middle East*, 175–91, Leuven: Leuven University Press.
Sewell, W. H. (2005), *Logics of History: Social Theory and Social Transformation*, Chicago: University of Chicago Press.
Smith, L. and V. Mazzucato (2009), 'Constructing Houses, Building Relationships: Migrant Investments in Houses', *Tijdschrift voor Economische en Sociale Geografie*, 100 (5): 662–73.
Swidler, A. (2001), *Talk of Love: How Culture Matters*, Chicago: University of Chicago Press.
Tipple, G., D. Korboe, G. Garrod, and K. Willis (1999), 'Housing Supply in Ghana: A Study of Accra, Kumasi, and Berekum', *Progress in Planning*, 51: 253–324.
Van der Geest, S. (1998), '*Yebisa wo fie*: Growing Old and Building a House in the Akan Culture of Ghana', *Journal of Cross-Cultural Gerontology*, 13: 333–59.
Van Dongen, E. (2008), '"That Was Your Time … This Time Is Ours": Memories and Intergenerational Conflicts in South Africa', in E. Alber, S. Van der Geest, and S. R. Whyte (eds), *Generations in Africa: Connections and Conflicts*, 183–206, Münster: Lit Verlag.

Discussion questions

1. What do houses and property ownership mean to you? What role do they play in your own narrative of success or belonging to a place?
2. What are some of the reasons why migrants might revise their life story repeatedly? Do you think they are more or less likely to have changing narratives of place and self than non-migrants?
3. What happens during the ageing process that may prompt re-evaluations of belonging to a place or a sense of success?
4. Why might narratives take longer to catch up with practices? Which change more rapidly?
5. In what ways can emplacement and belonging occur through social relations?

2

'We will be able to get there – what? – a life!' The Congolese in Kampala Narrating Migration through Time and Space

Ruslan Zaripov

Introduction

Most migration takes place by land, across borders from one country to another, sometimes in search of a better life, but often to escape from danger. Africa is no exception to this, with massive migratory flows in the context of tribal wars, political instability and natural disasters. This chapter turns our attention to Central Africa, and in particular to migrants around the Congo area, a region that has long been torn by conflict.

While much research in recent decades has approached narrative in terms of wider themes such as identity, authorship or genre, there currently appears to be less interest in the way stories are expressed through different languages and in the cultural traditions in which they are embedded. In particular, when analysing real accounts of migration, we believe it is important to take into consideration the linguistic, sociolinguistic and sociocultural dimensions that shape people's storytelling traditions and perhaps also condition their lived experiences of the narrated events.

Along these lines, this chapter begins with an explanation of the historical and linguistic background to current migration from the Congo, paying special attention to the languages and cultures of Central Africa and the way time and space are conceptualized there. An analysis of time and space in four migration narratives is then presented. These are discussed in terms of tenses, temporal deixis and time conceptualization in Bantu languages, and then analysed with regard to spatial deictics and locatives. This is then complemented by a multimodal analysis, showing how the storytellers' body language serves to emphasize their words by measuring the spatio-temporal distance from the human centre(s). Our discussion brings out some of the characteristic ways in which times and spaces seem to be fused in these narratives, and offers a contextualized interpretation of this merging process.

Background considerations

Historical and linguistic background

The region that forms the background to this study comprises the territory of the present-day Democratic Republic of the Congo (DRC), as well as the countries bordering it on the east, especially Uganda. The DRC is the second largest African country after Algeria.

Linguistically speaking, the area offers a mixed pattern. Its official language is French, but the DRC also has four national languages – Kikongo (ISO 639-3 code: KON), Lingala (ISO 639-3 code: LIN), Congolese Swahili (ISO 639-3 code: SWC) and Tshiluba, also known as Luba-Kasai (ISO 639-3 code: LUA) – all of which belong to the Bantu group of the Niger-Congo language family. This linguistic dominance can be explained in terms of Bantu migration, a process of expansion of Bantu-speaking people from around the territory of the present-day Cameroon towards the East and South. After the ancestors of the present-day Bantu people mastered iron forging, equipped by their strong iron weapons and tools, the Bantu conquered almost all of Central, Eastern and Southern Africa. This process began in the second millennium BCE and ended around 1500 CE, and as a result, most of the people south of the line between Cameroon and Kenya nowadays speak Bantu languages (Vansina 1995).

Since all national languages of the DRC belong to the Bantu language family, they are quite similar in grammatical terms (based on the nominal classes system) and in their core vocabulary. However, although also a Bantu language, Swahili does not historically belong to the Congo basin. It originated on the East African coast around tenth century CE as a result of increased commercial activities between coastal Bantu tribes and traders from the Arabian peninsula, and it possesses a significant vocabulary of Arabic origin, since until the 1960s this language played a key role in the formation of Swahili language and culture (Gintsburg 2018). Swahili was first introduced into the eastern part of the present-day DRC in the last quarter of the nineteenth century by Zanzibari traders. Driven by increased demand for slaves and ivory in the Middle East and depletion of the supply of both from the regions neighbouring the Sultanate of Zanzibar, these traders crossed the East African hinterland and the Great Lakes kingdoms (Rwanda, Buganda), and entered the Congo around 1870 (Page 1974). Thanks to their firearms, which were unknown to the Congolese, they soon established large domains, controlled through a chain of trading stations established on the ground. By far the biggest of these domains was that of Tippu Tip, a rich trader from Zanzibar, which stretched from present-day Lubumbashi to Kisangani. This division remains to our day: Swahili is widespread in Kisangani – along with Lingala – but hardly further to the West. Manyema province, the citadel of Tippu Tip, is the only province in the present-day DRC where Swahili is the native language, and not a second one.

The rule of Tippu Tip was interrupted in the late nineteenth century by the establishment of Leopold II's Congo Free State at the Berlin Conference of 1884. Leopold II carried out this project with significant help from H. M. Stanley, whose expeditions he had secretly subsidized. Stanley was a close friend of Tippu Tip and eventually convinced him to abandon his domain and return to Zanzibar.

However, the new rulers kept some of Tippu Tip's administrators in the new Belgian administration, as they spoke Swahili, the only language present on the ground which had a writing system (based on the Arabic alphabet). Since Swahili is a Bantu language, it was better understood by the speakers of other local Bantu languages than French, and this decision cemented the presence of Swahili in this area. Later on, Christian missionaries transcribed this language into the Latin alphabet, for the purpose of translating the Bible into Swahili, and soon thereafter, Swahili was recognized as one of the four national languages of the Congo. Through the succession of the above factors, by the time Congo declared independence from Belgium in 1960, Swahili had become the well-established *lingua franca* across the whole eastern part of the Congo (from Kisangani eastwards).

However, the story did not stop there. From 1965 to 1997, the DRC was governed by Mobutu Sese Seko, who renamed the country Zaire. His long term in power was characterized by harsh dictatorial rule, widespread corruption and nepotism. Coming from the western part of the Congo, Mobutu favoured Lingala against other national languages but could not change the existing linguistic status quo. During his rule, Lingala became the language of communication of the Zairean army and police. Another important change dating from the Mobutu period is that there is now a national consensus in the DRC that Lingala is the first and the most important among the national languages (Bocamba 2019). One of the reasons for this universally shared belief is that the Swahili-speaking area stretches far beyond the DRC. It is the most widely spoken language of Africa, but in the DRC it is only spoken by the easterners, which means that it is more widespread outside of the DRC than inside, and thus is seen as an international, 'outside' language, as opposed to Lingala, a major language that is truly 'ours'.

The most important achievement of Mobutu's period was that his long rule cemented the notion of the Congo as a nation in the minds of the people. One can say that he is the father of the Congolese nation. Throughout his rule, administrators were sent to serve away from their tribal areas, settled there and married local people. This created a situation where people in our days move and settle across the Congo without being discriminated against by the locals: their belonging to the Congo grants them free access across the land (Bokamba 2019). Mobutu was overthrown in 1997 by Laurent-Désiré Kabila, who in turn was followed by his son Joseph Kabila. This family originates from the Swahili-speaking province of Katanga in the south-east of the DRC. The period from 1997 to the present day has been characterized by wars, political turbulence and increased violence, as well as by more intense participation in Congolese politics by the regional powers, especially Rwanda and Uganda. One important consequence of the Joseph Kabila period was that Swahili eventually replaced Lingala as the language of communication in the police, although Lingala has remained the language of the army.

The political turmoil took a heavy human toll. The mineral-rich east of the Congo has suffered from killings and kidnappings, as well as sexual violence, which is widely used as a method of warfare. This havoc has been caused in large part by the abundance of local and foreign armed militias – some researchers estimate their total number in the Eastern DRC from around 70 to more than 100 different groups. Local groups include dozens of organizations belonging to the *Mai Mai* and *Raia Mutomboki* local self-defence movements. The most important foreign armed groups are the radical Christian-inspired Lord's Resistance Army and the Islamist Allied Democratic Forces (both of Ugandan origin) in the north-east, as well as factions of the ex-Rwandese *génocidaires* known as the *Forces Démocratiques pour la Libération du Rwanda* (FDLR) in the South Kivu and North Kivu provinces (Stearns 2012).

For all these reasons, as well as other broader phenomena found across large areas of Africa, large numbers of people have left the Congo over the last thirty years, many of them settling in neighbouring Uganda, Burundi and Rwanda, while others have moved on to Kenya or further afield to Europe or South Africa.

This study focuses on Uganda, where the history of the development of Swahili is different. Formed by the British as the Uganda Protectorate, around the Kingdom of Buganda, its postcolonial history is marked by a struggle to overcome the dominance of the Ganda people, the tribe that gave the name to this country. They are the biggest ethnic group in Uganda (16.5 per cent of the population, according to the 2014 census) and their language – Luganda (ISO 639-3 code: LUG) – is a true *lingua franca* not only in the Central Province, including the capital, Kampala, but also in many other parts of the country. One might mention that the first president of independent Uganda, the *kabaka* (Ganda traditional king) Mutesa II, only ruled for three years, from 1963 to 1966, and was then deposed by the Prime Minister A. M. Obote for fear of the Ganda taking the upper hand in Uganda. Since that time, no Ganda has reached this position (Kavuma-Kaggwa 2013).

Since British times, Swahili has been used for training of the African conscripts in the KAR (King's African Rifles), and it is still in use in the army and police. In Uganda, the use of Swahili was especially important during the rule of Idi Amin Dada, an ex-KAR, in 1972–9. After the Civil war of the 1980–6, the new President Museveni (in power from 1986 to date) pushed for adoption of the new Constitution adding Swahili as the national language (English had always been the official language since independence). Although Swahili is not a native language to any Ugandan ethnic group, and is less widespread than Luganda, the latter is opposed by the majority of non-Luganda speakers in the country. This led to the acceptance of Swahili as a neutral 'compromise' language. The curious fact is that many Ganda people do not like Swahili, fearing this giant language might threaten their language and culture. The image in Figure 2.1 is one of the rare manifestations of the official status of Swahili in Uganda.

Time and space in narratives on migrations

The importance of time and space in narrative has long been a subject for analysis, although most previous work focuses on literature (Ricoeur 1984) or other canonical forms of storytelling in different cultures. In the field of conversational narrative, some researchers have explored how these categories are controlled by the narrator as a way of providing his/her audience with the temporal and spatial coordinates to trace the progress of the story (Labov and Waletsky 1967). The representation of time relations can thus be seen as one of the resources used in personal narratives 'to imbue life events

Figure 2.1 A Ugandan shilling note, bearing inscriptions in English and Swahili.

with a temporal and logic order' (Ochs and Capps 2001: 2), while spatial orientation can also be understood as having a similar organizing function. In view of this, the representations of time and space may well be particularly significant in the narratives of people whose lives have been marked by migratory pressures (De Fina and Tseng 2017). For example, Baynham (2003) argued that the time-space orientation ought not to be seen as a mere backdrop for the events of a narrative and proposed a constitutive, performative understanding of space-time relations in migrants' narratives. Perrino (2005) explored narratives told by Senegalese migrants to Italy, showing how these migrants manage configurations of time and space strategically to create empathy for their characters by eroding distinctions between the storyworld (past) and the storytelling world (present). In a rather different sense, De Fina (2003) analysed how space coordinates, rather than time, form a fundamental axis in narratives of disorientation told by migrants about their border-crossing experiences, while other researchers opened up the question of 'fuzzy' or 'indeterminate' time contours (Herman 2002). These authors' interpretations suggest that the space-time configurations that surface in migrants' narratives may reflect a degree of psychological confusion due to displacement and/or trauma, rather than providing evidence of accomplished storytelling strategies.

At the same time, on a more macro level, the importance of addressing the social construction of time in specific socio-structural contexts is increasingly being recognized (Saldaña 2003), and this includes not just the immediate interactional context that arises between narrators and listeners, but also the more profound differences that mark the way time (and, we may assume, also space) are conceptualized and represented in different cultures. The resources available in our language(s) and the conceptualizations found in the prevailing worldview, cultural framework or religion probably go a long way to configure our basic understanding of time: time in rural Africa is clearly not the same as time in New York. In the most subjective sense, it is a matter of everyday experience that 'our experience of time rarely if ever coincides with what the clock tells us' (Melucci 1996 cited in McKie, Gregory and Bowlby 2002: 904), but if we add traumatic events and long journeys to the mix, it is likely that people's understanding of time will diverge strongly from linear regularity.

To complicate matters further, as De Fina noted (2003), the category of time has been found to be highly enmeshed with that of space in many contexts. For this reason, sociologists such as Adam (2000) propose the use of the concept of 'timescapes' to encompass quantitative time and the connections between space and time, while Perrino (2005) uses the Bakhtinian notion of chronotopes to unpack migrant narratives, showing how migrants exploit present-past relations, current and past context to create complex temporal and spatial configurations.

In this chapter, we adopt an exploratory approach to narratives by Congolese migrants, in which we try to shed light on the temporal and spatial dimension of the storytelling from our knowledge of the African languages used, as well as the participants' background culture. The next section will provide a brief overview of the conceptualization of time and space in Bantu languages and cultures.

On the concept of space and time among the Bantu people

Although it is inevitable that this chapter will be coloured by the concepts of time and space that exist in Western cultures inspired by Greek thought, as the author of this chapter is the product of these cultures, a special attempt will be made here to understand how time and space are represented by the Congolese migrants in their narrations. A few words are in order here to outline how Bantu people express the spatio-temporal aspect of their lives, so as to make a preliminary attempt to apply this in the analysis of their narratives, as a complement to the Western perspective. I will use here the term Bantu because Swahili is a Bantu language and therefore shares with other Bantu languages some similarities on the structural level. I will also use the term African, although in no way is it my purpose to overgeneralize and present Africa as a homogenous culture.

Space: African cultures are based on the idea of community. The notion of space, therefore, is strongly influenced by the sense of belonging to a particular group of people. A human being is placed in the centre of the world order and, in this sense, plays the role of the reference point for measuring both time and space.

In addition, in African cultures, space and time are often perceived as an inseparable phenomenon. For instance, Alexis Kagame, a philosopher from Rwanda, introduced the notion of *hantu*[1] that implies three kinds of places (spaces) and times that are both physical and metaphysical: (1) locality or space/time occupied by the object; (2) localization of space/time and (3) external place/time. This notion corresponds with the complex system of locatives existing in the Bantu languages. Table 2.1 offers an overview of locatives in Swahili.

Time: it has been noticed by numerous researchers who worked with African languages and African cultures that one of the most striking characteristics of a great number of African languages, including Bantu languages, is the fact that the process of measuring is almost never abstract, that is, time is not measured in abstract units but rather in events and seasons (Booth 1975; Evans-Pritchard 1940; Mbiti 1971).

In addition, Bantu languages, like a great number of African languages, are characterized by a well-developed system of past and present tenses and a rather

Table 2.1 Locatives in Swahili[2]

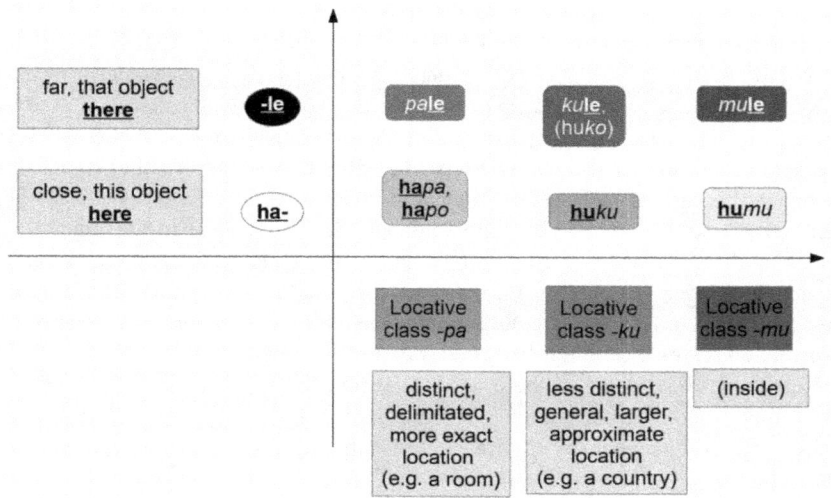

Table 2.2 System of tenses in Swahili[3]

Tense	Formant	Example	Translation
Past imperfect	-li-	Niliongea	I talked (often a repetitive action)
Past preterite	-me-	Nimeongea	I have talked (action already done)
Narrative mode	-ka-	Nikaongea	I usually talk/I used to talk
Present	-na- / -a-	Ninaongea / naongea	I talk
Future	-ta-	Nitaongea	I will talk

schematic one for future tenses. The table above (Table 2.2) illustrates this: we see that while there are two past tenses, one present tense, and one tense that can be used to cover both past and present events, only one tense is used to refer to the future.

In this connection, it is of interest that the Kenyan philosopher John Mbiti argued that in the Bantu languages there are two major categories of time. The first, called *zamani*, is distant past, the 'graveyard of time' (Mbiti 1990: 21) or the events that are not linked to the present, but rather serve as existential foundation, tightly linked to mythology and ancestral beliefs. The second one, called *sasa*, is about present, something that is 'about to occur, or in the process of realisation or recently experienced' (Mbiti 1990: 22). Mbiti did not define future as a separate category but rather sees it as part of *sasa*. Booth, in his turn, suggests that time in African culture is always directed not to the future but to the past (Booth 1975). It is the past, therefore, that serves the reference point for an African person.

Data and method

The oral narratives used in this study were collected in February 2021 by the author from four Swahili-speaking Congolese migrants – two men and two women – residing in Kampala, Uganda, with the help of Zoom online conferencing software (I used the 'record' function). It is important to mention that although all my informants are native speakers of Swahili, lexically, the variety of Swahili they speak is rather poor. Most probably, this can be explained by their low socio-economic status, as well as their remoteness from the heartland of the Swahili language and culture in Tanzania. While collecting these interviews, I used prompts in order to make sure that these narratives would not diverge too much from the main topic, namely migration. The length of the recorded narratives was 15–30 minutes. The table below (Table 2.3) contains the information on the informants that is relevant for this chapter[4].

To analyse the content of these narratives from the spatio-temporal perspective, I will apply the theory of alignment in oral narratives of displacement and, where appropriate, complement my analysis with insights from the African perspective on space and time.

Three of my four informants crossed the DRC-Ugandan border between Mahagi (DRC) and Paidha (Uganda) (Figure 2.2).

Linguistic analysis

While narrating their experiences of migrating from the DRC to Uganda and crossing the DRC–Ugandan border, by and large, the interviewees resorted to ways of constructing space and time resembling those described by De Fina (2003), Baynham (2003, 2006), Haviland (2005) and Liebscher and O'Cain (2005). Just like Mexican immigrants, who now live in the United States, or Western Germans who relocated to East Germany, the Congolese immigrants in Kampala have recourse to the full scale of spatial and temporal deixis, including tenses of the verb, to position themselves in the complex array of times and spaces involved in the fabric of their narrative, and use alignment to maintain the coordination between the spatio-temporal aspect of the events discussed in their stories and the act of telling.

Table 2.3 Information on the interviewees

No.	Name	Gender	Age	Religion	Home town in Congo	Year of arrival to Uganda
1	Zainabu	F	56	Muslim	Mungbwalo	2019
2	Marc	M	54	Christian	Rutshuru	2007
3	Jacques	M	24	Christian	Bunia	2006
4	Marie	F	25	Christian	Bunia	2020

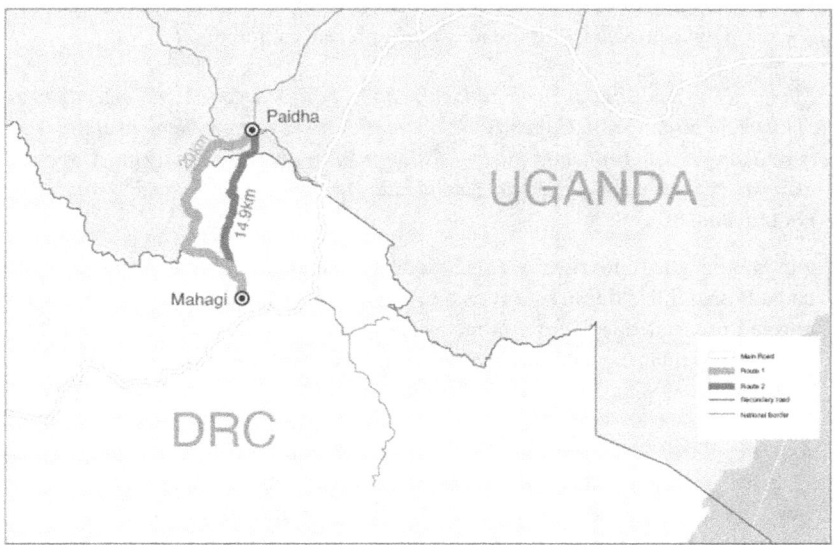

Figure 2.2 Mahagi – Paidha route used by the majority of Congolese refugees to escape from the DRC to Uganda.

Temporal aspects

Past events are retold in the present tense

When talking about the present time, the interviewees most often use the word *sasa* (now), especially if it is opposed to some moment in the past. This word came very frequently in the interviews. To illustrate, below are small extracts from the interview with Marc. About the nature of his work in Kampala, Marc says:

> <u>*Hapa*</u>[5] *Kampala? Mimi kazi nilifanya hapa Kampala. Nawasaidia* maçons *kujenga, aide maçon, lakini* **sasa***, sawa, wananipatia hiyo.. kilo hamsini kubeba ya ciment nipeleke nakakutosha mpaka* <u>*kule*</u>*. Sasa maisha inakuwa nguvu sana kuweza.*
>
> <u>Here</u> in Kampala? Me, the work I did in Kampala. I help masons, I'm an *aide maçon*, but **now**, okay, they give me that.. to carry [bags with] cement, 50 kgs, so I carry it until <u>**there**</u>… Now, life becomes very difficult to bear.

One peculiarity I noticed was that, as the story progresses, the narrator gradually 'enters' the story (past events) and starts to recount them in the present tense as if they were happening at the time of the narration.

In the following extract, the interviewee, Jacques, is talking about past events, but when he gets involved in the story, the past becomes present. And in the summarizing end of the story, when referring to the actions as opposed to the result of the story as it is at the present moment, the interviewee 'returns' to the present moment, and his past is now strongly contrasted with the now of his present moment:

Mama ashakufa, sasa ilikuwa tunabaki na mama mdogo. Mama vile mdogo alikuwa na bwana yake. **Hape<u>nd</u>i**[6] *tu… – nini? – tukae na yeye. Tena akatufukiza, hata akatufukuza,* **tu<u>na</u>enda** *huko… fasi… tuko tu hivyo. Nyuma yake, yeye vile akatoka. Uyu vile mama akaenda. Saa hii hata hatujui, yeye alienda na bwana yake hatujui hata. Tuko tu.*

Our mother died, now, we remained with her small sister. That maternal aunt had a husband. He **doesn't want** us to… – what? – that we stay with him. So he rejected us, even chased from home, we **go** there.. places.. we are just there like this. Behind that, she left. That *mama* went. Until now, we don't know, she went with her man, we don't even know. We are just there.

As we can see, in the beginning of the story the narrator is using the past tense, making us understand that the events he is talking about happened in the past. However, as he progresses, he gradually dwells in the time of the story, and his time becomes exactly that, that is, he is talking about past events as if they were happening now. This is his new *now*. To return to the verbal perspective of the narrative to the moment of narrating, that is, the present (Gimenez 2010), the narrator restores his timeline according to the present moment, that is, he starts using past for past events.

Jacques left Kampala for *Bunia* at the end of the clashes in the DRC that had forced him to flee, only to have to run again soon thereafter. When asked if he wanted to go back to *Bunia*, he responded in the affirmative, which was rare in the interviews.

We see the same situation in the interview with Zainabu – the present time of the story becomes the *now* of the narrative:

Mama alikuwa Mande, nilienda Beni. Beni mbaya, **wa<u>na</u>kata** *watu,* **wa<u>na</u>chinja** *watu, nikaona maisha ni ngumu, nikaenda Mungbwalo.*

My mother was a Mande, I went to *Beni*. *Beni* bad. They **cut** (present tense) people, they **slice** people, I saw life as difficult, so I went to *Mungbwalo*.

In another interview, Marc describes how he was campaigning for Jean-Pierre Bemba in the 2006 DRC Presidential elections, and he was then attacked and detained by armed supporters of Joseph Kabila (upon which his father was killed), which eventually made him flee the DRC for Uganda:

Wakanifunga kama hivi (showing his arms behind his back), *wakanipeleka, nikabeba vitu, ku pori* **<u>huku</u>***. Wao walikuwa watu ya – nani?..* (indistinct). **Wa<u>na</u>nichukua** *ku pori. Tukaenda ku pori, nikaikaa* **<u>kule</u>** *kama wiki tatu. Kukakuja soda moja hivi, akanisaidia.*

They tied me like this (showing his arms behind his back), they took me, I carried my things, to the jungle there. These were people of – who?.. (indistinct). So they

take me to the jungle. We went to the jungle, I stayed there for like 3 weeks. Then came a soldier like this, he helped me.

Again, we can see that, gradually as the narrator plunges into the story, he slips into present tense. This time he corrects himself very quickly and continues in the past.

Use of future tense to narrate past events: future tense comes regularly but less frequently when talking about events that *would* have happened in the future of that time they are talking about, as evidenced in the following extract from the interview with Jacques, when he is justifying why their mother and maternal aunt left them in *Paidha* (Uganda) and went back to *Bunia* (DRC):

Bamama wangu, bamama bakatuacha **pale***, banapima kurudia* **kule** *Bunia. Bakaenda tena. Habakufika Bunia. Balitembea ma-côté ya* **kule** *yote. Sisi tulikuwa tulibangojea tu* **hapa***,* **pale** **wanatuacha***. Balikuwa balishapata* **pale** *marafiki. Kwa siku nyingine, balikuwa bameshamaliza* **pale***. Bakaacha* **pale***, bakarudia. Kwenda kupona kama* **wataweza** *kupata moyen. Imepita kama miezi tano hivi bakarudia. Bakasema* **hakuna** *tena moyen. Mwenyewe* **iko** *yule* **anaweza** *kusaidia,* **iko** *kule Kampala.* **Tunaweza** *kwenda* **kule***.* **Tutaweza** *kupata – nini? – maisha. Twende* **kule***!*

Our mother and her sister, they left us **there**, they tried to go back. They went again. They never reached *Bunia*. They walked all sides **there**. As for us, we were **here** waiting for them, **there** where they **leave** us. They had got friends **there**. Another day, they finished their business **there**. They left **there**, they returned. To try to find out whether they **will be able** to get some means. Around 5 months passed, and they came back. They said there **are** no means. The one who **is** supposed to help, he **is** there in Kampala. We **can** go **there**. We **will be able** to get **there** – what? – a life. Let's go **there**!

At some point, the interviewee positions himself in the moment his relatives went off, so the time becomes present ('waiting for them where they **leave** us'). Then, as his relatives leave, but the story is not yet concluded (for the listener), the narrator is using the future to formulate his mother's prospects of finding some means back in the DRC (to try to find out whether they **will be able** to get some means). Back there, this was the future, after all. Next, as Jacques' relatives are sharing their plans with him, he uses the future tense again, this time supposedly quoting his mother ('we will be able to get there a life'). In the same paragraph, again, as the narrator quotes direct speech of his returning relatives, he is already deliberately using the present tense all across the phrase.

The narrator is building the tissue of time around himself, ending up by positioning himself in the time of the story (it becomes present). Some storylines, still unconcluded (still untold) at the moment of narration, are presented in the future tense, to be concluded at the end of the story.

Past is never a truly accomplished past: interestingly, when interviewees compare past events with the present, they seem to never fully go to the distant past in their narratives, that is, their past appears to be never truly accomplished. For instance, when Marc contrasts his life circumstances in the past against the present coronavirus crisis, he uses the adjectives *leo* (today) and *sasa* (now) to indicate the present moment:

> *Maisha i**ka**kuwa nguvu, mpaka **leo**. Zaidi **sasa** – nani?.. – corona i**ka**kuja. Ndio i**na**tuleta shida **sasa** kubwa sana. Kila kita iko down.*
>
> Life was difficult, until **today**. More than that, **now** – what?.. – corona came. Really, it brings us a lot of difficulties **now**. Everything is down.

African insight: Curiously, this resonates with the ideas of Mbiti (1990), who, on the material of the Bantu languages, argues that an African person (meaning, of course, a Bantu-speaking person) builds his story moving towards the past and not towards the future. The natural opposite of *sasa* is the Swahili word *zamani*. However, this did not feature in the interviews. One possible explanation is that *zamani* means 'a (very) long time ago', while the events narrated took place relatively recently. It can also be that the traumatic experiences lived by the interviewees in the Congo and leading to their fleeing to Uganda are not yet *zamani* (resolutely finished past, page definitely turned) for them, they are still 'living' these events. Obviously, the migration stories narrated by the Congolese migrants living in Uganda, despite the fact that they took place years ago, have still not become part of *zamani*. Instead, they remain part of *sasa* – their current life.

Units of time are always borrowings: Curiously, all my informants had difficulties when they were asked about precise dates related to their lives. First of all, this concerned questions about the number of years lived in Uganda, the year of coming to Uganda, and the like. At times, the informants used French or English numerals, sometimes, a combination of Swahili and French or English and, on several occasions, just a simple reference. Consider the following examples:

1. Zainabu says the date in English and then confirms it, using a less complex but, at the same time, more practical system of counting:

> *Mimi nimefika Uganda, nimeingia Uganda **twenty nineteen**, mwaka ya juzi ile ya jana, na inaanza, a-ha.*
>
> I came to Uganda, I entered Uganda in **2019**, the year of behind the last year (showing the thumb behind the back), and it starts, a-ha.

2. Jacques resorted to French to tell the date of his arrival in Uganda:

> *Tulikuja hapa, ilikuwa **deux mille cinq**. **Deux mille cinq – deux mille six**.*
>
> We came here [to Uganda], it was **2005. 2005–2006**.[7]

3. Marc was trying to produce a complex number in Swahili, then skipped to English, only to finish it in Swahili:

> ***Elfu mbili… mia… two thousand… mpaka hii elfu mbili na saba***
>
> **Two thousand… hundreds…** (in Swahili) **two thousand..** (in English).. until that **two thousand and seven** (in Swahili).

4. Finally, Marie failed to say number 2020 when asked which year she entered Uganda, and only said it was the year which just ended:

Mwaka hii imeisha ile

This year that has ended.

African insight: This inconsistency in counting time could probably best be explained using some ideas suggested by African philosophers, as well as experts in African cultures. In the introductory section, we saw that one of the striking characteristics of Africa, and of the Bantu language, is lack of use of abstract units to measure time. Confusing as it might seem, this can be explained by the fact that an African person would measure time not in abstract units but rather in real events because events are concrete, and years are abstract and therefore make no sense (Booth 1975). In the narratives collected from the Congolese refugees living in Kampala, this lack of abstract units manifested itself in a peculiar way: with the exception of counting units,[8] none of my informants used the abstract units of time that exist in Swahili. Instead, the informants used borrowings from English and French. We can assume, therefore, that this confusion of numbers can be interpreted as an example of mixing of the indigenous concept of time, where concrete events are used as measuring units, with the borrowed ones, where abstract units of time are preferred.

Spatial aspects

In their narratives, the interviewees constantly switch between the two axes of spatial deixis: here (*hapa*, *huku*) and there (*kule, pale,* etc.), where 'here' is typically not their actual location but the one of the story.

It has been noticed that the interviewees use a broad spectrum of locatives offered by Swahili; however, only the word *hapa* (and much more rarely, *huku*) figures in all the interviews as a definite 'here', while the rest of them seem not to have a definite connotation and are used by the interviewees quite randomly to define shades of 'there'. Since English does not possess such an elaborate locative system as Swahili, I used the word 'here' to translate *hapa/hapo* and *huku*, and 'there' for the rest of the locatives.

There* becomes *here: similarly to dwelling in the time of the story, the interviewees often became so deeply involved, even entrenched, in the story that gradually they entered into its space, and the *here* of the story becomes the *here* of the narrative.

At the beginning of the interview, the interviewees quite coherently position themselves in Kampala. For example, this is how Jacques begins his story of their crossing of the DRC-Ugandan border:

Tukapima kuja tukarudia, twende **kule** *Bunia. Wakati tulirudia* **pale** *Bunia, vita tena ikarudia. ukarudi. Tukakurudia* **hapa** *Kampala.*

We decided to go back, let's go **there** to Bunia. When we came back **there** to Bunia, the war came back again, it returned. So we returned **here** to Kampala.

But then, at some point, the space of the story becomes the space of the narrative, the new *here*. For instance, this is how Jacques narrates his experience of migrating from Congo to Uganda:

*Tulikuwa tulitoka Bunia, tulikala Fataki, tulikala bafasi mingi, iko fasi nyingine inaitwa Nderere **pale**, **pale** gari ikakufa. Tungoja motokari, ikakamataka kama semaine kama sita hivyo bila motocari. Tikukuja **pale**, tulikala tu **pale**. Ah, tukakuta **pale** motocari ikakuja. Tulikuwa tukafika **pale**... ah... Paidha, kufika **hapa** Paidha.*

We left Bunia, we stayed in Fataki, we stayed in many places, there is another place called Nderere **there**, **there** the car died. We waited for the car, it took like around 6 weeks, **there** without a car. When we reached **there**, we just stayed **there**. Ah, we waited for a car **there**, and it came. We reached **there**... ah... Paidha, reached **here** Paidha.

We see in this passage, as Jacques is gradually plunging into the story, the space of the story – Paidha (Figure 2.2) – becomes his current *here*, the *here* of the story.

In some instances, it comes as a glimpse, as Jacques quickly realizes where they are at the moment of narration (Kampala):

*Bamama wangu, bamama bakatuacha **pale**, banapima kurudia **kule** Bunia. Bakaenda tena. Habakufika Bunia. Balitembea ma-côté ya **kule** yote. Sisi tulikuwa tulibangojea tu **hapa**, **pale** wanatuacha. Balikuwa balishapata **pale** marafiki.*

Our mother and her sister, they left us **there**, they tried to go back. They went again. They never reached Bunia. They walked all sides **there**. As for us, we were **here** waiting for them, **there** where they leave us. They had got friends **there**.

As we can clearly see, the interviewees did not only position themselves in the time of the story, but also in its place.

Here becomes there: consequently, as a distant place (the place of the story) becomes the place of the story/narration, the real here (Kampala), as opposed to this new *here*, becomes *there*.

In a different extract from the same interview with Jacques, he refers to Kampala (when talking about him travelling from the Congo) as **there**:

*Tumebaki tu na nguo yenyewe tulikuwa naye, na ma-**sacoche** ya mgongo. Pale, tukabaki pale Paidha, vile Paidha tulikala pale. Bamama wangu, bamama bakatuacha pale, banapima kurudia kule Bunia. Bakaenda tena. Habakufika Bunia. Balitembea ma-côté ya kule yote. Bakasema hakuna tena moyen. Mwenyewe iko yule anaweza kusaidia, iko **kule** Kampala. Tunaweza kwenda **kule**. Tutaweza kupata – nini? – maisha. Twende **kule**.*

We remained with only the clothes that we were wearing, and our backpacks. So there we remained there in Paidha, and we stayed there. Our mother and her sister, they left us there, they tried to go back. They went again. They never reached *Bunia* (indistinct word). They walked all sides there. They said there are no means. The one who is supposed to help, he is **there** in Kampala. We can go **there**. We shall be able to get – what? – a life. Let's go **there**.

When starting a story, Jacques is obviously aware that he is *here* in Kampala. Gradually, as he is taken back to the events of their past, time-space warps and starts revolving around that time and place: the time and the place of the action becomes the present time (*now*) and place (*here*), all the other times and spaces becoming secondary compared to it. Hence, Kampala, as seen from *Paidha*, becomes *there*.

African insight: from the perspective of the African or the Bantu culture, the shades of *here,* that is, the choice between *hapa* and *huku,* and *there,* that is, the choice between *pale* and *kule* (Table 2.1), appear to be of less importance, to the narrator at least, as long as he/she shows the approximate distance. We see here, again, that space is perceived in terms of community and not individually, that is, the narrator is more interested in the rough delimitating of space, as belonging not to him/her, as an individual, but rather as him/her a representative of a community.

Multimodal analysis

I will now support the linguistic analysis of the oral narratives with elements of multimodal analysis. Taking multimodality in consideration while analysing oral narratives is of special importance in the case of African culture, where the non-verbal, visual aspect is of special importance (Gintsburg, Galván Moreno and Finnegan 2021). Almost all the interviewees demonstrated well-developed facial expressions and gestures, perhaps to compensate for their relatively poor vocabulary in Swahili, which I mentioned earlier. Non-verbal markers were also used when the Congolese informants could not finish the phrase because they were lacking the appropriate word. In this case, they left the phrase uncompleted and added an assertive gesture to replace the missing word. In addition, some gestures were used to emphasize the meaning, for example, when they felt that the word they used was not expressive enough, to compensate, they would clap hands or snap fingers, or make a brushing movement with the hand in front of themselves. Sometimes this would be additionally accompanied by another non-verbal marker, like clicking the tongue, or an interjection such as 'hmm', 'Aha' or the like.[9]

Following Goodwin (2003), a non-verbal mark – a facial expression, humming or a pointing gesture – is used to mutually contextualize what is being discussed in a conversation. In addition, the heavy use of pointing gestures registered in the narratives I collected is similar to that of the non-verbal language used by the members of African diaspora in Soqotra, who extensively resort to pointing gestures in order to better convey the meaning when lacking proper vocabulary (Gintsburg and Esposito 2022).

Below I will discuss some of the gestures, facial expressions and lip and head movements pertaining to space and time that I was able to register.

Head and face as reference point for spatio-temporal dimensions: one striking feature was that the interviewees used a lot of head movements. For example, past events frequently came with a typical 'sealing' head movement behind, sometimes slightly turning it to the right or to the left. The movement seems to dub a similar hand gesture showing behind the shoulder, and meaning 'back that time', 'back there' or anything associated with returning to some place. On the contrary, the head movement forward (again, slightly bent to the right or to the left) means 'over there'. This gesture is rarely temporal. Head forward or sideways is also used to show directions (sometimes, lips are further stretched forward, forming an arrow).

For instance, Marie, when asked where her husband was going to find a job, used her lips to show the direction towards *Kireka*, a neighbourhood in Kampala (Figure 2.3).

However, sometimes this lip movement was also used when showing temporal direction. The same informant, Marie, when she was trying to say that she had come to Uganda last year (2020), used the same stretching lips sideways gesture, as if showing that point of time when she arrived (Figure 2.4).

Time and space go sideways, through me: however, time (events) and past places can go also from one side to another. In this case, when referring to some past events or places, the interviewee would pass the hand across the body to the other side: that is, if shown with the left hand, the gesture would go across the body to the right, and vice versa. One example is this extract from the interview with Zainabu. At some point she starts using the left hand. And some of the gestures become 'mirrored' (Figure 2.5).

Figure 2.3 Marie uses her lips to show the direction.

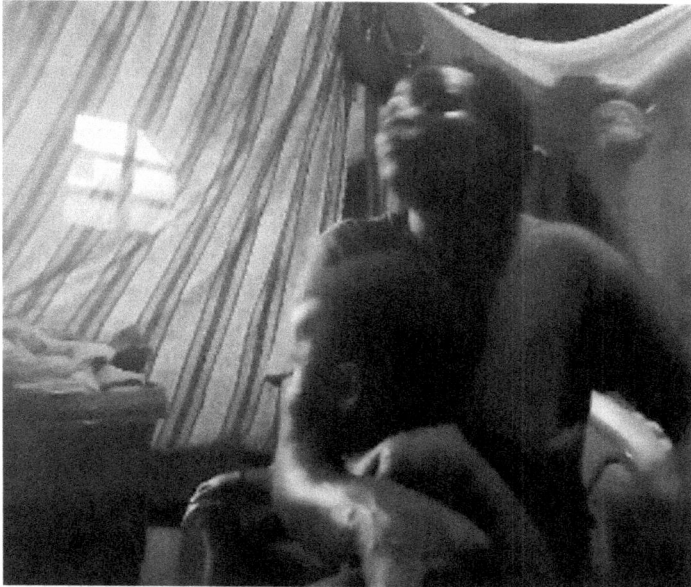

Figure 2.4 Marie explains when she arrived in Uganda.

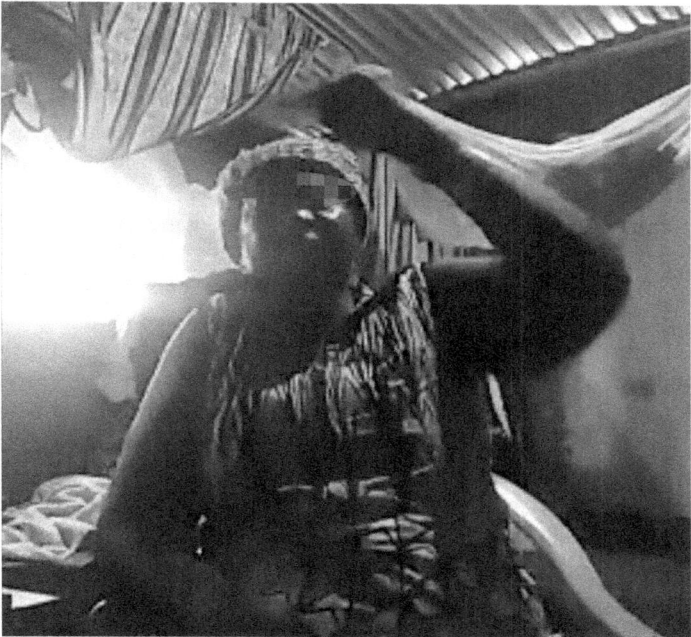

Figure 2.5 Zaynabu shows with her left hand across her body to the right that she returned to the native tribe of her mother.

African insight: in the Bantu culture, everything is related to real events and not to the hypothetical abstract units of time and place. In terms of time, everything relevant has to be linked to *sasa* but also grow from *zamani*. In terms of space, everything has to be seen through *here* in order to be connected to there. We see, therefore, that hand and head body movements are clearly used to measure the distance between *sasa* and *hapa* and *zamani* and *kule*.

Moreover, the off-the-body gestures used by the interviewees to complement the verbal contents of their narratives can be interpreted through the lens of Kagame's philosophy of the Bantu people, which places the human, or *mantu*, in the centre of the universe. Everything is therefore measured using the human as the point of reference.

Conclusion

Our aim in analysing this material was to apply insights from African approaches to representing time and space in contrast to their Western equivalents, factoring in our knowledge of the specific resources available in Bantu languages, and our interpretation of the body language used by the participants. First, we can observe that in general, linguistically speaking, the narrators used tenses and deictics that are comparable to those described in other languages/used by migrants in different linguistic and cultural contexts (De Fina 2003; Perrino 2005). However, it was striking that the mixing of times and places was particularly strong when these narrators became intensely involved in traumatic episodes from their migratory trajectories, which perhaps points to the effects of traumatic experiences that are still 'present' to the narrators. Here, as in the case of De Fina's border crossings (2003: 389), we were able to observe how the evident 'ambiguities, uncertainties in time and space (…) index the immigrants' lack of control over their own displacement in the material world'. The frequent confusion of times and places, and the 'making present' of past events or distant places, would seem to point to a degree of intense involvement, rather than to a deliberate narrative strategy intended to elicit sympathy.

At the same time, our insights from African languages, particularly concerning the linguistic contrast between a 'finished' past and a 'present' past, helped us to see how the journeys of displacement still remain very much part of the narrators' present lives. If we examine this from the perspective of African culture, we should recall Mbiti's thesis that there are only two categories of tense in the Bantu/African culture: *zamani* – distant past, fully completed events; and *sasa* – present, non-completed events that are related to the present. In terms of this division, the absence of adjectives/adverbs related to the distant past and the evident confusion of tenses might mean that the experiences narrated by the narrators had not yet been fully lived, and should therefore be assigned to the category of *sasa*. On the other hand, the seemingly incoherent use of locative deixis could perhaps be explained by the fact that the Bantu culture is a collectivist or non-individualistic culture, so when the narrator uses locatives inconsistently, this could be because his/her point of reference is not that of an individual but rather that of the community he/she represents.

On the level of multimodal communication, gestures here are emphatic, often conveying the same message through at least two channels simultaneously, and these interviewees used many pointing gestures whose function, we can assume, was to contextualize the narrative in the here and now, and complement its verbal component. Mirroring the mixing of tenses with its tendency to 'make present' past events, the participants' gestures act as a further affordance in a symbolic system that brings the narrated incidents into the present time and space. In the course of the analysis, it became increasingly clear that time and space can sometimes be fused and are shown with the same gestures (see Gintsburg and Esposito 2022). As Perrino noted (2005), the present-past relations, and the current context and past context undergo a process of blending to create merged temporo-spatial configurations. Like the migrants in Le Houérou (this volume) and Gintsburg and Breeze (this volume), rather than negotiating separate timetables and maps, these narrators inhabit 'timescapes' (Adam 2000) or 'chronotopes' (Perrino 2005) from which they may not easily extricate themselves, even should they desire to do so. In this context, it would be important for Western narrative researchers to open their minds to alternative ways of conceptualizing time and space, and to engage in dialogue with other experts, including linguists, anthropologists and psychologists, to develop a deeper understanding of the impact of migration on non-Western people.

Notes

1 The word *mahali* and its archaic form *pahali* (notice the use of the locative class pa- in **pahali**) designate 'place/space' in Swahili. *Ahantu* has the same meaning in Kinyarwanda.
2 Of the resulting locatives, the most popular for 'here' was *hapa*, with *huku/huko* coming rarer. For 'there' *kule* was more popular than *pale*, and *huko* non-existent. The word *huko* above (in brackets) is an exception in Swahili grammar. It should normally be used as a synonym to *huku* but for some reason it is rather similar in use to *kule*.
3 The following brief clarifications on the system of tenses in Swahili are in order here.
(1) The narrative mode is not a past tense per se, as it is used to enumerate, list habitual actions, regardless of tense, generally with a time marker or context (e.g. I **usually** wake up, brush my teeth, take a shower, etc., *or* I used **in the past** to wake up, brush my teeth, etc.). However, it has been noticed that the interviewees tend to use it exclusively to list actions in the past. It might be a specific feature of the Congolese Swahili.
(2) Sometimes the interviewees did not distinguish between past imperfect and past preterite, using them interchangeably – a common phenomenon in the Congolese Swahili that the author often noticed during his stay in the DRC.
4 For the purposes of protection of personal information of these people, who continue to live in Uganda in vulnerable situation, the names used in this chapter are fictional.
5 For locatives across the Swahili and English texts, I used bold and underscore, to distinguish them from other words (space, time) highlighted (only by bold, without underscore).
6 For the tenses, only the forms reflecting specific temporal structures, I used bold and underscore.
7 Another curious example from Jacques: **Semaine** *(kama)* **sita** – '(about) six weeks', where **semaine** is a French borrowing and **sita** is an Arabic borrowing.

8 In Swahili, only numbers from one to five are of Swahili origin. All other numbers, including zero, are borrowings from Arabic (here, sometimes the interviewees also used French or English numbers). An exception is number 8 (*nane*), which is clearly a Bantu word: it is formed by reduplication of 4 (*nne*) – a phenomenon also found in other Bantu languages.
9 In this chapter I adhere to Eastman's classification of interjections in Swahili that have a complex status and can be used as independent verbal expressions, verbal expressions that accompany gestures to intensify the meaning and as gestures (Eastman 1992).

References

Adam, B. (2000), 'The Temporal Gaze: The Challenge for Social Theory in the Context of GM Food', *British Journal of Sociology*, 51: 125–42.

Baynham, M. (2003), 'Narratives in Space and Time: Beyond "Backdrop" Accounts of Narrative Orientation', *Narrative Inquiry*, 13 (2): 347–66.

Baynham, M. (2006), *'Performing Self, Family and Community in Moroccan Narratives of Migration and Settlement'*, in A. De Fina, D. Schiffrin, and M. Bamberg (eds), *Discourse and Identity*, 352–76, Cambridge: Cambridge University Press.

Bocamba, E. G. (2019), 'Nationalism and the Emergence of Lingala as a Supranational Language in DR Congo', *World Englishes*, 38 (1–2): 53–6.

Booth, N. (1975), 'Time and Change in African Traditional Thought', *Journal of Religion in Africa*, 7 (2): 81–91.

De Fina, A. (2003), 'Crossing Borders: Time, Space and Disorientation in Narrative', *Narrative Inquiry*, 13 (2): 367–91.

De Fina, A. and A. Tseng (2017), 'Narrative in the Study of Migrants', in S. Canagarajah (ed.), *Routledge Handbook of Migration and Language*, 381–96, London: Routledge.

Eastman, C. (1992), 'Swahili Interjections: Blurring Language-Use/Gesture-Use Boundaries', *Journal of Pragmatics*, 18 (2–3): 273–87.

Evans-Pritchard, E. E. (1940), *The Nuer: A Description of the Modes of Livelihood and Political Institutions of a Nilotic People*, Oxford: Oxford University Press.

Gimenez, J. C. (2010), 'Narrative Analysis in Linguistic Research', in L. Litosseliti (ed.), *Research Methods in Linguistics*, 198–215, London: Continuum.

Gintsburg, S. (2018), 'Arabic Language in Zanzibar: Past, Present, and Future', *Journal of World Languages*, 5 (2): 81–100.

Gintsburg, S. and E. Esposito (2022), 'The Asymmetric Linguistic Identities of African Soqotris: A Triadic Interaction', in F. Al Rashdi and S. Rao Mehta (eds), *Language and Identity in the Arab World*, London: Routledge.

Gintsburg, S., L. Galván Moreno, and R. Finnegan (2021), 'Voice in a Narrative: A Trialog with Ruth Finnegan', *Frontiers of Narrative Research*, 7 (1): 1–20.

Goodwin, C. (2003), 'Pointing as Situated Practice', in Kita S. (ed.), *Pointing: Where Language, Culture, and Cognition Meet*, 217–41, Mahwah, NJ: Psychology Press.

Haviland, J. (2005), 'Dreams of Blood: Zinacantecs in Oregon', in M. Baynham and A. De Fina (eds), *Dislocations/Relocations: Narratives of Displacement*, 91–127, Manchester: St Jerome Publishing.

Herman, D. (2002), *Story Logic. Problems and Possibilities of Narrative*, Lincoln, NE: University of Nebraska Press.

Kagame, A. (1976), *La Philosophie Bantu Comparée*, Paris: Présence africaine.
Kavuma-Kaggwa, J. M. (2013), 'Tracing the Life, Legacy of Sir Edward Muteesa II', *The Independent – Kampala*, 15th March. Available online: https://www.independent.co.ug/tracing-life-legacy-sir-edward-muteesa-ii/ (accessed 19 November 2021).
Labov, W. and J. Waletzky (1967), 'Narrative Analysis: Oral Versions of Personal Experience', in J. Helm (ed.), *Essays on the Verbal and Visual Arts*, 12–44, Seattle: University of Washington Press.
Liebscher, G. and J. Dailey-O'Cain (2005), 'West Germans Moving East: Place, Political Space and Positioning in Conversational Practices', in M. Baynham and A. De Fina (eds), *Dislocations/Relocations: Narratives of Displacement*, 61–85, Manchester: St Jerome Publishing.
Mbiti, J. (1971), *New Testament Eschatology in an African Background: A Study of the Encounter between New Testament Theology and African Traditional Concepts*, Oxford: Oxford University Press.
Mbiti, J. (1990), *African Religions and Philosophy*, Oxford: Heineman.
McKie, L., S. Gregory and S. Bowlby (2002), 'Shadow Times the Temporal and Spatial Frameworks and Experiences of Caring and Working', *Sociology*, 36 (4): 897–924.
Melucci, A. (1996), 'Youth, Time and Social Movements', *Young*, 4 (2): 3–14.
Ochs, E. and L. Capps (2001), *Living Narrative: Creating Lives in Everyday Storytelling*, Cambridge, MA: Harvard University Press.
Page, M. (1974), 'The Manyema Hordes of Tippu Tip: A Case Study in Social Stratification and the Slave Trade in Eastern Africa', *The International Journal of African Historical Studies*, 7 (1): 69–84.
Perrino, S. (2005), 'Participant Transposition in Senegalese Oral Narrative', *Narrative Inquiry*, 15 (2): 345–75.
Perrino, S. (2015), 'Chronotopes: Time and Space in Oral Narrative', in A. De Fina and A. Georgakopoulou (eds), *The Handbook of Narrative Analysis*, 149–59, Oxford: Blackwell.
Ricoeur, P. (1984), *Time and Narrative*, Chicago: University of Chicago Press.
Saldaña, J. (2003), *Longitudinal Qualitative Research: Analyzing Change through Time*, Walnut Creek: AltaMira.
Stearns, J. (2012), *Dancing in the Glory of Monsters: The Collapse of the Congo and the Great War of Africa*, New York: Public Affairs.
Vansina, J. (1995), *New Linguistic Evidence and 'The Bantu Expansion'*, Cambridge: Cambridge University Press.

Discussion questions

1. What is the role of Swahili in East and Central Africa and how it is linked to the internal African migrations?
2. What are some interesting spatio-temporal aspects of Swahili and other Bantu languages?
3. Give at least two examples of alignment in the Congolese narratives from this chapter.
4. If we use what is called 'African insight', how else we could interpret spatio/temporal inconsistencies in the narratives of the Congolese migrants discussed in this chapter?
5. How could the multimodal aspect of narratives be used to better understand these narratives?

3

Exile, Time and Gender: Time Negation and Temporal Projection among Refugees from the Horn of Africa

Fabienne Le Houérou

Introduction

The Horn of Africa, especially Ethiopia, Eritrea and Sudan, has produced millions of refugees, from the struggles for independence in the 1960s, through the civil wars of the 1980s to our own days. These forced migrations originated from the political turmoil in the region. In the context of the Eritrean war of independence that began in 1961 and dragged on over three decades, ending with Eritrean independence in 1994, refugees from Ethiopia flooded into neighbouring Sudan, while many then made their way onwards to Egypt (Le Houérou 2006a, b, c). At around the same time, during the second Sudanese civil war (1983 to 2005), many Sudanese refugees also fled to Egypt as the Sudan People's Liberation Army (South Sudan) fought the central Sudanese government in a conflict that soon spread to the Nuba Mountains, the Blue Nile and Darfur. By the time South Sudan gained independence from Sudan on 9 July 2011, almost two million people had died as a result of war, famine and disease over the twenty-two years of conflict, and four million people in southern Sudan had been displaced at least once (and many repeatedly) in the course of the war.

Against this background, this chapter focuses on the experience of female refugees from Ethiopia and the Sudan, focusing on their own narratives of displacement, self-loss and self-reinvention. The analysis is based on filmed field research conducted by the author in Egypt and Sudan from 2000 to 2006, first of all, two ethnographic documentaries: (1) *Four and a Half* (2006) and (2) *Nomads and Pharaohs* (2005).[1] In an approach based on Bergson and Deleuze and Guattari, the emotional dimension of hardship in exile is explored. Following Bergson's analysis of time duration as non-rational and highly impacted by emotions, and the rhizome model developed by Deleuze and Guattari as a heuristic tool embracing time and space, I tease out the implications of exile for gender roles and gender identity. My account documents the emergence of a feeling of *strangeness to oneself* ('étrangeté à soi'), time negation, self-rejection, self-incongruity and self-disregard among Ethiopian women refugees in Sudan, and compares these with the motifs of self-respect, self-reinvention and new gender roles in the context of Ethiopian and Sudanese women's lives in Egypt. Building on refugee narratives, this chapter thus examines the gender roles and gender reorientations imposed on/taken up by women refugees in their host countries and places of refuge.

Theoretical framework

The analytical methodology for this research was inspired by two major French philosophers who published important studies related to time and space. Bergson (1859–1941) first introduced his notion of duration in his doctoral thesis *Time and Free Will: An Essay on the Immediate Data of Consciousness* ([1889] 1910), in which he assumed that time perception is essentially related to a multiplicity of conscious states. The sense of duration is impacted by experiences of many kinds, including efforts, passions, stress and pain. Regarding these states of consciousness, Bergson stresses that

> it is usually admitted that states of consciousness, sensations, feelings, passions, efforts, are capable of growth and diminution; we are even told that a sensation can be said to be twice, thrice, four times as intense as another sensation of the same kind.
>
> (Bergson 1910: 1)

This is important for our understanding of time since emotional intensity, as evoked by Bergson, can alter, duplicate, develop or negate the sensation of duration. The perception of time is an aspect of the human being's inner life, and is neither a unity nor a quantitative multiplicity: duration is heterogeneous, so that its parts cannot be juxtaposed as a succession of different segments. In his view, duration is ineffable and can only be represented indirectly through multiple images that never reveal a complete picture.

Bergson's concepts of duration and multiplicity were later taken up by Deleuze (1925–95) and Guattari (1930–92), who build on similar foundations but go further in the direction of erasing the distinction between space and time. Their concept of rhizome effectively merges these two categories: any point of a rhizome can be connected to any other, while the notion that causality can be traced along chronological lines is rejected, as are binary choices and the hierarchical conception of knowledge (Deleuze and Guttari ([1980] 1987), see also Heynders, this volume). Deleuze and Guattari's notion thus posits a blurring of the distinction between space and time: as Deleuze and Guattari put it, the social world is structurally constructed on a horizontal interconnected level rather than a pyramidal one.

In the present context, the zone where my field research was carried out in Cairo and Khartoum could be considered a perfect image of the rhizome in a Deleuzian perspective. Arbaʿa wa Nuss, a neighbourhood in the outskirts of Cairo with predominantly marginalized refugee and migrant population, was organized as an underground space unreadable for the authorities. The horizontal structure was thus a counter-structure which allowed alternative, illicit realities to flourish. Here, time was constructed by the refugees on exiled ethnic territories in coherence with their gender identities and economic or cultural contexts, with multiple 'space-times' in operation at any given moment.

Let us examine this concept in more detail. In physics, *space* and *time* are associated with any mathematical model which fuses the three dimensions of space and the one dimension of time into a single four-dimensional phenomenon. For science, time is the same whatever the social and economic contexts are. By contrast, as we have seen, Bergson understood the human inner life as a kind of duration that is ineffable, which can only be represented indirectly, and which can only be grasped through the imagination. Time duration is thus dependent on emotional and subjective dimensions. Time during vacation is slightly different from time at work, as all of us might have experienced. The Deleuzian concept of the rhizome will be used here as a heuristic conceptual tool to explain the multiple links and interpenetration of *time* and *space* which intertwine to form an imbricative fabric, a rhizome, which we will use as a heuristic notion to describe this entanglement. In this chapter I posit that time in exile denotes a specific duration related to the living space of refuge. The intersection of the three elements is, in essence, conditioned by the emotional state of the forced migrants. Exiled communities experience the impact of time on an emotional level. In diverse geographical spaces, refugees feel that they are 'out of time' in their refugee context, as well as 'out of space'.

This chapter explores women's subjectivities related to space-time in the context of exile, look at how female refugees concentrate on special activities leading to time disorientation or time 'collapsing' or, at the opposite end of the spectrum, develop an acute conscious of time. My account relates different video experiences of fieldwork with women refugees in Sudan and Egypt to uncover spatial and temporal aspects of their exile from a gendered perspective. This field research among refugees in Sudan and Egypt made me reconsider the hypothesis that time's duration is constructed and 'felt' differently by men and women. My use of the notion of 'feeling' is intended here as a specific means of characterizing the subjective appreciation of duration. On the basis of these narratives from Africa and the Middle East, I examine the (possibly) universal paradigm of specific exiled durations and explore the sociocultural and gendered dimension of time in exile.

Field studies

Ethiopian narratives in exile in Sudan: Female disorientation and time negation

Narratives by Ethiopian refugees in a Muslim country such as Sudan drew on their own national historical references in their new Sudanese reality, referring to their national calendar to celebrate Ethiopian holidays on the periphery of Sudanese society's calendar and timetable. They listened to Ethiopian radio, and music, following a calendar and timetable that was disconnected from the Sudanese culture around them. When I was conducting a research programme in Khartoum in 2004, I found that women were unable to name the current Sudanese president and still mentioned their Ethiopian dictator Manguestu who had been overthrown long before (2004a, 2006a). This was a clear case of time negation in exile. However, Ethiopian women did show the capacity to adjust to the local employment market and become breadwinners for their families, reinventing their daily schedule according to new economic responsibilities, leading to what I have called a 'gender revolution in exile'.

During my field research among Ethiopian women refugees in Sudan, I realized how pertinent Bergson's hypothesis on time sensation being emotional was. In Gédaref province in Sudan I interviewed women who admitted that they were no longer concerned by time and who defined time as 'a man's interest'. They refused to listen to the news on the radio and voluntarily ignored everything that was politically related to their country's situation. They asserted that they wished to feed their children and were not concerned with anything unrelated to their survival strategies, to the point that they were ignoring the date and the year, and demonstrated a clear time negation. It seems that they were refusing to look at their past, and to remember the loss of their homes and families in their country of origin, and felt the need only to live the present moment. Most of the interviews took place during Omar Al-Bashir's presidency in Sudan, which was particularly rigorous regarding the imposition of the *Sharia* law, especially towards women and female refugees who did not belong to the Muslim faith. The Ethiopian women I interviewed were refugees and street tea sellers, who were at the bottom of the economic ladder of refugee occupations (Figure 3.1). In Sudan this kind of work made them the object of disrespect, denigration, mockery, contempt

Figure 3.1 Time negation: street tea sellers. Wadi Halfa, Sudan, 2006. Photo credit: Fabienne Le Houérou.

and sometimes odium. As street sellers, they conducted their daily activities on the pavements of Sudanese cities (as well as in refugee camps) and were often exposed to dangerous situations of sexual harassment. They lived on the margins and presented various signs of continuous fear in the context of ordinary street violence. The police were continuously arresting them or asking for *baksheesh* at the end of a working day.

This day-to-day aggressive context was associated with a clear denial of time, linked to a negation of their femininity. The Ethiopian refugee women used to wear Sudanese clothes, and to hide their faces with the traditional *thob*[2] (7 metre saree-like cloth), in a refusal to be elegant, to wear make-up or to expose anything that could be read as a sign of femininity, while feminine aspects like hairstyles were feared as a possible trigger for street harassment. Refusing to show any fashion sophistication was a survival strategy in order to be left 'in peace', to be left alone and escape any kind of street intimidation, social pressure or annoyance associated with their status as women refugees without any family protection. This is reminiscent of Hassan's (2020) findings concerning the role of the burqa in Pashtun society, pointing to an overwhelming need to avoid the male gaze. In a paternalist society the absence of male protection often leads to abuse, and a woman in exile in such situations is exceedingly vulnerable. During my fieldwork, I witnessed the humble status and absolute domination to which widows, unmarried women or divorced women were subjected in refugee camps, and clearly, all women were in an inferior position to men. Their survival strategy was to focus on the task they had to do, that is, to prepare tea and train themselves to escape the male gaze. To avoid any attractiveness, they chose to be invisible and do everything that could be done to be ignored. In that sense, any form of seduction or glamour was avoided. One of my informants in Sudan applied old frying oil as hydrating beauty cream. At the end of the day, she would gather the rest of the oil she had employed to prepare donuts to hydrate her legs. She applied oil on her legs and feet, and would also give herself a self-massage sitting on the pavement in the public view, causing a kind of disgust among the people passing by. One of my informants was still so strikingly beautiful that she was still attracting men in the streets who were drinking tea – they would sit around her for hours on any pretext, drinking tea, *karkade*[3] or coffee. Her strategy to avoid annoyance was to show humility, shyness and hide herself under many veils.

In Khartoum (Le Houérou 2004a, b; 2005a, b and c), sometimes the police would round women refugees up for no reason and put them in jail for *indecent behaviour*. Most of these women would make no projection for the future and expressed no remembrance of the past, focusing only on the present. The task of living and surviving through one particular moment was absorbing all their energy. I used to sit for hours saying nothing and filming. This act of filming for hours provided a window of observations on all social interactions. It seemed that in these women the fear of the present was blocking any future project. As many researchers have highlighted, in different academic studies, a *project* is a key notion that might position the migrants on an upcoming agenda (Polyzos 2017; Ma Mung 1999, 2000, 2009). Conversely, having no 'project' and taking refuge in time negation are characteristic in situations of great fear and hardship (see Breeze and Gintsburg, this volume). Here, this denial of time was also connected with the Sudanese political situation, and with the vulnerable situation of being an exiled woman and a human being devastated by fears. Fears of being raped or fears of being insulted, denigrated or humiliated were clearly associated with this. In one of my previous publications, I discuss this loss of time and the loss of Ethiopian and Eritrean history among Ethiopian and Eritrean refugees (Le Houérou 2006c). For this research, I used a questionnaire with 250 refugees in the urban neighbourhoods of Khartoum, Sudan, in 2001 and 2002, asking them about aspects related to conceptions of time and cultural events. I included questions on key historical events related to Ethiopian history, such as the battle of Adwa (1896), which is considered a significant historical marker in the Ethiopian highlanders' vision of history. The refugees we interviewed expressed interest in these topics and often considered it dignifying to be dealing with questions from their, that is, Ethiopian, history, rather than being consumed by immediate health and material needs (Le Houérou 2006c).

However, their responses on these questions also brought gendered differences to light. Most men responded with an acute consciousness of the cultural meaning of Adwa, whereas most women had forgotten the battle. The perception of historical time was thus conditioned by gender, as well as social and economic status. Being at the bottom of the economic and social ladder, women tea sellers seemed not to need to preserve historical memory and regarded such aspects as unimportant. Such representations of time are inspired by the group and thus remain collective (Halbwachs 1997), but different groups within society may invest them with different emotions and ultimately accord them different levels of importance.

In fact, my conclusion regarding the enquiry-driven question about 'time and exile' among Ethiopians and Eritreans in Sudan was that there is no universality among them surrounding the representation of time. Religious holidays are important social constructs given the prevalent conceptions of time. The Christian Ethiopians refugees' representation of time was based on Christian feasts. Whenever I made an appointment with refugees in Sudan, it was invariably in relation to the Sunday mass. There was a weekly rhythm and a linear perception of time, and even for the women tea sellers, the church remained a strong reference and benchmark. The historical conscious had more or less evaporated among these women, but they expressed their Ethiopianness and culture by respecting a precise Christian agenda and keeping their original Ethiopian cooking and social coffee traditions. These observations in Khartoum reflect the inner heuristic qualities of Bergson's theory that a particular shock (fears or traumatic events) may result in a *pathology of memory* (Bergson 1988). If we look at the relationship between trauma and memory and collective histories in Bergsonian terms (1988), we see that often at the origin of a forced migration event is a drama (individual or collective) that has effectively pushed people out of their countries of origin. Such a 'push factor' has a heavy psychological impact. While the representation of time and history admittedly will vary according to gender or social belonging, suffering abnormal pain (such as rape) has a noticeable effect on the process of loss or preservation of memory. Women refugees in Sudan focused their attention almost exclusively on the everyday effort of living the present time and were forgetting about the past. The strategy adopted by the most vulnerable portion of the refugee population (female head of household) was to take refuge in the void, the emptiness of time: time was a blank and each day was the first and last day. Remembering the lost country was perceived as a man's luxury when one had to face the daily burden of feeding a family unit.

Ethiopian narratives in exile in Egypt: Gender roles, time reinvention and temporal projection

Following the same project I extended my enquiry-driven research in Cairo among the Ethiopian and Eritrean refugees during the years 2001–4 with questionnaires distributed to 161 male and female refugees (Le Houérou 2006c). Most of these refugees had arrived in Cairo through Sudan and considered the stop in Cairo as a short interlude before further migrations to the West. Based on my interviews, 99 per cent of the refugees desired to leave Egypt. A research project supervised by Barbara Harrel-Bond at the Department of Forced Migrations and Refugee Studies (2003) concluded that there was a clear correlation between the permanence of movement and a life lived in a state of continuous fear. The impact of this fear has multiple consequences related to time perception and psychological damage. Most of the interviews were with Eritrean deserters who had escaped military service in Eritrea, and with young women employed as servants in wealthy Egyptian families in the richest neighbourhoods of Cairo. Pathology of memory and time negation here followed an opposite gendered pattern to that observed in Sudan. Men were more likely to be in a state of limbo and mental shock due to the sufferings endured during their Eritrean national service, while women, in contrast, revealed themselves as the *breadwinners* of the community. The young women of the communities shared apartments with the young deserters and were more active and integrated in the Egyptian working market. Most of the men were jobless and dependent on the women's economic activities, producing what I have characterized as a *gender revolution* (Le Houérou 2006c). Being integrated into the Egyptian labour market brought the women into close contact with the Egyptian reality, as they struggled for themselves to earn a living, while many of the young men suffered from post-traumatic stress disorders (PTSD) after the horrors they had faced in the Eritrean army and the flight out of Eritrea (Le Houérou 2020). Women provided the necessary links between their male partners and Egyptian society. The men expressed extreme pain and suffering, and many of them would narrate the negative effect of being lethargic. Sitting all day in front of the television, they expressed no desire to get out of their apartments. For their survival, they relied on their partners or female relatives, who were paying the rent, buying the food and meeting the medical expenses of everyday life. They spoke about their sense of humiliation at being 'dominated' by women economically and submitted to their charity in terms of *shame,* and used the term *revolution* to describe what had happened to them in Cairo. In that respect, the men were isolated and showed inward-looking attitudes. They seemed like prisoners: prisoners of themselves and prisoners of the fears related to their traumatic experiences in Eritrea during national service. They did not know the date, the time, or the month, and were in a situation of time distortion arising from a state of depression. Most psychologists would describe this state as showing PTSD symptoms, when the patient is lost in a disruptive representation of reality. Participatory observation confirmed the phenomenon of time distortion among these men (Le Houérou 2004c).

By contrast, the women were in touch with reality and were capable of projecting their lives in the future. Most of the young women were putting money aside with a project to finance a business when they returned to their home country. The women I interviewed mostly wanted to buy cars or buses in order to set up a transport company in the cities where they once belonged. As many scholars have observed (Erel, Reynolds and Kaptani 2018; Hack-Polay et al. 2021),[4] the creativity related to building a project introduces a positive energy, offering the migrant a dynamic time representation that transmits a vision of the future. By contrast, the young men retreated into themselves and would never express such temporal future projections. They were living the *instant* in a painful sense of eternity and were unable to create a project that would push them into the *hereafter* and *upcoming* moment.

In contrast, due to their work in opulent Egyptian families, the women were very careful about their appearance and were eager to choose elegant fashionable clothes. Being integrated through participation in the workforce was also placing them in a social role that was not available to the young men. I understood their coquetry as a sign of social alignment and assimilation. Going to the hairdresser or showing their henna tattoos as a feminine symbol was emblematic of their African feminist identity and constituted a clear symbol of the attention given to their appearance. This social representation of self (Goffman 1959) is far from being anecdotal or superficial – it shows the deep relationship of the self in the socio-space and space-time according to one's state of consciousness. The social impact of coquetry in the female migrant diaspora (Reddy 2016), like the hairstyle in African communities, is a social phenomenon in Migration Studies that has been explored since the 1970s. Beauty salons and the Afro-specific aesthetic market (Nutell 2007) are a significant social marker of the will to express cultural gender pride: a black beauty pride playing a positive role in their adaptation in the Egyptian labour market (Figure 3.2). Their foreignness as migrants from Abyssinia did not mean that they wanted to neglect their appearance – on the contrary, I witnessed, as a researcher, a sort of competition among the Abyssinian *nannies* to be as 'presentable' as possible. It was also perhaps because they were paying so much attention to their appearance that the wealthy Egyptian families declared a preferential taste for Ethiopian nannies, who were paid in dollars, unlike other nationalities who were paid in the local currency. It was frankly argued by one Egyptian informant that they appreciated the fact that the Ethiopian nursemaids were educated, knew how to write, were polite and more than clean, elegant and took care of themselves because this meant that they were adapted to take care of the Egyptian children. Formal physical appearance and salaries were thus interrelated.

Here, again, I would like to mention and underscore the connection between trauma and time representation and the issue of suffering as a major hindrance for temporal projection. As stated by Bergson, a *pathology of memory* (1939) is directly linked to painful experiences and puts the migrant in a situation of paralysis. This intellectual paralysis is connected to depression and may well lead to the negation of time.

Figure 3.2 Time and self-consciousness: Afro Beauty Salon, Cairo, 2004. Photo credit: Fabienne Le Houérou.

Sudanese narratives in exile in Egypt: Time negation

The same fieldwork project on the East African diasporas in Cairo in 2000–5 also led to some enquiry-driven research in Arbaʿa wa Nuss (*Four and a Half*), a Cairo suburban territory inhabited by Sudanese migrants (Le Houérou 2006b, c; 2008), as well as marginalized groups of Egyptian migrant population, predominantly from Upper Egypt. This research gave rise to the paper titled 'In that split second: reconstruction of self and invention of new professions by Darfour refugee women who live in Cairo' which I published in 2008 and the above-mentioned ethnographic film I produced in 2014 – *Four and a Half*. These different approaches to the topic (scientific, novelistic and cinematographic) illustrate the rhizome model of Deleuze and Guattari (1987): a single theme produces a variety of cultural products associating scientific knowledge with a fictional text and images in order to compose different variations around a unique subject.

The different results regarding our research in Arbaʿa wa Nuss highlight the great diversity of refugees' situations in terms of space. The Sudanese ethnic group presented original aspects related to the conscious of time. Time perception was distorted in comparison with the rest of the capital because the district where they lived was very far from the centre of Cairo and had its own rules conditioned by multiple marginality. Geographical, economic and ethnic marginalities compounded each other, and added together produced a singular territory with its own rules. The police did not enter the district and the government was almost absent, giving this place a feeling of being *out of time*, *out of Egypt* in a wild and chaotic space organized by community leaders and religious leaders.

The urban zone of Arbaʿa wa Nuss was a clear instantiation of a rhizome model of spatial organization. This neighbourhood was created by the Sudanese refugees and Southern Egyptians displaced in a chaotic illegal settlement (Figure 3.3). The Egyptian police was unaware of most unlawful activity in the district, while refugee networks were building up parallel authorities controlling the space. The territory of Arbaʿa wa Nuss had the morphology of a labyrinth criss-crossed by underground connections that was totally incomprehensible for a non-initiated observer. It thus constituted a classic example of the 'rabbit hole' structure posited by Deleuze and Guattari, with its horizontal underground structure and multiplicity of entries (Deleuze and Guattari 1987).

The situation of the South Sudanese refugees in Arbaʿa wa Nuss was completely different from the Abyssinian refugees' reality in Cairo. The low sociological and educational background of the South Sudanese refugees did not give them opportunities comparable to the Ethiopians. Sudanese refugees were employed as servants at a lower level and refunded in local money, and they suffered from disregard, scornful attitudes, discrimination and racism. Their 'primitivism' and rough nature were arguments mentioned by the wealthy Egyptian society to explain why they disliked engaging Sudanese women to take care of their children (we may compare their satisfaction with the 'superior' Ethiopian female servants). These refugees were employed as rough

Figure 3.3 Arbaʿa wa Nuss, a neighbourhood in Cairo which can be considered as a model of rhizome, a horizontal organization of time and space from the documentary film *Quatre et demi* (2012). Photo credit: Fabienne Le Houérou.

cleaners for heavy housework. In consequence they did not adopt the social strategy of presenting themselves with aesthetic care and concern. The primary need for food was – as for the Ethiopians in the Sudan – the main priority in their lives. Hairstyles were a luxurious waste. Moreover, their income was not at all comparable. While the Ethiopians in Cairo lived in relatively decent housing conditions, the South Sudanese conditions in Arbaʿa wa Nuss presented all the signs of extreme poverty. No drinking water was available, and electricity had not been installed. The district was regarded by the citizens of Cairo as one of the most dangerous areas of the capital and one of the poorest. In this perspective time/space/labour can be seen to be interrelated to impact on self-consciousness and gendered self-awareness. Extreme poverty and absence of insertion in the labour market thus also emerge as important factors related to time negation.[5]

Conclusion: Comparative exiles and a universal paradigm?

If we compare the different exiles in various geographical areas we will observe a common theme of time/space/labour interconnectedness. The Ethiopian women in Sudan showed no interest in aspects unrelated to their survival strategies, to the extent that they ignored the date and the year, demonstrating a clear time negation. Similar phenomena related to timelessness were noted with the traumatized young Ethiopian men in Cairo who experienced a state of time distortion, and the Sudanese at Arbaʿa wa Nuss, whose lives were out of synchronization with the Egyptian calendar.

Even though the Indian space here is out of the geographical scope of this publication, it is interesting to mention that in India very similar cultural aspects of duration have been observed in the Tibetan diaspora in the neighbourhood Majnu Ka Tilla (New Delhi), where Tibetan vacations, holidays and religious festivities are observed in the Indian context (Le Houérou 2018, 2019). Here, women also endorse new roles, have a new status and live according to mixed Indo-Tibetan rules. The diaspora also manages to impose their own holidays inside their geographical enclave in New Delhi so that the Indian shopkeepers are obliged to close their businesses during Buddhist holidays even if they are not believers when the community leaders request this (Le Houérou 2019). Being settled or living in a diasporic organization in rural or city surroundings are parameters that clearly influence the temporal agenda and the experience of time in many different contexts.

However, as stressed in the introduction, the poorest places where the refugees live are more likely to show evidence of a *time negation* pattern, whatever region of the world we are observing (Africa, the Middle East, Asia). In different geographical situations I observed that refugees experiencing extreme poverty are more prone to refuse temporal projections. The everyday struggle for elementary needs such as food and shelter has devastating consequences for people's mental dynamics and projections. The Sudanese refugees in Egypt whom I observed at Arbaʿa wa Nuss understood the organization of the year and seasons in a way that was very different from the calendar of the country where they were living, presenting a rhizome-like structural organization of space/time (Le Houérou 2008). By contrast, in the centre of the Egyptian capital, the wealthier and more successful Ethiopian and Eritrean women adjusted to the local employment market and became breadwinners for their families, reinventing their agenda according to their new economic responsibilities, leading to what I have called a *gender revolution in exile*. Of course, there are numerous elements of variation that place the migrants at the crossroads of myriad parameters. Gender, educational background, racial prejudice in the host country (*prejugés*), the *status ante* of the migrant, his/her health and his/her economic position, the geographical space of exile and the local labour market are all elements that, when combined, impact strongly on time representation. The emotional state of the migrant him/herself and the traumatic events prior to the migration have quite an important influence on time representation. It is also relevant that it is perhaps not meaningful to attempt to build a hierarchy that organizes these parameters systematically since they follow a multiple, heterogeneous pattern. As Deleuze and Guattari posit, to understand such phenomena there is no pivot or unity:

> Principle of multiplicity: it is only when the multiple is effectively treated as a substantive, 'multiplicity', that it ceases to have any relation to the One as subject or object, natural or spiritual reality, image and world. Multiplicities are rhizomatic, and expose arborescent pseudo-multiplicities for what they are. There is no unity to serve as a pivot in the object, or to divide in the subject. (…) A multiplicity has neither subject nor object, only determinations, magnitudes, and dimensions that cannot increase in number without the multiplicity changing in nature (the laws of combination therefore increase in number as the multiplicity grows).
> (Deleuze and Guattari [1980] 1987: 8)

The multiplicity of refugees' situations is an objective observable fact that should always be borne in mind. For example, refugee camps offer a model that is very different from that found with urban refugees: the space of the camp is a total space, in the sense analysed by Goffman when describing total institutions in *Asylum* (Goffman 1968). It is fully organized, with its own rules in a given space, defined by frontiers and forming *un monde à part*. In camps, refugees are completely dependent on international aid, and this dependency also has a dire influence on the refugees' representation of time (Le Houérou 2004a, b, c). In her book *Imposing Aid* (1986), Harrel-Bond long ago demonstrated that too much dependency on the international community can be counterproductive and have terrible consequences for the refugees, changing them into lethargic subjects incapable of being self-sufficient. Being institutionalized in this way can detach refugees from economic reality and from the perception of time, while being well integrated in the labour market is a universal element that integrates the subject into social reality. The ineffable nature of this reality, however, could also be seen in terms of the rhizome model, as described by Deleuze and Guattari in their essay *Mille plateaux* (1980).[6]

> A rhizome has no beginning or end; it is always in the middle, between things, interbeing, intermezzo. The tree is filiation, but the rhizome is alliance, uniquely alliance. The tree imposes the verb 'to be', but the fabric of the rhizome is the conjunction, 'and… and… and…' This conjunction carries enough force to

shake and uproot the verb 'to be'. Where are you going? Where are you coming from? What are you heading for? These are totally useless questions. Making a clean slate, starting or beginning again from ground zero, seeking a beginning or a foundation – all imply a false conception of voyage and movement.

(Deleuze and Guattari [1980] 1987: 25)

In this Deleuzian perspective, exile is linked with space and time, but with no measurable interconnectedness. It would be impossible to generalize a unique representation of time and space in exile. They are as many 'time-feelings' as there are humans or displaced humans, in different geographical zones, and the *pathology of memory* (Bergson) depends largely on rhizomatic elements. However, as we have seen, careful examination of the imbrications of time and space in specific settings can bring out underlying patterns that shape the way time and space are experienced in a given community, and in particular, enable us to glimpse the emotional dimension and gendered nature of these phenomena.

Notes

1 Both documentaries are available on YouTube. *Four and a Half* (in French): https://www.youtube.com/watch?v=ETF9T_5QcAM. *Nomads and Pharaohs* (in English): https://www.youtube.com/watch?v=m8yNaYDTYgM&t=9s.
2 *thob* (Arabic *thawb*) – 'a piece of cloth' or 'garment', worn in the Arab world by both men and women. In Sudan *thob* is either a white or coloured sleeveless garment worn by women, which is perceived as a symbol of a Sudanese woman.
3 *karkade,* or also known in Egypt and Sudan as Sudanese rose, is a variety of hibiscus plants. Dried *karkade* flowers are used to make herbal tea, which is very popular in the region.
4 Also see the report of the UNHCR: https://www.unhcr.org/innovation/7-art-initiatives-that-are-transforming-the-lives-of-refugees/.
5 This is similar to the situation of the African community in Soqotra, who, despite having a long history of living on this island, continue to stay segregated from the autochthonous population. African Soqotris remain living compactly in particular neighbourhoods and do the lowest paid jobs (Gintsburg and Esposito, 2022).
6 This essay was published in English in 1987 under the title *A Thousand Plateaus: Capitalism and Schizophrenia.*

References

Bergson, H. ([1889] 1910), *Time and Free Will: An Essay on the Immediate Data of Consciousness*, trans. F. L. Pogson, M. A., London: George Allen and Unwin.
Bergson, H. ([1939] 1988), *Matter and Memory*, trans. N. M. Paul and W. S. Palmer, New York: Zone Books.
Deleuze, G. and F. Guattari (1987 [1980]), *A Thousand Plateaus: Capitalism and Schizophrenia*, trans. B. Massumi, Minneapolis: University of Minnesota Press.

Erel, U., T. Reynolds, and E. Kaptani (2018), 'Migrant Mothers' Creative Interventions into Racialized Citizenship', *Ethnic and Racial Studies*, 41 (1): 55–72.
Gintsburg, S. and E. Esposito (2022), 'The Asymmetric Linguistic Identities of African Soqotris: A Triadic Interaction', in F. Al Rashdi and S. Rao Mehta (eds), *Language and Identity in the Arab World*, xxx, New York: Routledge.
Goffman, E. (1959), *The Presentation of Self in Everyday Life*, New York: Doubleday Anchor.
Goffman, E. (1968), *Asylums: Essays on the Social Situation of Mental Patients and Other Inmates*, London: Penguin Books.
Hack-Polay, D., A. B. Mahmoud, A. Rydzik, M. Rahman, P. A. Igwe, and G. Bosworth (2021), *Migration Practice as Creative Practice: An Interdisciplinary Exploration of Migration*, Bingley: Emerald Group Publishing.
Halbwachs, M. (1997), *La mémoire collective* [The Collective Memory], Paris: Éditions Albin Michel.
Harrel-Bond, B. (1986), *Imposing Aid*, Oxford: Oxford University Press.
Hassan, S. (2020), 'The Representation of Afghan Refugees. Corpus-assisted and Qualitative Discourse Studies', PhD diss., University of Navarra.
Le Houérou, F. (2004a), *Passagers d'un monde à l'autre, migrants forcés éthiopiens et érythréens* [Passengers Travelling from One World to Another: Forced Ethiopian and Eritrean Migrants], Paris: L'Harmattan.
Le Houérou, F. (2004b), 'La caméra à la croisée des chemins' [Camera on the Crossroad], *Actes de l'Histoire des Migrations*, 4: 103–26.
Le Houérou, F. (2004c), 'Exile and Loss of History among Ethiopian Diaspora in Khartoum', *Kolor, Journal on Moving Communities*, 4 (1): 33–48.
Le Houérou, F. (2005a), 'Diaspora in Cairo: Transit Territories and the Transit Condition. An Introduction', *Kolor: Journal on Moving Communities*, 5 (1): 3–6.
Le Houérou, F. (2005b), 'Living with Your Neighbour. Forced Migrants and Their Hosts in an Informal Area of Cairo, Arba 'a Wa Nuss', *Kolor: Journal on Moving Communities*, 5 (1): 37–49.
Le Houérou, F. (2005c), 'A la rencontre des mondes: l'épopée des réfugiés du Darfour' [Getting to Know Other Worlds: the Épopée of Refugee Women from Darfour], *Maghreb-Machrek*, 185: 103–26.
Le Houérou, F. (2006a), 'Les territoires usurpés des ex-réfugiés érythréens dans le nord-est soudanais' [The Usurped Territories of Former Refugees from Eritrea in the North-East of Sudan], *Bulletin de l'Association de Géographes Français*, 83 (1): 63–75.
Le Houérou, F. (2006b), 'Le drame de la place Mustapha Mahmoud au Caire raconté par Barbara Harrell-Bond' [The Drama of the Cairene Square of Mustapha Mahmous] *Recueil Alexandries, Collections Reflets*. Available online: http://terra.rezo.net/article553.html (accessed 3 July 2021).
Le Houérou, F. (2006c), *Forced Migrants and Host Societies in Egypt and Sudan*, Cairo: American University in Cairo Press.
Le Houérou, F. (2008), 'Poussières d'instants: la reconstruction de soi et l'invention de nouveaux métiers des femmes réfugiées du Darfour au Caire. Femmes et migrations' [In That Split Second: Reconstruction of Self and Invention of New Professions by Darfour Refugee Women who Live in Cairo], *Mouvement social*, 225: 81–99.
Le Houérou, F. (2018), 'The Tibetan Ethnic Enclave in New Delhi. A Visual Perspective', *Sociology Mind*, 8: 203–20.
Le Houérou, F. (2019), *Behind the Bridge. The Tibetan Diaspora in India 1959–2017*, Münster: Lit Verlag.

Le Houérou, F. (2020), 'Le transit de l'horreur: exilés abyssins en Égypte (1992–2019)' [The Transit of Horror: Abyssinian Refugees in Egypt], *Migrations Sociétés*, 179: 177–90.

Ma Mung, E. (1999), *Autonomie, Migrations et Altérité* [Autonomy, Migration and Alterity], Poitiers: Université de Poitiers.

Ma Mung, E. (2000), *La diaspora chinoise. Géographie d'une migration* [The Chinese Diaspora: A Geography of One Migration], Paris: Éditions Ophrys.

Ma Mung, E. (2009), 'Le point de vue de l'autonomie dans l'étude des migrations internationales: "penser de l'intérieur" les phénomènes de mobilité' [The Perspectives of the International Migrations Studies: The Mobility Phenomena – 'Thinking from Inside'], in F. Dureau and M.-A. Hily (eds), *Les mondes de la mobilité* [The Worlds of Mobility], 25–38, Rennes: Presses universitaires de Rennes.

Nutell, S. (2007), *Beautiful/Ugly: African and Diaspora Aesthetics*, Durham, NC: Duke University Press Book.

Parater, L. (2015), '7 Art Initiatives That Are Transforming the Lives of Refugees', UNHCR. Available online: https://www.unhcr.org/innovation/7-art-initiatives-that-are-transforming-the-lives-of-refugees/ (accessed 13 July 2021).

Polyzos, I. (2017), 'Autonomie et projet migratoire' [Autonomy and the Migration Project], *E-Migrinter*, 15. Available online: https://journals.openedition.org/e-migrinter/822 (accessed 13 July 2021).

Reddy, V. (2016), *Fashioning Diaspora: Beauty, Femininity, and South Asian American Culture*, Philadelphia: Temple University Press.

Discussion questions

1. French philosopher Bergson insisted on the importance of differentiating between time and space. What was his main argument?
2. How does the notion of rhizome developed by Deleuze Guattari define the relationship between time and space?
3. How can the life of protagonists of *Arba'a wa Nuss* be analysed through the notion of the rhizome?
4. How did Christian Ethiopian refugee women in predominantly Islamic Sudan survive using the strategy of time negation and how was this different from the case of the Christian Ethiopian women in Cairo?
5. How can the notion of rhizome be instrumental in gaining a better understanding of refugees' spatio/temporal life organization?

4

Und wir sind weggelaufen: Borders and Walls in Narratives of Forced Displacement– A Study with Middle Eastern Refugees' Visual Narratives in the German as a Second Language (DaZ) Classroom

Silvia Melo-Pfeifer

Introduction

The study of the integration of young refugees[1] has gained increasing attention, especially with regard to the role of educational institutions and the related acquisition of the host country's language. In Europe the growing number of refugees, as well as the different national responses, justify this rising interest since the migration phenomenon induces demographic changes, in general, and linguistic and educational changes, in particular. In Germany, the significant rise in the number of refugees in 2015 and 2016 led to diverse responses from the government. In relation to so-called refugee students, it must be recognized, as Hek states, that they 'are not a homogenous group, and have a range of different needs, experiences and expectations' (2005: 158). In this sense, as Taylor and Sidhu point out, migrants should not simply be merged with other migrants 'because of the forced departure from their home land' (2012: 42). Furthermore, despite the common factor of forced displacement, refugees might have lived border crossing very differently, and this might become a distinctive sign of the 'micro narratives' they might have and want to tell.

The aims of this study are twofold: first, I aim to analyse how refugee students enrolled in German as a second language (DaZ) visually represent borders and walls, both in their homelands and in Germany; second, I intend to reconstruct the negotiation of meaning of borders and walls in classroom interaction and their relationship to their narratives of forced displacement and resettlement, namely in terms of representations of times and spaces. To achieve these goals, I will engage in a theoretical discussion of the role of borders and walls in the narratives of migrants and refugees, as these elements are both physical and metaphorical expressions of transition, of crossing, of becoming and, at the same time, of leaving behind or moving ahead. So borders can be oriented towards the past, the present and the future. This chronology will orient the presentation of the empirical data.

Borders and walls: Non-spaces in the narrative construction of migrants and refugees

The concept of borders and walls requires a multidisciplinary approach since it is commonly associated with politics and the definition of geopolitical boundaries and national identities (Nail 2017). To define a border that fits with the themes of migration and forced displacement like those that frame this chapter, I decided to choose the definition of border by Anzaldúa (2007), as borders can be understood both metaphorically and in their materiality, being a metaphor for all types of crossing. Following this author, known for her emotional reconstruction and theorization of borderlands, 'borders are set up to define places that are safe and unsafe, to distinguish *us* from *them*. A border is a dividing line, a narrow strip along a steep edge' (Anzaldúa 2007: 25). Borders can therefore be understood as a liminal space where separation occurs and a non-space of transition, where 'becoming' can occur, which is not really connected to 'being' in that place. As a non-space, people can stay anonymous (Augé 1992). The border is a space characterized by its traversing, thus not connected to identity, time or space, but rather to what comes next, after the transition. It is a non-space because it is essentially the 'transit' from both sides (idem). So, the border should not be amalgamated to 'borderlands', places important because of their hybridity and the perspectives they open up to their residents (Anzaldúa 2007). 'Borderland' refers to living between countries, languages, cultures, spiritualties, sexualities. The borderland is 'a constant state of transition' (Anzaldúa 2007: 25). Crossing the border, in contrast, is a moment of transition, of trespassing and symbolic transgression, a time-place that may have no return, and is rather conceived as either one side or the other of the border. For this reason, the concept of border cannot be limited to the mainstream idea of demarcation of geographical nation states and cannot be apprehended statically (Nail 2016).

Following from Lefebvre (1992), (social) spaces are created through demarcation and the establishment of boundaries that lead to 'named places' (Lefebre 1991: 193). In the scope of this chapter, two particular places are important: (1) 'Boundaries and forbidden territories – spaces to which access is prohibited either relatively (neighbours and friends) or absolutely (neighbours and enemies)' (Lefebre 1991); and (2) 'Places of abode, whether permanent or temporary' (Lefebre 1991). These categories are important as 'forbidden territories', in the case of forced displacement, which can be both the territories of departure and the territories of arrival, as well as all in-between 'places of abode' during the journey from one to another.

Being a migrant or a refugee implies that someone has left their country or region of origin and crossed borders – by air, earth or water – to other countries. From this perspective, crossing borders might be seen as a moment of transition, the moment when one ceases to be in one place and enters another one, thus being directly connected to lived experiences (Gintsburg 2019), to embodiment and replacement. Borders are sometimes materialized through walls (these being merely terrestrial), making them more difficult to cross, making communication and contacts between both sides of the border harder. Walls might be seen as having a protective function for those situated within them, as a protection from the enemy, as in the walls protecting some fortified cities in medieval times. Walls might also be signs of divisive ideologies and separation of states, and be lived as a privation of freedom, such as in the case of citizens that escaped the limitations imposed by the Berlin Wall.

In the field of narrative analysis, De Fina explains that the border is a 'highly symbolic space in the retelling of immigration experiences' that is 'always presented as an imaginary line which exists in order to be crossed' (2003a: 380). Borders and walls are thus constitutive of the imaginary of escaping, overcoming boundaries and reaching out to new countries and destinations. They are constitutive of narratives of life-changing events: 'The migration process itself depends, in their case, on the successful crossing of the border. On the other hand, crossing the border represents the first immigration experience' (De Fina 2003b: 10). Crossing the border is seen as an element of paramount important in the migrants' journey: they tell researchers the experience even in cases when they are not asked to. This saliency of the border in the emigrant and refugee journey opens up the structuration of individual narratives in terms of both time and space: there is a before and after the border crossing; there is a here and there, referring to places left and newly inhabited places. The characters, another element in the narrative, also change: the people move from one side and from the other side of the border, opening new spaces for socialization and, therefore, for identity (re)construction (being able or not being able to cross the border). The same could be said about the plot: what happened before and after border crossing. Symbolically in terms of archetypal narrative construction, the border and the wall are the hurdles separating the protagonist from his/her dream or plan, the personal sacrifice (s)he has to go through to achieve acknowledgement and glory.

This chapter presents visual narratives of refugee students, told in the first person. As autobiographical narratives, they relate to individual stories whose 'importance is connected with the fact that in order to understand their own lives people put them into narrative form – and they do the same when they try to understand the lives of others' (Czarniawska 2004: 5). Because of the theme that was proposed to the participants in the study, reconstructing experiences and memories of borders and walls, the narrator is placed as the expert participant, being able to provide an accurate account of the factual events, embedded in emotions. As De Fina and Tseng put it, 'telling stories is a way of sharing and making sense of experiences in the recent or remote past, and of recounting important, emotional, or traumatic events and the minutiae of everyday life' (2017: 381). As stories can be told multimodally, we accept that these aspects might transfer to our corpus. Through these visual autobiographies, reconstructions of lived experiences or appropriation of told narratives, we aim at putting the authors at the centre of the stories they are called to tell, counterbalancing hegemonic discourses from a 'second-hand audience', that is, those who tend to build their representations and beliefs about border- and wall-crossing without either directly living it or witnessing it as first-hand audience. And indeed, according to the same authors, 'work on migrants has taken prominence precisely because a primary scholarly objective has been building knowledge about processes of displacement and relocation as lived by narrators and their stories' protagonists, thus offering a counterbalance to the often-negative views about marginalized social groups circulated through political discourse and the mainstream media' (De Fina and Tseng 2017: 382, also Smets et al. 2019).

In the available research (e.g. De Fina 2003a; Mezzadra and Neilson 2013; Nail 2017), scholars concur that borders and walls are constitutive of migrants' narratives. De Fina concedes that 'migration is connected discursively to being able to cross the border, in that talk about migrating immediately focuses on how the crossing took place' (2003a: 375, see also De Fina 2003b). Even if De Fina relates to the context of Mexican-American border crossing, it is clear that this life-changing event can be transposed to other contexts as well. Analysing how space/time connect in migrants' narratives, Baynham also acknowledges that 'the construction of space has been relatively intimate and small-scale, even in the contexts of dislocation and border crossing' (Baynham 2015: 131), meaning that, despite temporal and spatial distances, and the experience of dangerous and life-threatening 'border crossing', migrants' discourse on this transition in time and space is permeated by a sense of intimacy and a unique moment.

Methodological design

Context of data collection: German as a second language (DaZ) classroom

The empirical study was conducted in Hamburg in February 2018, in the scope of the international project *Amicae*, coordinated by l'Université du Maine (France), in February 2018 (Melo-Pfeifer and Wegnerski in press), following the idea that space is of paramount importance in many learning processes (see Benson 2021 for a recent account). As of December 2018, the distribution of refugees in this city was as follows: Afghanistan (749, corresponding to 15.7 per cent of the total), Syria (732, 15.3 per cent of the total), Iran (510, 10.7 per cent of the total), Iraq (378 or 7.9 per cent of the total) and Eritrea (187, 3.9 per cent). At the end of the same year, Hamburg had 305 unaccompanied minor refugees. As schooling for minors in Hamburg is compulsory upon registration (Daschner 2017: 18), Hamburg had 204 IVK classes – *Internationale Vorbereitungsklasse* (International Preparatory Class) – on 9 January 2019, with a total of 2,599 learners, this being the most common reception arrangement.

The IVK class researched in this study has eleven learners between sixteen and seventeen years old, both girls and boys, from Syria, Afghanistan, Iraq and Iran, preparing to join the mainstream classroom, in order to continue their studies and attain the *Schulabschluss*[2] diploma. So, despite the differences in terms of origins, they are all almost the same age and have the same purpose: to develop language skills to be able to continue their school path in Germany. Data were completely anonymized, because of two contextual issues: the first is that some students did not have their refugee status fully acknowledged; the second is that some of the students were unaccompanied minors, who could not themselves give their consent to have some of their personal information displayed for research purposes. In Table 4.1, I present some basic data, collected by the teacher, on the participants.

The religions represented were Christian, Muslim and Yezidi. In terms of German language skills, the students are at A2/B1 levels. J. Wegnerski, a master's student in Educational Sciences, a future teacher of English and Spanish as foreign languages for secondary school, was a volunteer teacher of DaZ (German as a second language) at

Table 4.1 Participants' data

Code	Gender	Age	Country of origin
S1	Female	17	Afghanistan
S2	Male	17	Syria
S3	Female	16	Iraq
S4	Female	17	Iraq
S5	Male	17	Afghanistan
S6	Female	16	Syria
S7	Female	17	Iraq
S8	Male	17	Iraq
S9	Male	17	Iraq
S10	Female	17	Afghanistan
S11	Male	17	Afghanistan

the school where the data was collected. She asked the head teacher to take a class to collect data for her master's thesis. The activities were planned for a special classroom unit designed to foster intercultural communicative competence (Wegnerski 2018).

With these assumptions in mind, Wegnerski developed a didactic project around the development of intercultural competence consisting of four course blocks, 8 hours in total. The aim of this teaching sequence was to reconstruct different representations of walls and borders in order to highlight the collective identities of the learners, while at the same time emphasizing their individuality and the individuality of their paths. The didactic method most used in the course was collaborative thinking-pairing-sharing (Lyman 1981), known for its potential for collaborative learning (positive interdependence between participants, sharing and co-construction of knowledge, etc.). The sessions were organized around two questions that guided the tasks and the collaborative work of the learners: (1) What are walls and borders? What functions do they serve? (2) Homeland versus Germany: different borders?

To answer the first question, the learners first produced drawings of walls and borders and presented them to the class. They then discussed them with the other students, engaging in processes of collaborative construction of representations of walls and borders and reflection on their personal and collective experiences with them. To answer the second question, they produced and presented posters as a group on the theme of walls or borders in their home countries and then discussed them with their peers. At the same time, they reflected on the protective and/or destructive value of walls and borders.

Data collection and analysis

Even though a range of materials was collected during the implementation of the project, we will focus, in the scope of this chapter, on the visual representations of borders and walls, understood as particular significant elements in the narratives of young refugees, and on the retelling of the content of the drawings. The visual material that will be the focus of this analysis was produced by the students and could be understood as memory snapshots, bits of narratives that are visually produced to prompt students' verbal reconstruction. In the context of this word, it is important to resort to visual narratives because the recalling of traumatic experiences is facilitated by non-verbal reconstruction and because students might not yet feel at ease enough with German to retell their stories. By using visual narratives as a source of data collection we could give students a multimodal voice (Melo-Pfeifer and Schmidt 2019) and make them actors within their own stories, which is not always the case when they have to use a second language, since this limits their narrative skills.

The analysis of the drawings includes a description of the elements present and their relationships (close to a multimodal analysis) as well as the learners' explanations. For the analysis of the interactions, I follow a content and discourse analysis of the selected extracts. Despite this quest for objectivity, it must be admitted that the contact with the data was not always easy, especially because of the emotional dimensions present in the material collected from the students who participated in our study. Table 4.2 presents a set of the data in order to explain the methodological paths followed in the empirical study.

In the first stage, I carried out a multimodal analysis of the drawings, describing the elements the student selected and how they are combined. In a second stage, I analysed the transmodal intertextuality in both modes of production (the drawn and

Table 4.2 A data set constituted by visual narrative and its verbal explanation (S5).

Visual narrative	Oral reconstruction
S5 *krieg* *reich* [drawing]	S5. I have represented protection. I painted a wall between two countries and in one country there is war and they are not rich and in one country there is no war and they are rich. And if there is no wall between these countries, then the criminals can go to other country. They are rich. They can also start war there.

the verbalized). Transmodal intertextuality refers to how different layers of meaning, depending on the mode, interact and are present or absent from one another. Drawing and telling are different modes with different 'narrative capitals' (Goodson 2015: 11). In the case of the methodological path followed in this chapter, the transition of modes and narratives simultaneously gains and loses meaning: the oral narrative that follows the drawn one can lead to reduction or expansion of drawn elements and information. Produced after the drawing, the written and oral narratives can be called 'explanation narratives' because they are based on a previous, visual one, this being the theme of the other. Nevertheless, they also acquire the status of narratives in the continuum of narratives being successively told, what could be called 'multimodal intertextuality'. Thus, 'they are not a mere verbal reconstitution and reconstruction of the visual narrative; in the same way, the visual narrative does not depend upon the written and oral narrative to be interpreted: the visual narrative is a multisemiotic ensemble with its own meaning' (Ferreira and Melo-Pfeifer 2017: 147, our translation).[3]

In order to structure the presentation and analysis of the corpus, I decided to crisscross the description of borders and walls with the temporality in which they are placed. This means that I will analyse the way students conceive of different borders, both material and immaterial, depending on three moments of their biographies:

1. *Before the forced displacement*: Under this category, I classified the borders and walls students identify in their lives before the displacement, which usually are presented by students as triggers for the need to leave or 'keep leaving'.
2. *During the forced displacement*: In this category I will focus on the borders and walls students perceived in their journey to Germany, meaning between the moment they left their countries, until they were received in Germany (which could be related to the temporary 'places of abode' referred to by Lefebvre 1991).
3. *In the resettlement situation*: In this category I have placed visual and discursive reconstructions that illustrate that borders and walls do not disappear on reaching a geographic goal, but rather convert into other forms of threat or protection. Borders in this category describe the present situation but are also oriented towards the future.

The classroom discourse was first recorded in German, transcribed in that language and afterwards translated into English. Syntactic features, common in DaZ interactions, which were deemed to impede the understanding of students' utterances in this chapter, were reviewed.

Data analysis

Perceptions of borders and walls before the forced displacement

In the task of drawing walls or borders, young refugees often depicted scenes of physical or symbolic violence, with physical walls having either a protective or threatening function. However, some also drew metaphorical walls with both contradictory functions. When it comes to borders/physical walls, students refer to personal experiences of fleeing and experiencing physical or symbolic violence:

> When I was in my country, there is, there was war. I fled to Germany and I saw many borders on the way and some were free for refugees and some were closed. And this was a wall for refugees.
>
> (S5)

As mentioned previously, borders and walls are not always physical. In the drawing in Figure 4.1, the student has depicted a family separation, in this case of two sisters. On both sides of the border (*Grenze* in German), the two sisters express their desire to be reunited – *Ich will zu meine Schwester gehen* (I want to go to my sister). The student also writes a definition of border: *Die Grenze für mich, ist zwischen meine Schwester und ich* (the border, for me, is between my sister and me). So, in this case, the border is represented as an obstacle, impeding family reunification.

In this drawing, placed in the story of what we could call micro-narratives (individual stories), the narrator represents, in a mirror effect, the two characters of the story, in a constraining situation: the sisters are placed on different sides of the border, looking at each other and saying exactly the same words. The desire for reunification is expressed by the sisters using the same semiotic resources: on both sides of the wall, there is a visual representation of the two sisters in two speech bubbles and the writing of *Ich will zu meine Schwester gehen* (I want to go to my sister). The same

Figure 4.1 A wall separating sisters (S6).

semiotic means are employed twice, a strategy of redundancy, that helps to convey the visual and oral message. In this representation, the border separates characters and discourses, and it acquires a predominant place in the drawing (being placed in the middle and represented with some details, like the wire), as this also helps to structure it in two clear definite parts. Also, importantly, to reflect time and space in this drawing we can see the present sadness of the children speaking (the sad face) and the reference to past situations of joyful contact (the sisters represented in the speech bubble are smiling). So, this drawing could be said to offer a simultaneous representation of past and present or, to be even more accurate, the co-representation of two past situations: being together (past 1) and crossing the border (past 2), both seen from the perspective of the present situation (being in Germany, in a DaZ classroom), which makes the case for juxtaposition of different orders of time (Baynham 2003) and spaces.

Situations of physical violence are depicted in Figures 4.2 and 4.3, the former showing a threatening (or protection-inhibiting) physical border and the latter a

Figure 4.2 The border between Iraq and Turkey (S7).

Figure 4.3 A protection wall (S1).

protective physical wall. Figure 4.2 shows a bombing, the death of a civilian and the destruction of houses.

The drawing illustrates the comparison between two named places, to recall Lefebvre's terminology (1992), one scene of peace (Turkey) and another of violence (Iraq), separated by a border, not referring particularly to an individual story, but rather to the depiction of a situation, which might also be called a generic narrative (and not a personal one as in the previous example). The contrast is visible in the representation of antithetical objects in both scenarios: life and death, the destroyed house and the undestroyed one. On the border, the student has written the following captions: 'safe country' and 'dangerous country'. Ironically, it seems that the narrator depicts one character only: the man with the happy face is the one dead at the border. The caption says: *dieser man ist in der Türkey, dann geht er in den Irak und in Irak is Krieg, dann ist er gestorben* (this man is in Turkey, then he goes to Iraq, in Iraq there is a war, then he dies). The history is articulated around three moments: being in security in Turkey, moving to Iraq and crossing the border and dying, articulating a sequence of events, in time and space. This highlights Baynham's thesis of space, together with time, as defining characteristic of narrative (2003: 364), rather than time alone. Even with few linguistic resources, the use of verbal modes *ist, geht, ist gestorben* and the temporal repetition *dann* (then) and spatial markers *in der Turkey* (in Turkey), *in den Irak* (in Iraq) make it clear that the narrative orientation is constructed around time and space.

In terms of the visual spatiality of the drawing, a prominent area in the drawing is given to the explosion of a bomb, which causes the death of the newcomer. Border crossing is thus here connected to the idea of danger, as in De Fina's (2003a and 2003b) and Zaripov's (this volume) accounts. This is made graphically very explicit as the dead body is represented superposed on the border. Interestingly, a first attempt at representing the dead man was made on the side of the Turkish border. It was erased, as the marks still let us seen, and replaced over the border.

As in Figure 4.1, the visual representation of the border also divides the drawing in two parts: situations of security and insecurity. It is also important to analyse the different frames of the drawings: in this drawing, as the audience, we are placed almost on the same plane as the characters. In Figure 4.2, we find a mixture of the same plane and what seems to be an aerial view of the border. The transcription of the oral explanatory sequence of this drawing maintains its 'declarative content' and adds little information to the drawing. The student begins by describing his drawing and justifying his choice of country, a country at war (Iraq) and a country at peace (Turkey).

S7: (…) What I drew is between two countries.
Teacher: A wall between two countries.
S7: Yes. In one city, for example, I chose Iraq and Turkey. In Turkey it is not dangerous. But there yes.
S6: Yes it is/Of course it is.
Teacher: well that's okay. She sees it in a different way from yours (X).
S7: There we have no fear. There is no war here. But in Iraq, when you go to Iraq, then there is war and whoever goes there dies.
Teacher: And you drew in relation to which question? Protection
S7: Protection
Teacher: Protection, okay
S7: In Turkey all the houses are still (inaud.)(…) S7: The houses and that in Turkey are, then, not destroyed, they are still good. But in Iraq they are all destroyed (…)

Figure 4.3 again depicts a scene of war, with the wall functioning as *Schutz von Krieg* (protection from war). In the outer space, three people carrying weapons are shooting at two passers-by and blood is flowing. Shooters seem to be smiling, making the situation terrifying. In the indoor space, one person is protecting him/herself inside a house surrounded by a circular wall. Flowers are growing in the garden. This means that walls might protect life in this drawing, as represented by the person on the inside and the presence of nature. In terms of the grammar of this visual production, it is possible to see that the drawing is oriented in two parts: a left one and a right one.

As the student explains, in this case, the wall has a protective function and he expresses this using the first-person singular, as if it were a direct relationship to experience ('the wall protects me').

S1: So I drew a wall between a house and the outside where there is war.
L1: So for you, is a wall something positive or negative?
S1: For me the wall, for example, the wall protects me.

Figure 4.4 shows a couple, or at least a girl and a boy, separated by a wall. Both are in love and their faces are sad. You could think that this is a representation of the separation of lovers because of the war.

Our hypothesis of separation by war is contradicted by the author of the drawing who explains that it represents a symbolic border, that of the family, which prevents the lovers from coming together ('Because, then, a wall may not always be a wall'):

> L1: Okay, very nice. Very interesting. What did you draw?
> S10: Me? I drew, what is fear as a feeling, so, I drew two people. They are afraid for each other, they love each other, but they are afraid to become a couple. Because, then, a wall may not always be a wall. The family can also be a wall then. And she says, okay, you can't be together and all that. So, you love each other but you can't be together. Because of uh particular reasons and that
> L1: And that's fear for you?
> S10: Yes.
> L1: That you can't be with someone, even if you like them?
> S10: Yes.

After praising the presentation of the previous drawing (the discursive ritual for doing so being somewhat stereotypical!), the teacher asks the student to explain the meaning of his drawing. The student explains that it is a metaphorical wall ('The family can also be a wall then') and that families can separate people who love each other for other particular reasons and thus provoke fear in lovers, as is apparently the case for

Figure 4.4 A couple in love separated by a wall (S10).

the student who responds positively to the teacher's two questions: 'And that is fear for you?' and 'That you can't be with someone, even if you like them?' Again, the representation of the symbolic wall structures the drawing in two parts, left and right, with each lover placed irremediably on one side.

Perceptions of borders and walls during the forced displacement

The next two extracts deal with the experience of fleeing and the students' journeys to Germany. These extracts are not represented through visual narratives because they arose in the context of previous descriptions of the visual material, but did not directly relate to them any more. These can be regarded as extensions of the discussions triggered by the visual representations.

The following extract expresses the uncertainties and anxieties experienced in the country of origin due to the violent situation. Student 2 recounts his passage through Turkey, a first place of abode, where he also experienced conflicts between Turks and Arabs, due to the reception of refugees.

> S2: We were always afraid. You don't know when you die or when you live. And we wrote the words security and places of security. For example, like here in Germany. Or when I was in Turkey, there was also some security, but not like here in Germany, because there were also problems with Turks and Arabs and that.
> L1: Did you have a fight?
> S2: Yes, there was a lot of that. They don't want foreigners to come either. And we had written fear of being alone. Fear of being alone.
> L1: OK, but in your home countries or where exactly? Or at school? Or at home? Or in Germany?
> S2: OK, so for example, I'm now in Germany and I don't have anyone here. Only my family, otherwise nobody else.
> L1: You have us too (smiling). Have you written anything else?

In this excerpt, in which he evokes the theme of fear, the student expresses the constant fear of loneliness ('And we had written fear of loneliness. Fear of being alone') to which the teacher responds in a very empathetic way, both verbally and non-verbally ('You have us too (smiling)'). The fear of loneliness is linked to the loss of social ties with the people who were part of the network in his home country ('I am now in Germany and I have nobody here. Only my family, otherwise no one else'). Two places are named: Turkey, as a place of temporary abode, with 'some security', and Germany, constructed as more permanent and with more security. Even if just recalled, we can see that the student had the experience of crossing several borders until coming to Germany, from what we could describe as extreme insecurity in the home country ('you don't know when you die or when you live'), the semi-secure space of transition, between two borders (between home country and Germany), and the experience of living in security (Germany). The reaching of security, crossing the border to security, comes at heavy personal and emotional cost, including the loss of social ties: the fear of being alone, and the feeling of having 'nobody else' beyond the family.

The second extract deals with the journey from the country of origin to Germany and the situation at the Hungarian border, again making the successive border crossing clear. To do this, four places are named: 'my country', Turkey, Hungary and Germany, even if not in strict chronological order.

> S5: Fear of war. I wrote fear of war. In my country there is a war and because of that we fled to Germany. And I was afraid of the walls. In the way and we were in 'Hungria'.
> L1: You were hungry.
> S5: Yes. And the police officers were ...
> S8: No, they were in Hungary.
> S5: ... They fired their guns at us
> L1: In Hungary?
> S5: In Hungary, right.
> L1: Ah okay.
> S5: And we fled. And I felt scared in front of a kind of wall in Hungary.
> L1: Okay. In front of the border. Hungary. Okay.
> S5: Yes, right.
> S3: (...). We went on foot to Turkey. In Turkey, they don't want to have foreigners. (inaud.)

At the start, the student's statement leads to incomprehension on the part of the teacher, who confuses 'Hungarian' with 'hunger', thinking that it is a transfer from English. The linguistic misunderstanding is picked up and corrected by another student, which again shows the classmates' collaboration and interest in the topics being discussed, as well as their desire to participate in the interactions. Pupil S5 recounts the confrontations with the Hungarian police at the border ('They fired their guns at us'), aligned with other accounts of confrontation in border-crossing situation (De Fina 2003a and 2003b, Zaripov this volume). Another pupil also explains that they left Turkey because of rising anti-migration sentiment ('We walked to Turkey. In Turkey they don't want to have foreigners'), corroborating the content in the first excerpt in this section. The student expresses the feeling that they had to leave Turkey because of growing instability related to the reception of 'foreigners' (growing racism or xenophobia), making it clear that lives could be in danger. So, between borders, placed in different dangerous situations (the eminence of death), the students frame border-crossing 'as an enterprise that implies a loss of freedom and the need to put oneself in the hands of others. It also implies fighting against feelings of fear and anxiety that stem from the lack of knowledge about and control over events' (De Fina 2003b: 53).

Perception of borders and walls during resettlement in Germany

When the teacher asks learners to name walls and borders, the metaphorical nature of these terms is immediately apparent:

– 'Jobcenter' is protection for us, because they give us money. And time to learn, until we learn German (S9);

- 'Here we have Frau Merkel. She protects us' (S8);
- 'The last point is the German language, a difficult language' (S7).

It is important to note that these metaphorical walls can be material or immaterial, institutional or non-institutional, personal or impersonal, positive or negative. Thus, the 'jobcenter', being a material and institutional wall, has a positive value. The German Chancellor, as a material and personal wall, also has a positive connotation. Only the language has a rather negative connotation, being considered difficult, thus metaphorically imposing a border between the students and their integration.

In the following excerpt, which focuses on the differences between the school experience in the country of origin and in Germany, the student explains that school means protection, but only in Germany because the school experience in Syria is associated with fear and both physical ('the wooden ruler in your hands', often cited by students) and symbolic punishments ('so you have to write something'):

> S1: Yes, we talked about school, which is the opposite in Germany to what it is in our countries. Here you don't have to wear a uniform. And when we don't do the homework, then we don't get any punishment. But when you repeat it, then you have to write something down. And you don't get a wooden ruler in your hands.
> L1: Does that mean that school is a kind of wall for you? That's fear, isn't it?
> S1: No, that's protection.
> L1: A kind of protection?
> S1: Yes.
> S2: Here in Germany the school is very different from here. Because, for example, in Syria, I was afraid to go to school. Not to be beaten, like this. Or when you come too late, you are beaten.
> L1: But here, you like going to school?
> S2: Yes. Sometimes I'm happy.
> SuS: (laughs).
> S2: But only sometimes.

Figure 4.5 shows a second symbolic wall, but this time one offering protection: the school diploma they are trying to obtain, in order to be able to pursue their studies.

During the explanatory interaction, the student explains that he has drawn a protection situation. As the learner has difficulties in naming the object in question ('Protection is for me, how to say it, diploma') and in explaining why he considers the diploma to be a protection, the teacher anticipates his words and participates in the co-construction of the meaning of the drawing:

> S3: Yes, I have the protection theme. I drew a sheet of paper. Protection is for me, how to say it, diploma (*Schulabschluss*).
> L1: To have the diploma.
> S3: To have the diploma.
> L1: Okay, that means, if you have a diploma, then that's a kind of protection for you, that you have security for your future, what happens after (school).
> S3: Yes.

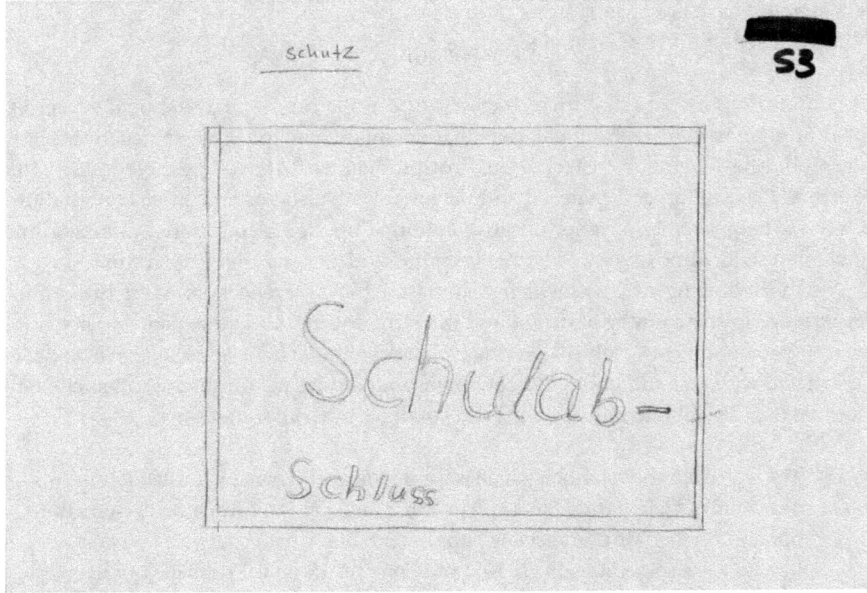

Figure 4.5 The school diploma as a protection (*Schutz*) (S3).

School, as a space and time in which the development of (linguistic) skills takes place, is seen as a springboard to a future different from the past.

Conclusion

In our multimodal description of drawings and discussion of interactional sequences, the wall and the border appear as the in-between (peace or war), a non-space that serves to protect or separate. They are non-spaces that make contrast between both sites visible. Interestingly, because of that task design, students structure their drawings around the visual representation of the border or the wall, when these are physical (except Figure 4.4), and produce complex visual and oral accounts of times and spaces that sometimes seem to overlap, and other times to be in concurrence. The 'here-and-now' and the 'then-and-there' (Baynham 2003) are complex entities in the visual narratives and, in terms of their oral explication, they might be appropriated individually or collaboratively. The experiences of border crossing, living between borders and going through successive border crossing, are shared in the classroom interaction, and they build a common fund of experience, defining a common trajectory through times and spaces. In my corpus, the focus on the representation of borders and walls structures the presentation of spatiality and temporality and, therefore, the bits of personal or appropriated stories being told.

As a summary, we can say that refugee students perceive walls as protections or threats, depending on the narrative temporality they are placed in, and that these walls can be symbolic or physical. Most of the walls and borders drawn seem to be related to direct experience of situations of physical or symbolic violence in the countries of origin. We could thus say that the border is not just separating places and characters, but also separating times. Borders tend to be negatively thematized and walls seen rather in protective terms. Given the Middle Eastern origins of some of the students, this might also have a cross-linguistic explanation: in Arabic, the 'wall' comes from stem *ḥwṭ* – (1) to protect; (2) to surround. The word 'ocean' – *muḥīṭ* is related to it – surrounds the earth. Its synonym *jidār* is semantically related to stem *jdr* – (1) to become a foundation and (2) to grow roots. These two words have a clear positive connection. On the contrary, the word 'borders' (always in plural) is related to the stem *ḥdd* – (1) to prevent, to hinder, to forbid and (2) to be sharp, to be pointed.[4]

In pedagogical terms, it was possible to observe the mediating value of the discussion on walls and borders in the development of intercultural competence, through the hybridization of functions and representations assumed by those two elements, which reflect physical, psychological and emotional boundaries. Talking about borders and walls in the classroom also allows students to challenge their own and others' perspectives about border crossing, living between borders and going through successive border crossings, in their singular path towards Germany. The classroom thus becomes a space of linguistic and cultural complicity, a very space of intimacy, where students talk about fears and anxieties and where they feel a member of a collective and individual at the same time, that is, a person inserted in a collective venture but with single individual stories.

The narrative work around displacement and resettlement was based on the questioning and interpretation of memory (memory and experiences as resources, as starting points and themes for discussion): learners talk about the past (before and during the war, before and during the border crossing) in order to be part of the present (understand the host society, build a sense of what is happening to them) and to imagine a future (getting a diploma). To conclude, it seems that the work on memory becomes a work of (re)signification, and importantly, one that involves re-inscribing oneself in space and time.

In terms of perspectives for further development, it would be important to analyse experiences of border crossing and expectations in the host country from a developmental perspective, comparing qualitative information in terms of biographical data (origin, age, gender, etc.). Another hypothesis would be to turn this research into a quantitative study, in which issues surrounding the anonymization of personal information would not limit the possibilities of analysing the relationship between different variables. We could hypothesize that the experiences of border crossing and the subjective vision around physical and symbolic borders might be heavily influenced by the students' biographical paths, which we could not fully cover in this study.

Notes

1 In the context of this chapter, we adopt the term 'refugee' to refer to individuals 'with (or whose parents have) recognized refugee status, Exceptional Leave to Remain, other formal status, or who are asylum seekers' (Hek 2005: 158). That said, while this is seemingly an anodyne and bureaucratic definition, it must be acknowledged that

the definition of 'refugee' may well highlight a stratification of their status and value, with regard to country of origin, race, class, gender, religion, language(s), political affiliations and prior educational experiences (Taylor and Sidhu 2012). We therefore recognize that the term is politically and ideologically charged and acquires different values depending on national and international agendas.

2   Students in Germany receive their school-leaving certificate after successfully completing education at school. This certificate is part of the so-called qualifying system, whereby the issuing institution enables the student's further educational or vocational career. Without such a certificate, students are not entitled to pursue further studies. Some diplomas give access to university, and others to professional training.

3   See also Breeze (2014) on how image and text may anchor, complement or contradict each other.

4   Explanation provided by Gintsburg, in interpersonal correspondence.

References

Anzaldúa, G. ([1987] 2007), *Borderlands. La Frontera. The New Mestiza*, San Francisco: Aunt Lute Books.

Augé, M. (1992), *Non-lieux, introduction à une anthropologie de la surmodernité*, Paris: Le Seuil.

Baynham, M. (2003), 'Narratives in Space and Time: Beyond "backdrop" Accounts of Narrative Orientation', *Narrative Inquiry*, 13 (2): 347–66.

Baynham, M. (2015), 'Narrative and Space/Time', in A. De Fina and A. Georgakopoulou (eds), *The Handbook of Narrative Analysis*, 119–39, Hoboken, NJ: John Wiley & Sons.

Benson, P. (2021), *Language Learning Environments. Spatial Perspectives on SLA*, Bristol: Multilingual Matters.

Breeze, R. (2014), 'Multimodal Analysis of Controversy in the Media', in G. Thompson and L. Alba Juez (eds), *Evaluation in Context*, 303–20, Amsterdam and Philadelphia: John Benjamins.

Czarniawska, B. (2004), *Narratives in Social Science Research*, London: Sage.

Daschner, P. (2017), 'Flüchtlinge in der Schule. Daten, Rahmenbedingungen und Perspektiven. Ein Überblick', in N. Mcelvany, A. Jungermann, W. Bos, and H. G. Holtappels (eds), *Ankommen in der Schule. Chancen und Herausforderungen bei der Integration von Kindern und Jugendlichen mit Fluchterfahrung*, 11–25, Münster: Waxmann.

De Fina, A. (2003a), 'Crossing Borders: Time, Space and Disorientation in Narrative', *Narrative Inquiry*, 13 (2): 1–25, 367–91.

De Fina, A. (2003b), *Identity in Narrative. A Study of Immigrant Discourse*, Amsterdam: John Benjamins Publishing Company.

De Fina, A. and A. Tseng (2017), 'Narrative in the Study of Migrants', in S. Canagarajah (ed.), *The Routledge Handbook of Migration and Language*, 381–95, London: Routledge.

Gintsburg, S. (2019), 'Identity, Place, Space, and Rhymes during a Pilgrimage to the Shrine of Moulay Abdessalam, Morocco', *Journal of Religion in Africa*, 48: 1–27.

Goodson, I. (2015), *Narrativas em educação: a vida e a voz dos professores*, Porto: Porto Editora.

Hek, R. (2005), 'The Role of Education in the Settlement of Young Refugees in the UK: The Experiences of Young Refugees', *Practice*, 17 (3): 157–71.

Lefebvre, H. (1991), *The Production of Space*, Oxford: Blackwell.

Lyman, F. (1981), 'The Responsive Classroom Discussion', in A. S. Anderson (ed.), *Mainstreaming Digest*, College Park, MD: University of Maryland College of Education.

Melo-Pfeifer, S. and T. Ferreira (2017), '"*Diz-me lá o que é que tu desenhaste aqui!*" – Narrativas visuais de crianças lusodescendentes na Alemanha acerca do Português e a sua co-interpretação em sala de aula', in S. Melo-Pfeifer and A. R. Simões (eds), *Plurilinguismo Vivido, Plurilinguismo Desenhado: Estudos Sobre a Relação dos Sujeitos com as Línguas*, 129–51, Santarém: Escola Superior de Educação de Santarém.

Melo-Pfeifer, S. and A. Schmidt (2019), 'Integration as Portrayed in Visual Narratives by Young Refugees in Germany', in P. Kalaja and S. Melo-Pfeifer (eds), *Visualising Multilingual Lives: More than Words*, 53–72, Clevedon: Multilingual Matters.

Melo-Pfeifer, S. and M. Thölkes (2021), 'Wie soll ich das Kind bewerten ?' Between Standardization and Differentiation in the Assessment of Refugee Students. A Qualitative Study of Foreign Language Teachers' Representations in Germany', in G. Levine and D. Mallows (eds), *Language Learning of Migrants in Europe: Theoretical, Empirical, Policy, and Pedagogical Issues*, Berlin: Springer.

Melo-Pfeifer, S. and J. Wegnerski (in press, 2021), '*Ich bin nach Deutschland geflüchtet und ich habe viele Grenzen unterwegs gesehen*»: visions et représentations de frontières et de murs par des jeunes réfugiés en Allemagne', in I. Audras (ed.), *Dispositifs et pratiques d'accueil d'élèves migrants en Europe: outils et leviers pour la formation d'enseignants*, Rennes: Presses Universitaires de Rennes.

Melo-Pfeifer, S., L. Loges, and M. Thölkes (in press, 2021), '*Willkommenskultur* à l'école ? Dispositifs d'accueil de jeunes réfugiés dans le système scolaire allemand: la diversification des publics à l'épreuve des traditions scolaires et disciplinaires', in I. Audras (ed.), *Dispositifs et pratiques d'accueil d'élèves migrants en Europe: outils et leviers pour la formation d'enseignants*, Rennes: Presses Universitaires de Rennes.

Mezzadra, S. and B. Neilson (2013), *Border as Method, or, the Multiplication of Labor*, Durham, NC and London: Duke University Press.

Nail, T. (2017), *Theory of the Border*, Oxford: Oxford University Press.

Smets, K., J. Mazzocchetti, L. Gerstmans, and L. Mostmans (2019), 'Beyond Victimhood: Reflecting on Migrant-Victim Representations with Afghan, Iraqi, and Syrian Asylum Seekers and Refugees in Belgium', in L. d'Haenens, W. Joris, and F. Heinderyckx (eds), *Images of Immigrants and Refugees in Western Europe: Media Representations, Public Opinion and Refugees' Experiences*, 177–98, Leuven: Leuven University Press. https://www.jstor.org/stable/pdf/j.ctvh1dkhm.12.pdf?refreqid=excelsior%3Abc84b8c80fff3cb2387e429d3226a5b1.

Taylor, S. and R. Sidhu (2012), 'Supporting Refugee Students in Schools: What Constitutes Inclusive Education?', *International Journal of Inclusive Education*, 16 (1): 39–56.

Wegnerski, J. (2018), Interkulturelles Lernen in der Internationalen Vorbereitungsklasse: eine Fallstudie an einer Hamburger Stadtteilschule, Hamburg: Universität Hamburg (master thesis).

Discussion questions

1. Would you agree that 'walls and borders' could be so-called non-spaces, as argued in this section of the chapter? Justify.
2. Can you think of other non-spaces that could be investigated in the relationship between migration and refugees? What would you like to research about those non-spaces?

3. Which relationship is it possible to establish between 'walls and borders' and 'space studies'?
4. What other research methods on migration and refugee studies do you know? Which ones do you think are (more) suited to research children's experiences of immigration and seeking refuge?
5. How would you make use of children's drawings if you had a research project in this area or were working with refugee children?
6. Try out your analytic competencies of multimodal productions by presenting your own analysis of the drawing in Figure 4.1 and combining it with the explanation the author provides.

Children's Narratives about Their Journey from the Middle East to Hungary

Ildikó Schmidt

Introduction

The aim of this chapter is to show how the text of life story interviews can be interpreted as narratives-in-interaction; how the narrative is organized in time and space segments and how social space is built up through them; and in which ways the macroprocesses of the world are realized in micro events. In describing microprocesses, the voicing activity of the speaker is particularly important since examining the characteristics of speech provides insight into the narrator's emotional attitude to his or her own story, which reflects as well as giving meaning on the macro level. The interlocutor's perception of the voice takes place primarily through speech, but it remains a question how much of a role the linguistic expression itself plays in understanding the story. Examining narrative units in this way provides an opportunity to find connections between language use, memory function and lived experiences.

The results of the analysis have social applications, with a view to the promotion of school integration after the immigrants' arrival in Hungary. On a more theoretical level, the description of changes in linguistic expression sheds light on how spoken language performance develops with a high degree of emotional involvement in multilingual children. These insights could be useful for therapists and counsellors in their practice with migrant children.

Theoretical perspectives

The narrative turn of the 1960s started from the perspective of structuralism mainly in the fields of literary theory (Bakhtin 1981; Barthes 1975; Genette 1980), folklore (Propp 1968) and sociolinguistics (Labov 1972; Labov and Waletzky 1967). With the advent of poststructuralism from the 1980s onwards, other directions in narrative research began to replace the earlier theoretical discourse. Different approaches examined narrative practices from different perspectives. These include the traditions of narrative analysis reflecting on narrative psychology (Bamberg 2012; McAdams 2001a, b) and developmental psychology (Freeman 1984; Gergen and Gergen 2001).

In the field of sociolinguistics, the social interactional approach to narratives emerged and researchers working in this paradigm began to focus more on the storytelling than on the stories themselves (Baynham and De Fina 2016; De Fina 2003; 2015). Narrative analysis has also gained more and more ground in applied linguistics research related to migration (Dörnyei and Ushioda 2011). With the increasing emergence of migration the phenomenon of super-diversity (Vertovec 2007) has been thematized in the field of critical sociolinguistics and related to the research on language use (Pennycook 2010; Rampton 2006), which has highlighted the characteristics of multilingual social spaces (Blommaert, Collins and Slembrouck 2005). To frame these ideas Blommaert (2007) developed sociolinguistic scale theory (Baynham 2011), which links global and local phenomena.

The present research is most related to linguistic ethnography among the classic approaches to narrative (cf. Baynham 2011). In this approach, instead of considering the narrative as monologue, we understand narratives to emerge in interactional co-construction. In the interview context, the lived experiences are manifested in dynamically co-constructed speech events (Baynham 2011). The events told during the interaction between the interviewer and the teller are called by Georgakopoulou (2007: ii) 'narratives-in-interaction'. A special characteristic of the narratives recorded in the interview situations is that it is difficult to interpret the created stories only by observing narrative units within the scope of classical, canonical, prototypical organization since there the emphasis was on narrative form. In narratives that unfold in interaction, the narrator does not present in a monologue what he or she is saying but tends to concentrate on his or her interlocutor. This necessarily evokes self-reflection because the narrator has moved away in time from the event, which involves other reference points in the development of the narrative. During the creation of narratives, the individual language use – and through that the realized voicing activity – is given a special role in interview situations. As a result of the interaction, a dialogically organized storytelling develops, which gives the story owner the opportunity to find the voice related to the message of the story in collaboration with his or her conversation partner.

The power of narratives lies in those characteristics by which they are able to travel in space and time alongside those people who are involved in the communication, in both interactive or literary narratives. Bakhtin's theory of literary chronotope highlights the inseparable relationship between space and time (Bakhtin (Bahtyin) 1976: 258). In literary chronotopes, the features of spatiality and temporality melt together in a thoughtful and concrete whole. The characteristics of time are manifested in space, and space is perceived and measured through time. The artistic chronotope is characterized by the intersections and the features of these lines (Bahtyin 1976: 258; Bakhtin 1981: 86). Bakhtin's notion of chronotope has been applied in sociolinguistic research by Agha (2015), who shifts its original focus to spoken language use. The same phenomenon was adapted to the analysis of oral narrative by Perrino (2015). The phenomenon of retrospectivity is closely related to chronotopes (Freeman 2015): the power of retrospectivity lies in recollection, which takes place through the amalgamation of time and space, more precisely in the blurring of an event that has taken place in the past (Freeman 1984) with the recollection of the past. There is thus a moment in the past, on the one hand, and a moment of recollection of the past, on the other hand, which is the storytelling itself.

According to Perrino (2015), these two aspects belong to two chronotopes that have inseparable spatial and temporal relationships. However, the space and time features of the two chronotopes come together again to form an inseparable unit that gives the cross-chronotope alignment (Agha 2007). The participating chronotopes are intertwined through memory and appear in specific language use phenomena during narration. These can manifest in spatio-temporal deixis through grammar and lexical units (Perrino 2015), specific units of time such as times of day and their changes, which are units that indicate the passing of time span.

The form of verbs in the system of verb tenses and aspects related to the given language through time also shows the mode related to the meaning of the verb, which leads to the way of orienting oneself in space. The time factor arising from the subject of the speaker is the rate of the speech, which determines and forms a bridge between the past and the time of the narration. As the temporal bridging takes place, the spatial connection also appears since it draws the listener into the space of the storytelling through the act of recollection. Parallel to this, the other element of the chronotope becomes apparent, that is, the spatial one, and at the same time the connection between the two chronotopes is realized. The spatial aspect of the chronotope accumulates as the story progresses over time, through the changes of the sites, the course of events and the persons who dialogue in the story, and who assign the new locations.

Chronotopes can refer to the same event, yet the linguistic expression of the space/time segment that emerges at the time of narration dominates and determines the action quality of past events. On the other hand, it also determines the language use that can be perceived when the reminiscence emerges, and its change gives to the interlocutor an extra emotional meaning. This effect is amplified when there is a significant difference between the nature of the narrated events and the narrative mode: that is, the narrated event is painful, emotionally and physically stressful, while the narrative mode is lean, monotonous and simplistic (Rosenthal 1991).

Migration and narrative analysis

The major social processes of mobility and migration are now global in nature. To capture their implications more clearly, sociolinguistics has borrowed the notion of scale from social theory, more precisely from social geography. The metaphor of scale gives the idea of images, which are more vertically organized than horizontally, forming a continuum of layered scales (Blommaert 2007). The social changes stemming from globalization create the macro-conditions that could be captured in microprocesses. Scale theory, through its spatial and temporal features, attempts to describe the sociolinguistic phenomenon between macro and micro levels (Blommaert, Collins and Slembrouck 2005). The narrative analysis of everyday (micro) events can exploit scale theory from the spatio-temporal perspective.

In the mappings of migration resulting from globalization, cultural geography has shown us that mobility, borderlands and exile are strongly associated with such spatial images, which are determining in defining spatial perception. Baynham (2015: 123) goes further down this path and refers to de Certeau, when he states that

> 'every story is a travel story, a spatial practice.' Nowhere is this more obvious than in migration stories, where displacement and mobility in time/space constitute the narrative action.

Deducing from the idea thematized in the quote, that is, the concept of travel as a spatial practice, research using the methodology of narrative analysis has become increasingly prevalent in migration research due to its spatio-temporal interrelations (Baynham and De Fina 2016). Emigration is the boundary line between the old and new life, through which remembrance leads forming a bridge between the abandoned past and the present that is forming.

The literature related to the narrative analysis methodology mainly examines adult migrant groups, giving rise to a range of studies which De Fina and Tseng (2017: 385) classify into the following subgroups: language learning, community membership and storytelling focusing on migrants. From the rich literature repertoire, I highlight Nyiri's (2001) research because of its relevance to Hungary: he examines the narrative of Chinese immigrants in Hungarian and Japanese comparison. Another special case of migration is the group of asylum seekers: Blommaert (2001) who carried out research using narrative analysis among African asylum seekers, Hatoss (2012) with Sudanese refugees living in Australia, Jacquemet (2005) on refugees' narrative performance and Maryns and Blommaert (2001) on the changes in the narrative resources used by asylum seekers.

Narrative analysis using data from children and young people is found less frequently than research focusing on adults. In two interesting examples, Pastor (2010) explores the 'fitting in' narrative of adolescents living in Madrid, while De Fina, Paternostro and Amoruso (2019) show the case of community practice formed by asylum-seeking minors and teachers in Italy. Within the same project, De Fina, Paternostro and Amoruso (2020) discuss the role of storytelling in relation to the sharing of traumatic experiences by unaccompanied asylum-seeking minors entering Italy.

The research conducted among children often uses a combination of visual methods and narrative analysis embodied in visual narrative. Visual methods mostly give insights into the settlement experiences, representations of social integration, language learning experiences and multilingual or plurilingual portraits in France by Clerc (2009) and Leconte (2009), in Germany by Melo-Pfeier (this volume), Melo-Pfeifer and Schmidt (2019) and in Canada's French part, in Quebec, by Razafimandimbimanana (2009). This brief review of the literature provides insight concerning where the present study is located within the main theoretical areas, and what research results precede it.

Methods and the research participants

I recorded a lifetime interview with the children involved in the research, in which they talked about the time spent in their country of origin. They talked about their family, their parents, their close and distant relatives, the daily routine of their lives there and their school. They described what languages and language variants they spoke with which family member. They then recounted how the family got to leave their home, and what motivated them in their decision. They reported on the path of their flight, their arrival in Hungary, their integration at the different places of residence and their school experiences. They described in detail their relationship with the Hungarian language and people, their experiences with different educational institutions and their integration into everyday school life. Below, I describe information from the interviews that is closely related to the topic of the chapter.

The interviews were recorded in Hungarian, which is the language the children acquired after their immigration. Both of the children are multilingual with a diverse linguistic repertoire, which stems, on the one hand, from the characteristics of the language use practices related to the family's origin, and, on the other hand, their migration experience, in which their linguistic resources have expanded to include Hungarian.

During the interviews I learned the following information from the children and their parents. The siblings are of Afghan descent but were born in Iran. There are three siblings but only two of them go to the Kígyó Street school. At the beginning of the interviews, Fariba was sixteen years old and Amir was ten years old. At that time, they had been living in Hungary for a year and a half, so Fariba arrived at the age of 14.5 and Amir at the age of 7.5. The family speaks Persian at home. The children attended school in Iran before the family's migration.

The mother was born in Iran to Pashto-speaking parents from Herat, Afghanistan. She attended school in Iran, so Iranian Persian became her dominant language. The father grew up in Bamiyan, where Dari is spoken and then moved to Iran as a young adult. The parents speak Persian to each other. This information was related in the interview and also confirmed when heard on informal occasions that the father speaks Dari and the mother's parents speak Pashto. The parents can communicate at a very basic level in Hungarian and English, but they were still learning Hungarian. During the interviews, their Hungarian spoken language level became visible. While the mother communicates in Hungarian at A2 level, it can be deduced from the possibility of the father's communication capacity that he is at A1 level. Regarding the parents' knowledge of English, it was observed during the interviews that utterances in Hungarian were supplemented with English words when the given word was not known in Hungarian. However, only certain linguistic elements, mainly certain words, were used in English, that is, they did not completely switch between the languages (Extract 1:13). However, had it been easier for them to express themselves in English, they would probably have switched languages because the need for communication seemed to be a strong motive for them, which was obvious from the high degree of emotional involvement.

Extract 1

1. Interviewer: *Irán Törökország az a Türkiye* (Iran Turkey is that one the Turkey)
2. Father: *Türkiye* (Turkey)
3. I: *az 10 nap* (it's 10 days)

4. I: *10 nap vagy 10 óra?* (10 days or 10 hours)
5. Mother: *pieda 10 óra, 10 óra* (*pieda*[1] 10 hours)
6. I: *A nap az a hétfő, kedd, szerda* (The day is Monday, Tuesday, Wednesday)
7. M: *Nem, nem nem óra* (No, no no hour)
8. I: *Óra* (hour)
9. M: *10 óra gyalog* (10 hours on foot)
10. F: *Türkiye, Yunan, Yunan* (Turkey, Yunan, Yunan)
11. I: *Mi az a Yunan?* (What is that Yunan?)
12. F: *Irán Türkiye 10 óra* (Iran Turkey 10 hours)
13. M: *Autó **go** Türkiye* (Car go Turkey)
14. I: *Akkor Törökországban autó* (Then in Turkey car)
15. F: *Türkiye Yunan, Türkiye Yunan* (Turkey Yunan, Turkey Yunan)
16. I: *Mi az a Yunan?* (What is that Yunan?)
17. M: *Yunan, Yunan* (Yunan, Yunan)
18. I: *Ez egy város?* (Is that a town?)
19. F: *Naaa, Yunan* (No, Yunan)
20. M: *Nem* (No)
21. I: *Nem, nem város, nem értem, angolul? Megtudjuk mindjárt (keresik a szótárban a mobilon) Ja, Görögország... Jó, jó, jó! Törökország, Görögország, ott autóval..* (No, it's not a town, I don't understand, in English? We'll know it in a second (they are looking it up in a dictionary on their mobile phone) OK, Greece... Ok, Ok, Ok! Turkey, Greece, then by car.)

According to the parents' accounts, the children spoke Iranian Persian, or Farsi, at school at their place of birth and the family also spoke Dari, or Afghan Persian, and Pashto, an Iranian language widely spoken in Afghanistan and Pakistan, at home. The two children, however, call the languages that they speak at home Persian and the one they spoke at school Farsi, that is, they do not differentiate between Dari and Pashto, two related but independent languages, but they do juxtapose Farsi as a language of instruction at school against them. Summarizing this information, I came to the conclusion that the siblings switched between Farsi, Pashto and Dari, depending on which parent or family member living in Iran they were speaking to. The family has a rich social life in Hungary, especially with the Afghans living there, and so Amir and Fariba have the opportunity to use their language and practise the customs related to their community life. When they first arrived in Hungary, they lived in a rural town where their application for asylum was launched. According to Hungarian law, they could immediately join the education system so they started studying at the local school. The teachers at the school have extensive experience in integration and the children said that they enjoyed attending this school. While there, they started to get acquainted with the Hungarian language, which they did not know at all before.

After a few months, they moved to Budapest and lived in church-run community housing. They continued their studies at a school close to where they lived. They were traumatically affected by the change of school because they had to suffer a high degree of exclusion from their classmates, teachers and the school management as well. Amir spoke Hungarian well enough by then, and was relatively well protected from bullying. Fariba, on the other hand, was more vulnerable due to her weaker language competence in Hungarian, and she became reserved and cried a lot. Due to poor school conditions, the family decided to change school again with the help of social workers at their community centre. Thus, they started the following year at the institution they were attending during the interviews. It is an inclusive school with immigrant children in every class, so the teaching staff are more experienced at teaching students with different language backgrounds.

The data was recorded in Hungarian, which the children did not speak before their arrival in Hungary. The datapool shows that they are making good progress in the process of language acquisition, as in a year and a half they have learned to use the Hungarian language effectively in all situations that occur in everyday life. In addition, they can take part in the subject classes on a substantive basis. The difficulty here is mainly writing and reading in Hungarian, which is confirmed by the children's self-assessment and the teacher's reports. Amir's speech and oral communication strategies are at a level close to that of monolingual Hungarian speakers. Fariba responds well to her interlocutor but her speech, while fluent, still lags far behind native speakers in terms of language accuracy. However, this does not affect her self-expression, and it is easy to understand what she means and wants to communicate.

In terms of content, what was said by the two children and the parents is the same. Each of the stations on the route is in the same order (Extract 1:10–19; Extract 2:25, 34; Extract 3:38), and the difficulties and problems experienced along the way are also consistent (Extract 1:9; Extract 2:25–27; Extract 3:39–42).

Extract 2
Fariba

22. Interviewer: *És milyen volt az az út?* (How was the trip?)
23. Fariba: *Nagyon nehéz volt nagyon, nagyon. Nem tudtunk aludni.* (It was very difficult, very. We couldn't sleep.)
24. I: *Mik történtek ott?* (What happened?)
25. F: *Hát… (Well…) Elmondom, hogy milyen volt. Nem tudtuk aludni este, nem tudtunk, csak gyalo, mi ez gyalogni* (I tell you tell you what was it like. We couldn't sleep, we couldn't, we just wa, how do you say walking.)
26. I: *Gyalogoltunk.* (Walking.)
27. F: *Gyalogoltunk, és olyan nehéz volt. Este gyalogoltunk, és reggel* (We walked, and it was very difficult. We walked in the evening, and morning…)
28. I: *Éjszaka?* (During the night?)
29. F: *Igen, éjszaka.* (Yes, during the night.)
30. F: *Akkor nekünk úgy mondták, mi nagyon sok pénzt adtunk az a ember, hogy velünk jöjjön, adtunk neki pénzt,* (And then they told us <my parents> that we gave lots of money to that man, that he guides us, so we gave him money)
31. I: *fizettetek* (you paid him)
32. F: *ige, adtunk neki pénzt, és mondtuk, légy szíves mi jobban, mint a más ember. Nagyon sok pénz volt. Nagyon sok.* (yes, we gave him money, and we asked him, please take care of us better than the others. Lots of money, really a lot.)
33. I: *Mhm.. értem.* (Yes, I see.)
34. F: *És utána, utána nekünk, amikor Törökországba mentünk, elkezdi, hogy nem ismerem téged, és vagy amikor meghívtunk neki, hogy légy szíves itt van egy férfi,*

elkezdi, hogy én nem kaptam semmi pénzt, nem tudunk veled mit csinálni, és az ő az, aki Törökországban volt, én sem nem ismerem az embert. De ő azt mondta, hogy ezzel az emberrel lehet menni, (And then, after we went to Turkey, he started telling, that he doesn't know us, and when we called him, that here we are, he repeated that he hasn't received any money, that was another man to whom we gave the money. Not him who is here in Turkey. But he said that he doesn't know that man. And we could travel with him)

Extract 3
Amir

35. Interviewer: *Te és hogy jöttetek Magyarországra?* (And how did you get Hungary?)
36. Amir: *Mhm.. Hár öö kettő hónap három hónapra sikerült jönni.* (Well.. 2 months 3 months we succeeded to arrive.)
37. I: *És hogyan utaztatok?* (And how did you travel?)
38. A: *Hát, öö Iránból, Iránból Törökországig sétáltunk, egy, egy.. és utána Törökországból hajóval elmentünk Athénba, és Athénről gyalogoltam Maktóniába, és onnan is sétál.. gyalogoltam Szerbiába, és Szerbiából ott egy kicsit autóval mentünk, azután elmentünk, elmentünk gyalog, gyalogon és Debrecenbe jöttünk.* (So... we... from Iran, from Iran we went to Turkey, a, a... and then after Turkey we went by boat to Athens, and from Athens we walked to Macedonia, and from there walked to Serbia and there we went by car, then we went, we went by foot, by foot and we came to Debrecen <in Hungary>)
39. I: *Te és te hogy bírtad ezt a sok gyaloglást?* (How did you bear the walking?)
40. A: *Hát muszáj volt.* (Well it was a must.)
41. I: *Muszáj volt.* (It was a must)
42. A: *Nehéz volt, hát muszáj volt.* (It was difficult, yes... it was a must.)
43. I: *Te és hol aludtatok?* (And where did you sleep?)
44. A: *Hát, hotel, öö abbaba ott voltak házak ott* (Well... hotel, mmm in the in theeereee were houses there)
45. I: *Mhm.. És sok ember ment együtt vagy csak ti a szüleiddel, meg a testvéreiddel?* (Right.. And were you with many others together or just you with your parents and siblings?)
46. A: *Hát, mi mi mi csak 14-en voltunk. Az ilyen kis csoport volt. Öö...* (Well, what we we just were 14 of us. That like it is such little group. Mmm..)

Results

These data extracts lead us to the children's journey of flight. It is interesting to unpack what the extracts tell us about the relation of spatial perception, the temporal characteristics of speech and their linguistic expression. The interview excerpts examined in this chapter – the parents' and their two children's – tell us the story of the same event. The focus is on the sibling's texts, which can be seen as narratives-in-interaction.

Through the narratives related to displacement, the inseparability of space and time can be well observed, which supports and also marks Bakhtin's chronotope theory as a point of reference. The narrative features of recalling past events in the migration process provide a good example of cross-chronotope alignment. In the case I have presented, this is accomplished as follows. I consider it important to cover the circumstances of the data collection, that is, its time and place.

The venue is the children's school in the centre of Budapest (Hungary), which is not a private place for any of the participants, although it is obviously closer to the children as it is in their school. The data collection takes place in the afternoon, it is spring, the place is bright and sunny. The interviewer had previously met the children on one occasion as part of a class observation during fieldwork in the planning phase of the research. They do not know each other any more than that, and the interviewer is hearing the stories told during the two interviews for the first time. This is important because there is no reference to previous common conversations in the storytelling, and the nature of the information transfer reflects how much and in what way the speaker wants to communicate for the first time of the encounter. In this process, it is well observable how the two chronotopes are related to each other in the speech of both children. In response to the interviewer's question, the talk about what happened begins. Then they start answering, and Fariba says: *elmondom, hogy milyen volt.* (I tell you tell you what was it like) (Extract 2:25), Amir says: *Mhm.. Hár öö kettő hónap három hónapra sikerült jönni.* (Well.. 2 months, 3 months we succeeded to arrive) (Extract 3:36). Both children's opening sentences create a bridge between the present and the past with an introduction in the present tense before switching to the past tense. Fariba uses a simple present tense verb *elmondom* – (I tell you) and then switches to the past tense *volt* (was). Amir utters a temporal adverb referring to the present tense *kettő hónap három hónapra* (for two three months) and then comes the verb in past tense form *sikerült* (succeeded). Although grammatically this refers to the past, semantically the verb results in the present meaning, which is that they succeeded in arriving in Hungary where the present conversation is taking place. With these two short bridging sentences, the teller creates the cross-chronotope alignment.

Next to this phenomenon among the characteristics of the siblings' speech, I present the research results that can be related to telling the story of the migration journey. I have selected passages from both children's narratives that illustrate the phenomena manifested in their speech. When expressing temporal and spatial change, different parts of the narrative can be identified. The change is induced by the evolution of the story. It can be seen that the two children show similar characteristics in their language use and these are strongly related to the content of the narrative. Three interrelated features can be observed in the tempo of the speech, how detailed the narrative is and their forms of linguistic expression.

The tempo of the speech and the mode of narration

Gintsburg, Galván Moreno and Finnegan (2021) argue that the audio component of any narrative is essential and therefore can offer valuable insights that complement the textual analysis. This observation is true for my study as well: for instance, the changes in tempo can be felt at certain points in the story: slowdown and acceleration depending on what part of the lived events the narrator is describing. Along with the tempo changes, the length of the statements also changes. The slowing-down speech is accompanied by longer statements (Extract 2:30, 32, 34; Extract 3:38), within which contiguous passages of text organized into larger units are created. The narrative mode is explanatory in nature, and this effect is passed on by the interlocutor through complex sentences. Both of the children's storylines can easily be followed and understood. The slower-paced parts are linguistically well organized, with coherent use of vocabulary and grammar. Understanding the story is not hindered even by the fact that at some points they choose the wrong grammatical form, as the organization and tempo of the statements give the listener enough time to process the content.

In the faster-paced parts of the speech, the opposite seems to happen: shorter text units, and the unlikely appearance of chain-linked compound sentences can be observed (Extract 2:27; Extract 3:42). The segmentation of the sentences is not produced by syntactic connectors, but rather through the cognitive demand in editing the content, as the speakers are searching for words and grammar (Extract 2: 25; Extract 3:44). Thus we can see statements that are quick and short, which give the feeling that the speakers have closed their passage of thoughts and do not want to talk about them any more (Extract 2:29; Extract 3:40). At these points, it can be perceived that the content of what they have to say shapes the characteristics of language production. With this strategy the children usually cover up painful, traumatic experiences, such as when Amir describes the fatigue of walking – *nehéz volt, hát muszáj volt* (It was difficult, yes... it was a must) (Extract 3:42), or when he can no longer talk about the sleeping conditions.

Linguistic expression

In the area of Hungarian language production, there are also large differences in certain stages of the interviews that can be observed in the selected extracts. In terms of linguistic expression, there is a sharp separation between those parts where natural language use can be heard and those where speech production deteriorates as a result of emotional involvement.

These phenomena become visible when Amir talks about where they slept along the way. His speech becomes hesitant, he stumbles. He cannot use proper grammatical forms *abbaba* (in that/in those) (Extract 3:44), but we can deduce from the lexical elements (hotel – hotel, there were houses there) (Extract 3:44) what he meant. It is difficult to understand what he says as the linguistic expression disintegrates in his statements. The stuttering and searching for linguistic elements is characterized by the following turn of phrase *mi mi mi csak 14-en voltunk* (what we we just were 14 of us) (Extract 3:46).

In the case of Fariba, it can also be observed that the use of the most basic linguistic elements, lexical units and grammatical marking shows a decline on such occasions. A good example of this is that a basic lexical item *gyalogol* (walk) cannot be recalled. After the interviewer helps her out, the next line is perfectly formulated *gyalogoltunk* (we walked) (Extract 1:25). This happens again in line 27 in the *este* (evening) and at *éjszaka* (night): these words are obviously also familiar to her. The other striking change in language use is that she repeats the units of utterances, giving them a hesitant tone. The repeated elements *nem tudtuk…, nem tudtunk* (we couldn't…, we couldn't) are in the past tense, but the dual transitive mode in the verb conjugation system which exists in Hungarian is misused. This grammatical form is common in the demonstrated function in the Hungarian language and is also known at a basic speaker level. Fariba uses it in other situations in the interview without any problems.

From this we can conclude that there is a momentary regression in the children's speech, which is related to the topic and their emotional involvement. Due to the decline in linguistic expression, the emotional tone of their speech becomes more dominant in making the listener understand the message. Given that both children speak Hungarian at a high level, and the compensation strategies taking place to avoid pronunciation and language-specific distractions work well, it was still possible to understand what they thought. At the same time, the changes in language performance do not show specific features related to the Hungarian language such as disfluency or use of discourse markers. Through this, it becomes apparent that in the narrative parts, a strong emotional involvement is presumably present, as the momentary level regression to one typical of the earlier phases of language acquisition can be observed in the statements of the non-native speaker.

We can see the traumatizing events breaking to the surface through the emotional motivation of short- and fast-paced speech organization. However, these processes could be noticed not only in the tempo of their speech, but also in the formation of basic language units. In this case, regression has a significantly stronger effect due to the disruption of coherence between content and form because the interlocutor is also hindered from identifying the meaning.

Discussion

I was able to gain insights into the reality of migration through the experiences of children and their parents, which clearly reflect the relationship between macro- and microprocesses described in social scale theory (Blommaert 2007), in this case the process of migration. The narrated event is a turning point in the participants' lives after which they cannot continue their old life, in other words, there is no way of going back to their previous life. The passages of migration and the experience of one's own internal processes bring a profound change in an individual's life which indicates the way ahead. Children perceive such situations as out of their control, which is reinforced by the fact that the parents decide about them and their lives since children are not in a decision-making position. On the other hand, as has been demonstrated by Melo-Pfeifer (this volume), such children suffer the consequences and bear them on an individual level. When confronting traumatic experiences, children often lack the necessary support from their parents because they are not present at all times, and so such children have to deal with the feeling of abandonment and loneliness on their own.

The narration of events from the past and the reliving of these events years later highlight the importance of the organization of space/time, that is, the characteristics of cross-chronotope alignment especially as enabled through the features of grammar and lexical elements. From the tempo and the linguistic organization of the speech units, the difficulties experienced by the storytellers become tangible. The weight of recollection and the atmosphere created by the re-narration become perceptible through the tissue of the dialogue texts. The description of the traumatic elements affects the interlocutor through the voicing activity, which comes about in the organic development of the narrative.

In light of the results, the question arises as to how the circumstances of the narration of the story affect the narrative. In the case of interviews, the story is outlined through a dialogue between the interviewer and the teller. During the interaction the narrative is built up dynamically, with a role for the audience, who in this case is an active participant in the conversation. This is supported by the observations by Gintsburg, Galván Moreno and Finnegan (2021), who argue that the role of the audience in the narrative is of key importance even though it is routinely underestimated. Even if the interviewer's questions are asked in a restrained, supportive, facilitating manner, it is obvious that the teller reflects on the interviewer's questions. Thus it is likely that the result would be a different narrative if the speaker presented his story in the form of a monologue in front of an audience. Having children in a monologue-like situation might not even succeed in generating any narration, simply because children often need guidance in developing their story. As evidence, we see that the boy relied so much on the interaction and feedback from the interviewer that he might have not talked about these events at all if he had not perceived interest in him and his story from the listener's side.

One important issue that has emerged from this study concerns the children's perception of the school's attitude towards their stories. Some parts of the research material suggest that the children have never really talked in school about these stories because they have not been asked about them. In their understanding, this occurs because of a lack of interest from the others. In the teachers' interviews, however, the informants state that they do not want to ask the children about their experiences: if they want to talk about them, they are happy to listen to them, but they do not consider it a good approach to ask them directly. This is completely misunderstood by the children and taken as indifference towards them and their history.

The other aspect of the narrative that emerges in the interaction is the linguistic dimension analysed above. Through dialogical collaboration, the children are helped to recall language elements through the interviewer's scaffolding, the most important role of which is to support rather than replace the missing units, since the children actually were able to use these elements in other situations showing a high level of proficiency. It became apparent that their linguistic regression is momentary and induced by the topic of the narration. Due to their emotionally overwhelmed state, the interlocutor plays a key role in reducing the effects of regression in language use and influences the development of narrative through interaction.

Further use of the results can be seen in that the specific cases presented here will promote, on the one hand, deeper understanding of the behavioural motives of those involved in integration processes. On the other hand, the characteristics of spoken language performance in an emotionally overwhelmed state shed light on which directions of language development would be most effective for students who may have been traumatized due to past experiences. Specifically, this might be relevant in those situations in school when the students need to perform verbally, for example, talking in front of the others, answering questions during lessons or writing tests. Throughout their language development, the children need to become aware of their own functioning mechanisms and know that under certain types of emotional pressure their capacity for linguistic expression might deteriorate. They also need to acquire compensation strategies, which would help them to minimize momentary language regression or even avoid it. They have to learn to identify the context when their capacity declines and to mobilize these compensation strategies. Such strategies would include a combination of communicative techniques like slowing down the tempo, controlling cognitive functions by concentrating on the subject of the conversation, and using certain language elements that can be automatically activated, such as chunks, collocations or formulaic phrases.

Note

1 *pieda* (Pashto), 'on foot'. The mother first comes with this expression in Pashto but soon, with the help of the interviewer, corrects herself and finds the correct expression in Hungarian.

References

Agha, A. (2007), 'Recombination Selves in Mass Mediated Spacetime', *Language and Communication*, 27: 320–35.
Agha, A. (2015), 'Chronotopic Formulations and Kinship Behaviors in Social History', *Anthropological Quarterly*, 88 (2): 401–15.
Bakhtin, M. M. (Bahtyin) (1976), *A szó esztétikája*, Budapest: Gondolat.
Bakhtin, M. M. (1981), *The Dialogic Imagination: Four Essays*, trans. C. Emerson, and M. Holquist, Austin: University of Texas Press.
Bamberg, M. (2012), 'Narrative Analysis', in H. Cooper (ed.), *APA Handbook of Research Methods in Psychology: Vol. 2*, 77–94, Washington, DC: American Psychological Association Press.
Barthes, R. ([1966] 1975), 'An Introduction to the Structural Analysis of Narrative', *New Literary History*, 6 (2): 237–72.
Baynham, M. (2011), 'Narrative Analysis', in K. Hyland and B. Paltridge (eds), *Continuum Companion to Discourse Analysis*, 69–84, London: Continuum.
Baynham, M. (2015), 'Narrative and Space/Time', in A. De Fina and A. Georgakopoulou (eds), *The Handbook of Narrative Analysis*, 119–39, Hoboken, NJ: Wiley-Blackwell.
Baynham, M., and A. De Fina (2016), 'Narrative Analysis in Migrant and Transnational Contexts', in M. Martin-Jones and D. Martin (eds), *Researching Multilingualism*, 31–44, London: Routledge.
Blommaert, J. (2001), 'Investigating Narrative Inequality: African Asylum Seekers' Stories in Belgium', *Discourse & Society*, 12: 413–49.
Blommaert, J. (2007), 'Sociolinguistic Scales', *Intercultural Pragmatics*, 4: 1–19.

Blommaert, J., J. Collins, and S. Slembrouck (2005), 'Spaces of Multilingualism', *Language & Communication*, 25: 197–216.
Clerc, S. (2009), 'Les dessins d'apprentissage d'élèves nouvellement arrivés en France: vecteurs d'un apprendre autrement?', in M. Molinié (ed.), *Le dessin feflexif*, 119–40, Cergy-Pontoise: Université de Cergy-Pontoise.
Dörnyei, Z. and E. Ushioda (2011), *Teaching and Researching Motivation*, Harlow: Pearson Education.
De Fina, A. (2003), 'Crossing Borders: Time, Space and Disorientation in Narrative', *Narrative Inquiry*, 13 (2): 367–91.
De Fina, A. and A. Georgakopoulou (2015), 'Introduction', in A. De Fina and A. Georgakopoulou (eds), *The Handbook of Narrative Analysis*, 1–17, Hoboken NJ: Wiley-Blackwell.
De Fina, A. and A. Tseng (2017), 'Narrative in the Study of Migrants', in S. Canagarajah (ed.), *The Routledge Handbook of Migration and Language*, 381–96, London: Routledge.
De Fina, A., G. Paternostro, and M. Amoruso (2019), 'Odysseus the Traveler: Appropriation of a Chronotope in a Community of Practice', *Language and Communication*, 70: 71–81.
De Fina, A., G. Paternostro, and M. Amoruso (2020), 'Learning How to Tell, Learning How to Ask: Reciprocity and Storytelling as a Community Process', *Applied Linguistics*, 41 (3): 352–69.
Freeman, M. (1984), 'History, Narrative, Life-span Developmental Knowledge', *Human Development*, 27: 1–19.
Freeman, M. (2015), 'Narrative as a Mode of Understanding: Method, Theory, Praxis', in A. De Fina and A. Georgakopoulou (eds), *The Handbook of Narrative Analysis*, 21–37, Hoboken, NJ: Wiley-Blackwell.
Genette, G. (1980), *Narrative Discourse*, Oxford: Blackwell.
Georgakopoulou, A. (2007), *Small Stories, Interaction and Identities*, Amsterdam: John Benjamins.
Gergen, K. J. and M. M. Gergen (2001), 'A narratívumok és az én mint viszonyrendszer', in J. László and B. Thomka (eds), *Narratív pszichológia. Narratívák 5*, 77–120, Budapest: Kijárat Kiadó.
Gintsburg, S., L. Galván Moreno, and R. Finnegan (2021), 'Voice in a Narrative: A Trialogue with Ruth Finnegan', *Frontiers of Narrative Studies*, 7 (1): 1–20.
Hatoss, A. (2012), 'Where Are You from? Identity Construction and Experiences of "Othering" in the Narratives of Sudanese Refugee-background Australians', *Discourse & Society*, 23 (1): 47–68.
Herman, D. (2009), *Basic Elements of Narrative*, Oxford: Wiley-Blackwell.
Jacquemet, M. (2005), 'The Registration Interview: Restricting Refugees' Narrative Performances', in M. Baynham and A. De Fina (eds), *Dislocations/Relocations: Narratives of Displacement*, 194–216, Manchester: St Jerome Publishing.
Labov, W. (1972), *Language in the Inner City: Studies in the Black English Vernacular*, Philadelphia: University of Pennsylvania Press.
Labov, W. and J. Waletzky (1967), 'Narrative Analysis', in J. Helm (ed.), *Essays on the Verbal and Visual Arts*, 12–44, Seattle: University of Washington Press.
Leconte, F. (2009), 'Quand le dessin fait discours: enquête auprès d'adolescents nouvellement arrivés en France sur leur vécu des langues', in M. Molinié (ed.), *Le dessin feflexif*, 87–115, Cergy-Pontoise: Université de Cergy-Pontoise.
Maryns, K. and J. Blommaert (2001), 'Stylistic and Thematic Shifting as a Narrative Resource', *Multilingual*, 20 (1): 61–84.

McAdams, D. P. (2001a), 'A történet jelentése az irodalomban és az életben', in J. László and B. Thomka (eds), *Narratív pszichológia. Narratívák 5*, 157–75, Budapest: Kijárat Kiadó.
McAdams, D. P. (2001a), 'The Psychology of Life Stories', *Review of General Psychology*, 5 (2): 100–22.
Melo-Pfeifer, S. and A. Schmidt (2019), 'Integration as Portrayed in Visual Narratives by Young Refugees in Germany', in S. Melo-Pfeifer and P. Kalaja (eds), *Visualising Multilingual Lives: More than Words*, 53–72, Bristol, Blue Ridge Summit: Multilingual Matters.
Nyiri, P. (2001), 'Expatriating Is Patriotic? The Discourse on "New Migrants" in the People's Republic of China and Identity Construction among Recent Migrants from the PRC', *Journal of Ethnic and Migration Studies*, 27 (4): 635–53.
Pastor Relano, A. M. (2010), 'Ethnic Categorization and Moral Agency in "Fitting in" Narratives among Madrid Immigrant Students', *Narrative Inquiry*, 20 (1): 82–105.
Pennycook, A. (2010), *Language as a Local Practice*, London: Routledge.
Perrino, S. (2015), 'Chronotopes. Time and Space in Oral Narrative', in A. De Fina and A. Georgakopoulou (eds), *The Handbook of Narrative Analysis*, 140–59, Hoboken, NJ: Wiley-Blackwell.
Propp, V. (1968), *Morphology of the Folktale*, Austin: University of Texas Press.
Rampton, B. (2006), *Language in Late Modernity: Interaction in an Urban School*, Cambridge: Cambridge University Press.
Razafimandimbimanana, E. (2009), 'Autoportraits d'enfants migrants plurilingues en classe d'accueil à Montréal: une démarche altéro-réflexive', in M. Molinié (ed.), *Le dessin feflexif*, 141–64, Cergy-Pontoise: Université de Cergy-Pontoise.
Rosenthal, G. (1991), 'German War Memories: Narrability and the Biographical and Social Functions of Remembering', *Oral History*, 19 (2): 34–41.
Vertovec, S. (2007), 'Super-diversity and Its Implications', *Ethnic and Racial Studies*, 30 (6): 1024–54.

Discussion questions

1. How are scale theory's macro- and microprocesses interpreted in the context of migration?
2. How does the cross-chronotope alignment take shape in the example presented in the chapter?
3. What linguistic background characterizes the research participants?
4. Which characteristics of speech provide insight into the narrator's emotional attitude to his or her own story?
5. Why is the description of changes in linguistic expression important?

6

Families on the Move: Spacetimes in Narratives of Language Socialization within Transnational Multilingual Moroccan Families in Spain

Adil Moustaoui Srhir

Introduction

The dynamics of globalization are in constant movement and so material and symbolic resources are in a permanent state of flux in which the space-time relationship may undergo changes (Giddens 1991). As Brah (1996) and Østergaard-Nielsen (2003) argued, individuals and communities in transnational and diasporic contexts create spaces connected between *here* and *there* through social, linguistic, communicative, religious, economic and political practices, forging an entire series of experiences, responses and expectations. One of the most complex and multifaceted spaces that have been the subject of scholarly debate across transnational and migration studies is the family. The growing number of transnational and multilingual families around the world in recent decades has generated academic interest in exploring not just how these families integrate into broader societies, but also what is happening within the family home environment. This includes questions such as the impact of transnational and multilingual experiences on family dynamics and everyday life; how families deal with new and ever-changing spaces and environments; and how they construct and renegotiate their identities, building social relations in different temporalities (Hua and Wei 2016).

As a transnational social space, the family provides and forms a *habitus*. According to Bourdieu (1983), the cultural and social capital that a person receives from his family implies the development of an original habitus, a set of dispositions and practices, encouraged by parental agency which operates as a regulatory mechanism for social practices that allow people to move with varying degrees of ease among different fields of competence (Bourdieu 1983; Bourdieu and Wacquant 1992). A habitus also provides the context in which capitals of various forms (economic, social, cultural) are valued and given meaning. Along these lines, Carrington and Luke (1997) consider that habitus is not only built and acquired in the home, but also shaped through a process of language socialization throughout life. This Bourdieuan consideration of the habitus in the home allows us to interpret how family members interact within the different interactional social spaces and times in which their relationships, practices and ideologies unfold. At the same time, it provides the conceptual tools necessary to analyse the role of language at the heart of these interactions and spaces. Even more, the transnational approach points to a significant change occurring in social life and practices in the sense that society is reformulated as multi-located social fields (Levitt and Schiller 2004), in which delocalized spaces are created that connect various scale-levels (Blommaert 2007; Dong and Blommaert 2011). These multi-located transnational social fields span borders and connect intertwined territorial scales and social space with overlapping power hierarchies. The family as a transnational social space thus provides an interesting context for exploring the tensions and ambiguities generated around the coexistence of a variety of linguistic resources, capitals, practices and ideologies – embedded in multiple scales, temporalities and spaces – that are prioritized and managed at home in a transnational context.

Based on the sociolinguistics of diaspora, this chapter aims to address the following issues: (1) the way in which multilingual transnational Moroccan families are faced with decisions about language and culture due to their participation in society; (2) the family ideologies, practices and management of heritage languages (HLs), inserted in certain temporalities and spatiality that affect language socialization, and their potentially positive impact on immigrant minority languages; (3) the temporalities and temporal factors that create new spaces for the transmission of the HLs within Moroccan families in a transnational context; and (4) the manner in which transnational family experiences can lead to situations of conflict due to the intersection of various agencies, ideologies and interests within the same family.

In order to answer these questions, I analyse the language socialization narratives in HLs within Moroccan families in Spain. In these narratives, I examine the nature of family language management in the home based on the linguistic biographies of migrant families of Moroccan origin. For this purpose, I consider family language ecology not just as 'a form of rationality, a reasoned organization of sociolinguistic regime at the scale-level of the family' (Blommaert 2018: 4) but also as a means of reproducing 'Moroccanness' with its Arabic, Amazigh and Muslim components, where space and temporal factors act as a key element in all these processes.

The chapter is organized into five sections. I first provide the theoretical background to space and time connected with family language practices, specifically in the transnational context, and also provides an overview of the research methodology. Then I describe the data collection process. This is followed by the analysis, focusing on the following: (1) how HLs are constructed as accommodated resources in *delocalized spaces*; (2) which family-specific temporalities create spaces for the transmission of HLs; and (3) how different family transnational experiences that occur in diverse spaces, scales and temporalities generate situations of conflict within families. The final section includes a discussion of the results and draws a series of conclusions.

Spatiality and temporality in language practices

Studies in social sciences argue that spatiality and temporality are a means for considering individuals within the dimensions of space and time in order to discern patterns in their everyday interactions. Scholars from social and other disciplines who have contributed to the spatial turn have posited that space is dynamic and socially and temporally constructed. Accordingly, many of these scholars target 'the processes involved in *spatialization* rather than the more static notion of *space* in order to examine human activities' (Higgins 2017: 102). Connecting space with language practices, Heidegger (1971) argues that through language and action, people regularly conflate spaces and places. In turn, Bourdieu focuses on meaning and action in order to argue that space can have no meaning aside from practice. Therefore, and as Bourdieu indicated, habitus constitutes and is constituted by actors' movement in space and the way that practices that emerge in some spaces interact in interdependent ways to inculcate and reinforce cultural knowledge and behaviours.

As Higgins (2020: 102) points out, 'in most applied linguistics research, space is acknowledged as a container for language', but in fact space should be considered in terms of the ongoing construction of human activity and practices. Although spatiality has been neglected in contemporary social theory, in recent decades the emergence of the concept of scale (Blommaert 2007) has enriched theoretical reflection on the spatial turn (Leitner and Miller 2007). Prinsloo (2017) claimed that 'the emergence of scales theory in sociolinguistics reflects this wider theoretical context, sometimes called "the spatial turn" in social theory, or the turn to the concept of "spacetime", that involves ideas about space and time as inextricably interconnected'. Based on these contemporary views, 'sociolinguists have started to see space not just as a neutral background but as agentive in sociolinguistic processes' (Prinsloo 2017: 4). Blommaert (2010: 80), in his essay on sociolinguistics of globalization, describes this new view arguing that 'languages and discourses move around, but they do so between spaces that are full of rules, norms, customs and conventions, and they get adapted to the rules, norms, customs and conventions of such places before moving further on their trajectories'. Yet Blommaert, Collins and Slembrouk (2005: 203) indicate that space is part of what we understand by 'context', which, as Gumperz (1982) and others have argued, is not a passive 'decor' but rather an active, agentive aspect of communication. However, space both shapes and is shaped by linguistic and communicative practices, and should therefore be seen as a site where power relations and inequalities are made visible, but where they can also be transformed in time.

Temporality is another relevant issue in language practices in society. As Blommaert, Collins and Slembrouk (2005: 203) discuss, each instance of human communication has 'an intrinsic temporality. Every communication event develops in some timeframe and in some space, and both, as we know, have effects on what happens and can happen'. In our research, temporality is understood in terms of how temporal factors impact on languages, practices and ideologies. The interest in this chapter lies explicitly in the complexities of family transnational experiences as rooted in temporal factors, associated with the move or what is known as 'the temporality of transnationalism'.

In this sense, consideration of the 'move' or what Heller (2011) referred to as the shift 'from stability to mobility' further contributes to the study of language practices and multilingualism in a post-structuralist and critical perspective. Heller makes a specific mention of the trajectories of social actors and linguistic and material resources in time and the way in which they cross and intersect with one another. Yet the mobility turn emphasizes the study of social processes and practices linked to forms of movement (of materials, people or capital) rather than phenomena linked to specific temporalities and geographical contexts (Prego Vázquez 2021).

The idea of spatiality and temporality is of particular interest to us, as in our research it extends to one particular key space and its temporalities, namely the family. Indeed, it is applied not only to linguistic socialization, but also to how HLs as resources are transmitted, developed and evolve, together with their underlying ideologies, practices and management within the transnational families in a number of social spaces and specific temporalities.

The home as spacetime for socialization on HLs

The home is one of the most complex and multifaceted spaces, and it has been the subject of scholarly debate across many disciplines. As Gieseking et al. (2014: 147) point out, the home is both a place and an idea and 'it resonates as a spatial metaphor in everyday conversations "home is where the heart is" or "there's no place like home"'. The home is also considered the locus of everyday family life and at the same time operates on a variety of overlapping scales that indicate how and where people have a sense of belonging. The home, although essentially cultural and social, is also a feature that escapes the boundaries of social and cultural structures because it is constantly being made and remade through our actions and practices. As such, it moves with us and is always open to other spaces. It is, first and foremost, a place for family interaction and the setting for personal intimate behaviours free from public interpellations. The home is also the place for the development of personal values and patterns of socialization and social reproduction within the family (Imrie 2014: 156). Yet the family is possibly one of the most private of spaces in which we navigate, and is considered by Fishman (1972) to be a private domain. Nevertheless, as Lanza and Lexander (2019) argue, this notion of 'the family as a private domain, requires to be critically discussed' and 'indeed can be challenged in light of current theoretical approaches to the study of space as applied to transnational families'. In this sense, Lanza (2020a: 180) maintains the notion of the family as a private space, indicating that 'we would need to argue that when it comes to communication, we can choose the language or languages we want to speak, express the ideologies or attitudes we have concerning different languages, and construct the identity(ies) we wish to construct through our own language choices'.

The exploration of the family as a transnational space has contributed to understanding the impact of declarations and alternate ways of feeling attachment in terms of how members experience the family as a transnational space, on occasions with conflicted or inconstant meanings, but also within specific temporalities (Imrie 2014;

De Fina 2012). Transnationalism is defined and understood as 'the process by which immigrants forge and sustain multistranded social relations that link together their societies of origin and settlement' (Basch, Schiller and Blanc 1994: 6), and is broadly referred to as 'multiple ties and interactions linking people, families, communities or institutions across the borders of nation-states' (Vertovec 1999; 2004). The paths that transnational individuals and families tread in order to sustain multistranded social relations that connect their societies of origin and settlement are in large part impelled by temporal factors of their move(s) (Hirsh and Lee 2018). Specifically, the focus is on how the inherent temporality associated with the move(s) at the very least affects decisions, actions and strategies regarding the use, learning, maintenance and/or loss of HLs in a diasporic context.

In accordance with this theoretical framework, the chapter is framed within an approach that understands family language management regarding HLs as ideology, practice and management (Spolsky 2012), and explores how they are (re)negotiated as different points in time. As family management occurs mainly in home, it responds particularly to 'what is actually done with language in day-to-day interactions; family members' beliefs and ideologies about language and language use; and their goals and efforts to shape language use and learning outcomes' (King et al. 2008: 909). My key argument in this chapter is that greater attention should be paid to the diverse experiences of transnational families, what parents do in terms of actions and practices, and the strategies they use to face the challenges of multilingualism in spacetimes in a transnational context. This is based on the idea that a family language management approach on a micro-scale allows us 'to uncover in detail the influencing forces behind such choices with a focus on culture-specific beliefs that may hamper language maintenance and may account for the differences in language maintenance and shift trends from one community to another' (Pérez Báez 2013: 31). As parents and children move through social and geographical spaces, they encounter different language ideologies and language regimes. Through language use and everyday actions, spatial practices contribute to the construction of (safe) family spaces that are recognizable to speakers. Finally, given that language management is a discursive construct (Blommaert 1996), this chapter is also framed from an explicit empirical analysis of family narratives. As Lanza (2002a: 177) states, 'narrative analysis has evolved over the years and transcended monologue focused stories to stories embedded in conversation, from big stories to small stories – from a focus on narrative as text to narrative as social practice'. In this sense, sociolinguistic approaches to studying migrant narratives allow me to understand the ways in which individuals and communities use languages and varieties to negotiate regimes of languages, identities, agencies and power in their social representation and positioning of the self in social relations and day-to-day experiences (De Fina and Georgakopoulou 2012; Golden and Lanza, 2019; Lanza 2013; Lanza, 2020b). Specifically, this chapter addresses the ideologies and agencies in migrant narratives related to the capitalization and transmission of HLs in transnational context and the consequences of their maintenance. The chapter focuses on how the intersection of multi-opposed agencies across times in migrant narratives can create conflicted situations in different scale-levels and space within transnational Moroccan families.

Participants and data collection

According to data from the Spanish Statistical Office (INE in its Spanish initials/1 January 2021), there are 869,661 people of Moroccan origin in Spain and 297,097 people with Spanish citizenship who were born in Morocco. Moreover, Moroccans make up the largest community of foreign origin in Spain.

A large proportion of the Moroccan population residing in Spain comes from the Rif region in northern Morocco, which is an Amazigh-speaking area (Bernabé López and Berriane 2004). The Rif region was an area of the Spanish protectorate, and therefore large numbers of people from this region are socialized to some degree in Spanish. Worthy of mention in this sense is that most of the transnational families I interviewed had a linguistic life trajectory in their country of origin marked by state linguistic policies that, at least until recently, failed to recognize the vernacular mother tongues of the country, specifically the so-called *Darija* (Moroccan Arabic), despite the fact that Amazigh (Berber) was recognized in 2011 as an official language. We are thus dealing with families who display complexity in their multilingual linguistic repertoire, which includes the local languages *Darija*, Amazigh and Standard Arabic, as well as the colonial and transnational languages, namely French and Spanish. Furthermore, these families attach different degrees of value to these languages, and have a particular understanding of the relationship between languages and power, in terms of their social, practical and functional status, both in their country of origin and in the host country. Moroccan families also pass on their religious practices and attend the local heritage schools or mosques, which act not only as places of worship but also as spaces in which to learn and reproduce the language and cultural practices of their country of origin.

The data analysed in this chapter was collected over five years in three qualitative studies begun in 2012. I conducted ten interviews and eight discussion groups (DGs) involving more than forty mothers and fathers of Moroccan origin in Madrid and peripheral locations in the Castilla la Mancha autonomous community, specifically the southern belt of the province of Toledo on the boundary with the region of Madrid. The interviews and DGs focused directly on the topic of family language management and their experiences and strategies regarding the transmission of their HLs. In addition to the interviews and discussion groups, I conducted an ethnographic study in an HL Islamic School managed by the Moroccan community in Fuenlabrada, a peripheral location situated in the south of the Madrid region. During my ethnographic work in this HL school, I interviewed mothers and fathers whose children attended Modern Standard Arabic and religion lessons. Some of the mothers interviewed are also involved in teaching these programmes. In all the narratives, which included both first- and second-generation migrants, the HL and its transmission emerged as a primary concern for the community in general, posing social, political, educational and even economic challenges.

Darija (see above) was the language used in all the interviews. It was chosen because it is a *lingua franca* that can be used among all the Moroccan linguistic communities.

Findings

HLs in *delocalized spaces*: Between transmission and accommodation

This section analyses how the HL is constructed as linguistic capital and social resource within the family, facilitating greater internal cohesion and consequently the integration of the children within the language communities, both in diaspora and back in the country of origin as delocalized spaces. I will explore also how the family language ideologies move from a continuum of interests and aspirations in spacetimes.

Example (1): Interview with Mouna (mother of a girl and a boy)

> Interviewer: Do you think that Arabic has other functions in your family? Is it simply used to communicate, or does it have other functions such as maintaining the link with your origins and the family in Morocco?
> Mouna: Yes. I want my children to know Arabic to communicate because (*c'est vrai*) it's true they need to interact because they have their cousins. Tomorrow, when we are no longer around, they ought to be able to communicate and maintain the link and be able to talk with their relatives. That's the main function. That's why I bought a house in Morocco, to give them these experiences and for my children to keep up their Arabic.
> Interviewer: To maintain the links.
> Mouna: Yes. (*Un lien*) a link and a tie with Morocco and they would never abandon their roots. It is also a valuable language, and although we speak *Darija*, it is another language that will be useful wherever you go and you can gain a lot from it.

Example (2) is a discussion group with first-generation male migrants residing in Madrid (the numbers correspond to the identification code of each informant)

> 2: How will a person know their relatives? Tell me. There are some who don't know their uncle, and ask their father: Hey Dad, what are my uncle and aunt's names? And Thingummy and little What's his name? And also there are those who ... because they know Arabic and every year you take them to Morocco and they visit the family and are in touch with society.
> 6: You know, you can read the posters, you know how to read and write Arabic and everything.
> 2: Imagine you die and when you die you leave an inheritance in Morocco, how is he going to manage it? He goes there and they cheat him and they give him a kicking and he comes back here again.
> [...]
> 3: I didn't say don't learn Arabic, I just wanted to know what the basic argument was.
> 2: Look, it's your mother tongue ... it's the language of religion; it really is the language of religion. On the Day of Judgement God will ask you about it.

In examples (1) and (2) there is a certain insistence that in order to gain access to different resources, the children of Moroccan families must acquire their mother tongue, learn Modern Standard Arabic and all those skills that will allow them to resolve communication situations in the country of origin. Language is understood and constructed as a relational resource and therefore as a way of structuring and facilitating relationships, such as accessing social knowledge, managing assets or accessing religious capital and knowledge in different spaces and scales. The child is therefore treated as a member of this language community and is expected to master the language in question through its transmission and teaching. These processes should establish the child in a territorial space other than that of her/his country of residence, together with a sense of identification and cohesion with the community of practice through sharing a language of origin. This converts the actual language into a linguistic and communicative resource to be used among family members and members of the wider community. The value that the fathers and mothers place on their languages and the market logic that they outline are reproduced through diverse scales in different spaces: (1) that of the host country, in which Arabic and Amazigh are linguistic resources of value within the family, resisting the dominance of Spanish; and (2) that of the country of origin, where both languages clearly occupy a highly significant position. In both examples the fathers and mothers assign and concede a high value to the HL in the context of diaspora, as social and economic capital, and as a linguistic resource for communicative and social purposes.

In both examples, we can see also how the mothers and fathers assign a relevant role to short and long stays in the country of origin in terms of language transmission as well as sociocultural and linguistic socialization.

When family temporalities create spaces for HL transmission

This section examines the temporal factors of the families' move(s) that create processes whereby parents forge and sustain multistranded social relations that link their societies of origin and settlement, and how these processes affect decisions, actions and strategies regarding language use, learning and the maintenance of HLs in a transnational context.

Example (3), interview with Mohamed, father of two boys.

Interviewer: This Moroccan atmosphere, doesn't it exist at home for instance?
Mohamed: We're trying now, but only now.
Interviewer: How do you go about it? Creating this atmosphere, like the one in Morocco, like that atmosphere in Morocco here in Spain, do you create it from time to time?
Mohamed: For example, when my nephews come, they start speaking Arabic and they speak a lot in Arabic. He speaks Arabic perfectly (in reference to his son). He speaks with the children. When there is a celebration, although Spanish is the predominant language, this is the problem I was telling you

about. As I told you before, some parents take their children and follow this strategy of taking the children and leaving them for a long time. This works well. These are the kind of solutions that must be implemented in order to maintain the language. When they go to Morocco, they speak Arabic as if they were true natives. What works with the children is that when they have vacations you take them and leave them there. You leave them there, so you don't speak to them in Spanish.

Interviewer: Ah, have you done that?

Mohamed: Yes, on one occasion.

Interviewer: You did.

Mohamed: Yes, there was one occasion, and it was from around June to September. He came back from Morocco Arabized and he would speak to you in perfect Arabic. He spoke to the children in Arabic and it worked very well. These are the solutions that are needed to maintain Arabic. The best way for the children is when they are on vacation you take them and leave them there and come back. You leave them there, so you don't speak Spanish to them. You leave them for three months for example there in Morocco and they will come back Arabized.

In this narrative, Mohamed recognizes that family visits and celebrations are temporary moments and factors that play an important role in creating spaces for linguistic socialization and language transmission in the home. Temporary visits by relatives and family celebrations are moments that are often ideal for creating environments and settings, albeit momentarily, that reproduce temporalities and spatialities related to the country of origin. Moreover, as Mohamed points out, the children use Arabic more intensely during these periods 'when my nephews come, they start speaking Arabic and they speak a lot in Arabic. He speaks Arabic perfectly (in reference to his son). He speaks with the children. When there is a celebration', 'When they go to Morocco, they speak Arabic as if they were true natives'. This example also illustrates how important it is for families to have strong roots in Moroccan culture. Despite residing in Madrid, and even though the children are being socialized in Spanish culture, family cohesion, close emotional bonds, unity and a sense of connectedness to Moroccan culture are transmitted through their collective participation in reunions and celebrations, considered as momentary temporalities that guarantee linguistic and cultural socialization through HLs. In this example, Mohamed insists on the need to practice the other temporal strategies for linguistic socialization, namely summer vacations and long stays in Morocco. He considers that they create spaces for immersion, linguistic practices in Arabic and the transmission of the original cultural values that the children were expected to adopt in full at home on their return to Spain: 'You leave them for three months for example there in Morocco and they will come back Arabized.' Likewise, according to Mohamed, long stays in Morocco allow children to disengage from the use of Spanish for a certain time, since if there is no one who knows this language in the children's environment in the country of origin, the use of Spanish could temporarily disappear during their stays in Morocco.

Example (4): Interview with Fouad, bilingual Riffian (Riffian/Moroccan Arabic) and father of two girls and a boy

> Fouad: since our first daughter was born (.) we have tried to talk only Riffian at home because our parents ((his and his wife's)) only speak Riffian.
> Interviewer: Only Riffian?
> Fouad: Only Riffian, so that there is communication with them when we go on holiday… so they can communicate with their grandparents. We started that way and the truth is that this strategy worked well. Then we started teaching them some Arabic here. When our second daughter was born, despite the health problems she has had, they learned to write in Arabic. Children like ours are lucky to have parents who studied in Morocco to a good educational level, as my wife and I did.

This narrative reveals that from the outset Fouad and his wife adopted the strategy of 'Riffian only', or 'one parent one language', at home, albeit accompanied by the teaching of Arabic, also in the home. The family management strategy was therefore to maintain bi/multilingualism in keeping with the profile of the parents, and also the grandparents who live in Morocco, which is also in line with the sociolinguistic regime of the Moroccan region of Rif. In turn, the mother tongue – which in the case of Fouad's family is Riffian – is considered to be a heritage language for family interaction in both Spain and the country of origin, and must therefore be passed on. Fouad gives a mini-narrative of the family's language trajectory in different temporalities related to the children's language socialization. He also describes the linguistic repertoire of the parents and their children prior to their starting school, the strategies deployed in passing on heritage languages, and the language usage options for interaction in the home and other spaces such as the Rif during vacation periods. Fouad's experience clearly shows how the crossover and intersection of various temporalities related to different linguistic socialization processes – family (here), and outside (Rif region/Morocco) – lead to an extensive repertoire of languages, varieties and the acquisition of linguistic competences. These linguistic competences and varieties are capitalized in the sense that some can be assessed and considered valid in certain communicative fields, temporalities and spaces, mainly the family home and the Rif, the region of origin, and the space preferred to spend holidays and stays in Morocco.

In examples (3) and (4), we see how social processes, events, practices and actions of the families are moved and developed on a continuum of layered temporalities and spaces, from the strictly national and local (here) to the transnational (there) (see also Gintsburg and Breeze, this volume). In both examples we observe how Fouad's and Mohamed's families create and construct different sociolinguistic scales (Blommaert 2007), in which the HLs and linguistic resources are transmitted and developed. The move from one scale to another (e.g. from the local to the translocal; from the momentary to the timeless) implies and presupposes access to different socializations and resources. At the same time, the move of the families on a continuum of multilingual, translocal and socio-spatially and temporally diverse scales allows them to elaborate and establish their own sociolinguistic regime in the transnational context.

Transnational family experiences and conflicted situations in spacetimes

This section considers how various family transnational experiences that occur in diverse spaces, scales and temporalities generate conflictive situations in which the parental model of socialization and language management are contested or fail to satisfy children's expectations and interests.

Example (5): Interview with Nassima, a mother of three children (two boys and one girl)

> Interviewer: Did you want to say something before?
> Nassima: I wanted to comment on something. We usually say that when the children are in Morocco they learn the language, Arabic, integrate and know how to behave. I have my children, thank God, they were all born here and thank God we speak the language, Arabic. However, we do not use *Fusha* (Modern Standard Arabic) very much at home. If I speak *Fusha* one day, they start making fun of me, Oh Mom speaks *Fusha*, she is a genius, you understand.
> Interviewer: You mean *Fusha*?
> Nassima: *Fusha*, if I speak and say something they start to
> Interviewer: You don't mean our *Darija*.
> Nassima: (*Laughing*) I tell them that it is necessary to introduce things like that in *Fusha*. What I have found here is my children in my opinion, they socialize with things quickly here more than when we are in Morocco.
> Interviewer: How? Can you explain that in more detail?
> Nassima: I mean social situations, because here, for example, the children adapt quickly to a lot of things. When they travel to Morocco, I realize that when I come back, I feel disappointed because my children haven't integrated.
> Interviewer: It's because they are on vacation.
> Nassima: Like here.
> Interviewer: The vacations are not the same.
> Nassima: The vacations.
> Interviewer: It's not like when there is school.
> Nassima: I get tired of being flexible and saying we are on vacation. I'm not happy when I come back even if I have been there for two months. It is the opposite of when they were little because I had to spend a lot of time (in Morocco) for them to learn many things. However, now that they are growing up and now as long as they are growing up they will tell me Mom, when we go to Morocco, we don't feel comfortable.

In example (5), Nassima recognizes that during family vacations and stays in Morocco, her Spanish-born children do not have a sense of integration in their country of origin. This occurs because the socialization model in Spain and which is familiar to her children differs from the models that may exist in Morocco, despite the fact that her children are fluent in *Darija* and have no communication difficulties in the country of origin. As a result of the awkwardness this situation generates, her children are reluctant to spend vacations or short stays in the country of origin: 'However, now that they are growing up and now as long as they are growing up they will tell me Mom, when we go to Morocco, we don't feel comfortable.' Furthermore, Nasima admits that this situation is becoming exacerbated as the children become older.

Example (6): Narrative by Nazha, mother of four children (three boys and one girl)

> Nazha: But Glory and Praise be to God, when they are in Morocco it's not the same as when they are here, they come here, I mean they are … .
> Interviewer: You mean the vacations.
> Nazha: Because my children were older when they came to Spain, in Morocco it was fine, thank God. When he came to Spain he was completely transformed. He doesn't pray as he should. I swear to God Almighty that in Morocco, he went to associations and participated in invocations, God bless the Almighty. However, the year he arrived in Spain the boy no longer prayed as he should and I started to argue with him. He started to go out with Christians and he prefers to spend time with them instead of with Moroccans. And he tells me that I have nothing to do with Moroccans. He has only Christian friends here, only European-Spanish friends. When we brought him here, he was twelve years old; at that time, he was twelve years old and not like when he was in Morocco. I mean I took him to the mosque to learn the Qur'an. I took him to the mosque here to learn the Qur'an – and I started teaching him at home. I don't know what could have happened for him to have changed from how he used to be. That is what I feel.

In example (6), the conflictive situation arises in a transnational context. Nazha employs an emotionally and religious socio-discursive frame to describe how her son, after settling in Madrid, embarked on process of rupture from Moroccan-ness in cultural, religious and sociolinguistic terms. The emergence of acts of agency produced by her son has affected the emotions and led to situations of conflict in terms of the family's social, cultural, religious and affective cohesion. This example clearly manifests how the transnational experience of Nazha's family stirred mixed-emotions in both the young people and their parents regarding the language socialization model and diverse forms of belonging in different temporalities. Within the context of these new and changing circumstances, the children started to see themselves as active and creative social agents who produce their own cultures and ideologies (Lanza 2007). During the interview, Nazha also describes how her son only speaks to her in Spanish, which is also the sole language he uses in the home. This situation has generated a sense of frustration for Nazha, who complains that she is often unable to follow the thread of the interactions with her son; she is unable to understand what he says and comments with his friends at home: 'I mean I took him to the mosque to learn the Qur'an. I took him to the mosque here to learn the Qur'an – and I started teaching him at home. I don't know what could have happened for him to have changed from how he used to be. That is what I feel.' Consequently, Nazha believes that her son is a family member who is linguistically and culturally positioned outside the community.

Example (7)

Nazha: Because with the others I don't have any problems (in reference to her older children); they are married thank God and have their own homes and I also have grandchildren. The last one I have had problems with. Because he speaks a lot of Spanish at home and especially on his cellular.
Interviewer: Hmm.
Nazha: Specifically in his personal relationships; I have to see who he talks to, who he talks to and who he is with. It gets on my nerves. Now I regret it and I regret it to the point that I start to cry. But next year, God willing, I will try to learn, to know what my son says, especially with his friends, the girls, sincerely, sincerely.

Examples (5), (6) and (7) reveal the manner and degree to which young people of Moroccan origin contest their parental model of socialization, and how the agency they develop in terms of ideologies, expectations and decisions affects language and cultural socialization models in which notions such as age, education, citizenship and cosmopolitanism are relevant. And as Baquedano López and Kattan (2007) argued, children are agents of change and have the potential to influence and reproduce established cultural and linguistic practices in temporalities when the agency is irrupted and activated in specific moments. In the same sense, Corsaro (2002) argues that children not only participate and reproduce family social order and sociolinguistic regimes, but also contribute to changes through their own (re)interpretation for an 'interpretive reproduction' account of the process of socialization. Both examples show how the irruption of the children's agency in adolescent years influences the patterns and models of language(s) socialization and habitus, leading to a loss of control by mothers and fathers. This occurs not only over the family language and cultural management at home but also over the social, cultural and religious order within the family, occasionally leading to conflicts between children and their parents.

Discussion and conclusion

This chapter has analysed how the tendency of fathers and mothers of Moroccan origin towards an 'authentic' conception and an essentialist interpretation of their heritage creates an integration of certain common markers of identification in specific spacetimes that navigate between ethnolinguistic and cultural aspects, and in particular between what is Arabic and what is Moroccan on a local, translocal and transnational scale. This also reflects the Moroccan community's tendency to associate itself with a linguistic, cultural and religious identity that is neither local nor national, but instead belongs to the country of origin. In all the narratives analysed here, the socio-spatial units are reordered within multiple power hierarchies that affect space and territory as well as the distribution of resources and the mobility of people in several times. Nevertheless, parents always valorize Moroccan HLs as resources and capital of use as they move across continents, countries and regions. These practices conform this transnational social space (Vertovec 2004), created primarily by the family, which contains a wide range of responses and solutions aiming to socialize the children in their home languages.

In their narratives, all the families interviewed – who all considered themselves as belonging to ethnic minorities – express the perception that they represent a distinctive culture and are anxious to retain their distinctiveness. 'This self-conscious identity relies crucially on contact with, and a certain understanding of, that which it is distinctive *in contrast to* – which is usually the majority or dominant group' (Hylland Eriksen 1992: 317). Therefore, success in maintaining the HLs of minority transnational Moroccan families depends on the mechanisms, strategies and managements they put in place during different temporalities with the aim of preserving their distinctiveness and differentiation from the dominant communities of host societies that might otherwise assimilate them.

The construction of the HLs that emerge from the transnational families' experiences analysed in this chapter must be considered as stemming from practices that take advantage of all the linguistic and semiotic resources that are believed to form the spatial repertoires (Canagarajah 2018; Pennycook and Otsuji 2014) that children of Moroccan origin gradually incorporate and add to their socialization and life trajectories. In this sense, both the linguistic and spatial transformations shed micro-social light on the transformation of individual linguistic resources, which are essential for their participation in their communities of practices on local, translocal and transnational scale-levels (Moustaoui and Llompart forthcoming).

The family narratives also reveal parents' expectations regarding the nature of their children's language skills in different spaces and times and how they should evolve. These expectations require parents to assume a high degree of responsibility and make considerable efforts in order to improve their children's language skills. Indeed, only the regular use of HLs in daily interactions in the home will guarantee their maintenance and children's possible subconscious acquisition of them. In addition, as examples (1), (2), (3) and (4) have shown, parents go to considerable lengths to make it possible for their children to speak the vehicular varieties, namely *Darija* and Riffian, by creating specific situations or conditions on different scale-levels and temporalities.

Another key issue suggested by this study is how family transnational experiences and moves generate the need to continuously reconstruct, renegotiate and change the family language repertoire, including parental language varieties. Repertoire management is conceived in the manner defined by Blommaert (2010), and is translated into the planning of the use of the language variation of Arabic, with its two repertoires: Moroccan and Standard Modern, and in the case of the Amazigh families, a wide repertoire of language and speech varieties. The Arabic language, in the case of the Muslim Moroccan diaspora, also fulfils functions related to the ability to carry out socio-religious practices framed in the Muslimness – often associated with the Arabic language – which is assumed to exist and will be inherited by the children over time (Moustaoui 2020).

The analysis of the spacetimes of language socialization within Moroccan transnational multilingual families indicates a reterritorialization of the spaces of interaction (Pennycook 2007) under the control of the family in which the languages (of migration, in diaspora, of origin and heritage) are capitalized and accommodated. The larger sociopolitical and sociocultural processes of the space and time that lie within the family point to the increasingly limited and diminishing capacity of the nation state to control linguistic and identity diversity on a microscale level in a context of globalization, transnationalism and the mobility of resources.

References

Baquedano-López, P. and S. Kattan, eds (2007), *Growing up in a Multilingual Community: Insights from Language Socialization*, Berlin: Walter de Gruyter.
Basch, L., S. G. Nina and C. S. Blanc (1994), *Nations Unbound: Transnational Projects, Postcolonial Predicaments, and Deterritorialized Nation-States*, Amsterdam: Gordon and Breach.
Bernabé, López G. and M. Berriane, (2004), *Atlas 2004 de la inmigración marroquí en España*, Madrid: UAM.
Blommaert, J. (1996), 'Language Planning as a Discourse on Language and Society: The Linguistic Ideology of a Scholarly Tradition', *Language Problems and Language Planning*, 20: 199–222.
Blommaert, J. (2007), 'Sociolinguistic Scales', *Intercultural Pragmatics*, 4 (1): 1–19.
Blommaert, J. (2010), *The Sociolinguistics of Globalization*, Cambridge: Cambridge University Press.
Blommaert, J. (2018), 'Family Language Planning as Sociolinguistic Biopower', *Tilburg Papers in Cultural Studies*, 216: 1–8.
Blommaert, J., J. Collins, and S. Slembrouk (2005), 'Spaces of Multilingualism', *Language & Communication*, 25: 197–216.
Bourdieu, P. (1983), 'The Field of Cultural Production, or the Economic World Reversed', *Poetics*, 12: 311–56.
Bourdieu, P. and L. Wacquant (1992), *An Introduction to Reflexive Sociology*, Chicago: University of Chicago Press.
Brah, A. (1996), *Cartographies of Diaspora. Contesting Identities*, London: Routledge.
Canagarajah, S. (2018), 'Translingual Practice as Spatial Repertoires: Expanding the Paradigm beyond Structuralist Orientations', *Applied Linguistics*, 39 (1): 31–54.
Carrington, V. and A. Luke (1997), 'Literacy and Bourdieu's Sociological Theory: A Reframing', *Language and Education*, 11 (6): 96–112.
Corsaro, W. (2002), *The Sociology of Childhood*, Thousand Oaks, CA: Sage and Pine Forge Press.
De Fina, A. (2012), 'Family Interaction and Engagement with the Heritage Language: A Case Study', *Multilingua*, 31 (4): 349–79.
De Fina, A. and A. Georgakopoulou (2012), *Analyzing Narrative: Discourse and Sociolinguistic Perspectives*, New York: Cambridge University Press.
Dong, J. K. and J. Blommaert (2011), 'Space, Scale and Accents: Constructing Migrant Identity in Beijing', in J. Collins, M. Baynham, and S. Slembrouk (eds), *Globalization and Language in Contact: Scale, Migration, and Communicative Practices*, 42–61, London: Continuum.

Fishman, J. (1972), *The Sociology of Language: An Interdisciplinary Social Science Approach to Language in Society*, Rowley, MA: Newbury House.

Giddens, A. (1991), *Modernity and Self Identity: Self and Identity in the Late Modern Age*, Cambridge: Cambridge University Press.

Gieseking, J. J., W. Mangold, C. Katz, S. Low, and S. Saegert (2014), *The People, Place, and Space Reader*, New York and London: Routledge.

Golden, A. and E. Lanza (2019), 'Language Learning and Literacy: The Multilingual Subject in Narratives of Older Immigrant Refugee Women', in S. Bagga-Gupta, A. Golden, L. Holm, H. P. Laursen, and A. Pitkänen-Huhta (eds), *Reconceptualizing Connections between Language, Literacy and Learning*, 253–76, Cham, Switzerland: Springer.

Guarnizo, L. E. (1997), 'The Emergence of a Transnational Social Formation and the Mirage of Return Migration among Dominican Transmigrants', *Identities*, 4 (2): 281–322.

Heidegger, M. (1971), *Poetry, Language, Thought*, London: Harper and Row.

Heller, M. (2011), *Paths to Post-nationalism: A Critical Ethnography of Language and Identity*, Oxford: Oxford University Press.

Higgins, C. (2017), 'Space, Place, and Language', in S. Canagarajah (ed.), *The Routledge Handbook of Migration and Language*, 102–16, London: Routledge.

Hirsch, T. and J. S. Lee (2018), 'Understanding the Complexities of Transnational Family Language Policy', *Journal of Multilingual and Multicultural Development*, 39 (10): 882–94.

Hua, Z. and L. Wei (2016), 'Transnational Experience, Aspiration and Family Language Policy', *Journal of Multilingual and Multicultural Development*, 37 (7): 655–66.

Hylland, E. (1992), 'Linguistic Hegemony and Minority Resistance', *Journal of Peace Research*, 29 (3): 313–32.

Imrie, R. (2014), 'Disability, Embodiment and the Meaning of the Home', in J. J. Gieseking, W. Mangold, C. Katz, S. Low, and S. Saegert (eds), *The People, Place, and Space Reader*, 156–61, London: Routledge.

King, K., L. Fogle, and A. Logan-Terry (2008), 'Family Language Policy', *Language and Linguistics Compass*, 2 (5): 907–22.

Lanza, E. (2007), 'Multilingualism and the Family', in P. Auer and L. Wei (eds), *Handbook of Multilingualism and Multilingual Communication*, 45–66, Berlin: Mouton de Gruyter.

Lanza, E. (2013), 'Empowering a Migrant Identity: Agency in Narratives of a Work Experience in Norway', *Sociolinguistic Studies*, 6 (2): 285–307.

Lanza, E. (2020a), 'Digital Storytelling: Multilingual Parents' Blogs and Vlogs as Narratives of Family Language Policy', in L. A. Kulbrandstad and G. Bordal Steien (eds), *Språkreiser. Festskrift til Anne Golden på 70-årsdagen*, 177–92, Oslo: Novus Forlag.

Lanza, E. (2020b), 'Urban Multilingualism and Family Language Policy', in G. Caliendo, R. Janssens, S. Slembrouck, and P. Van Avermaet (eds), *Urban Multilingualism in Europe: Bridging the Gap between Language Policies and Language Practices*, 121–39, Berlin: Mouton de Gruyter.

Lanza, E. and K. V. Lexander (2019), 'Family Language Practices in Multilingual Transcultural Families', in S. Montari and S. Quay (eds), *Multidisciplinary Perspectives on Multilingualism. The Fundamentals*, 229–51, Boston and Berlin: De Gruyter.

Leitner, H. and B. Miller (2007), 'Scale and the Limitations of Ontological Debate: A Commentary on Marston, Jones and Woodward', *Transactions of the Institute of British Geographers*, 32: 116–25.

Levitt, P. and N. Schiller (2004), 'Transnational Perspectives on Migration: Conceptualizing Simultaneity', *International Migration Review*, 38 (3): 1002–39.

Moustaoui Srhir, A. (2020), 'Making Children Multilingual. Family Language Policy and Parental Agency in Moroccan Transnational Families', *Journal of Multilingual and Multicultural Development*, 41 (1): 108–20.

Moustaoui Srhir, A. and J. Llompart Ebsert (forthcoming), 'Family, School and Intersectionality: The Language Regimentation of Multilingual Repertoires in Spanish Youth of Moroccan Origin in Spain', *Sociolinguistic Studies* (Special Issue Family language policy and the family sociolinguistic order in a neoliberal context).

Østergaard-Nielsen, E. (2003), 'The Politics of Migrants: Transnational Political Practices', *International Migration Review*, 37 (3): 760–86.

Pennycook, A. (2007), *Global Englishes and Transcultural Flows*, London: Routledge.

Pennycook, A. (2010), *Language as Local Practice*, London: Routledge.

Pennycook, A. and E. Otsuji (2014), 'Metrolingual Multitasking and Spatial Repertoires: Pizza Mo Two Minutes Coming', *Journal of Sociolinguistics*, 18: 161–84.

Pérez Báez, G. (2013), 'Family Language Policy, Transnationalism, and the Diaspora Community of San Lucas Quiaviní of Oaxaca, Mexico', *Language Policy*, 12: 27–45.

Prego Vázquez, G. (2021), 'Escalas Sociolingüísticas', in J. Pujolar and L. Martín Rojo (eds), *Claves para entender el multilingüismo contemporáneo*, 91–130, Zaragoza: Editorial UOC/Prensas de la Universidad de Zaragoza.

Prinsloo, M. (2017), 'Spatiotemporal Scales and the Study of Mobility', in S. Canagarajah (ed.), *The Routledge Handbook of Migration and Language*, 364–80, London: Routledge.

Purkarthofer, J. (2019), 'Building Expectations: Imagining Family Language Policy and Heteroglossic Social Spaces', *International Journal of Bilingualism*, 23 (3): 724–39.

Spolsky, B. (2012), 'Family Language Policy – the Critical Domain', *Journal of Multilingual and Multicultural Development*, 33 (1): 3–11.

Vertovec, S. (1999), 'Conceiving and Researching Transnationalism', *Ethnic and Racial Studies*, 22 (2): 447–62.

Vertovec, S. (2004), 'Migrant Transnationalism and Modes of Transformation', *International Migration Review*, 38 (3): 970–1001.

Discussion questions

1. What power hierarchies emerge in the process of the language socialization within Moroccan families in a context of minority and transnationalism?
2. How are HLs hierarchically stratified in a context in which notions such as delocalization, indexicality and scale-levels play an important role in the family language management developed in the diasporic context?
3. How does the complex multilingual repertoire of Moroccan families affect the design, negotiation and establishment of family language management in space-time?
4. How might the family language policy model be seen as an imposition of patterns of interaction and use of language(s) and consequently as an imposition of a sociolinguistic order within the family?

5. What new linguistic practices, such as translanguaging, are created and used by family members, as a result of the intersection of different language regimentation, scales levels, spaces and temporalities in language socialization? And how are these linguistic practices viewed, valued and considered by the parents and the children?
6. How do children and young people of Moroccan origin negotiate and renegotiate paths and identities for themselves that are more complex than the heritage positions ascribed to them by their parents in different space-times?

7

Circumscribed Transnational Spaces: Moroccan Immigrant Women in Rural Spain

Sarali Gintsburg and Ruth Breeze

Introduction

The recent waves of migration from Africa and the Middle East to Europe have given rise to an ample volume of research in areas as diverse as sociology, law, international relations, geography and global security. However, such studies tend to focus on members of the active population, mainly men, and young people in full-time education, probably because of the relative ease of contacting these groups. Despite the considerable presence of women in the migrant population, they tend to be less visible than their male counterparts and have attracted less research attention. However, this very invisibility suggests that female migrants have greater difficulty accessing public spaces and are accordingly less integrated into European societies. This problem seems to be particularly acute among women from the Muslim world, where various factors seem to hinder them from participating actively in the workplace and interacting with other members of the local society. In this chapter we help to redress this balance by using data from interviews with Moroccan women living in the rural Ribera area of Navarra, Spain. Our analysis proceeds from a consideration of the way these women represent themselves and their lives in space, taking the related dimension of time into account. In what follows, we first provide an overview of some theoretical reflections on the way people experience and represent space and time, and on the discursive cues that enable us to perceive how they are positioning themselves within the represented spaces. We then approach the interview material to examine how these women presented themselves and their lives as extending over private and public spaces, in both Spain and Morocco, and how these spaces were envisaged in gendered terms. Where appropriate, some consideration will also be given to temporal representations. In our conclusions, we discuss the implications that these findings may have and propose some lines for future research.

Social spaces and times

Since Durkheim, reflections in the social sciences have been guided by the awareness that the category of space depends on the particular society's way of configuring social grouping and the geographical use of space, just as time is simultaneously determined by the social rhythm prevailing in the group ([1912] 2003: 628). Homing in on the concept of space as such, Lefebvre (2009: 183–7) wrote that in human society all 'space is social: it involves assigning more or less appropriate places to social relations [… .] social space has thus always been a social product'. But these 'social spaces' can only continue to exist because they are accepted and reproduced by individuals over the years. Taking a discourse perspective on this, within a Vygotskian framework there is clearly no problem with the notion that private discourse is shaped by, and stems from, public discourse. In a broad sense, the meaning and structure of personal discourse on identity has to be looked at within a cultural context, and in relation to the larger normative system in which a person lives (Harré et al. 2009: 26). On this understanding, external social phenomena (customs, norms, conventions, laws) come to be internalized by individuals in their long process of formal schooling and informal socialization (Durkheim 1982), and these internalizations ultimately help to shape individuals' inner sense of space and time. Consequently, the personal understanding of space and time as expressed in discursive cues is clearly both an internalization and reproduction of external discourses and representations, and an attempt on the part of the individual to reflect on, make sense of and sometimes challenge those representations.

To understand this better, the notion of chronotope (Bakhtin 1981) could perhaps prove useful. This was designed to be used in literary analysis with a view to explaining the spatio-temporal aspect of literary production, but the chronotope concept is now being used in sociolinguistics in a number of cases to analyse narratives related to identity, 'foreignness' and migration (see Blommaert and De Fina 2017; Perrino 2015). While in the classic novel the concept of *chronos* was of great importance because, as we learn from Bakhtin, the event can only happen if there is time and space involved, sociolinguists using chronotope in the context of narrative research have noticed that although the role of time is, indeed, important, the role of space remains understudied (Baynham, De Fina and Georgakopoulou 2003). The vagueness of this term, coupled with the intuitive understanding that, on one hand, time is not always linear and, on the other hand, space is not always secondary, has led some scholars to rethink the notion of chronotope and its applicability outside the world of literature. The foregrounding of space rather than time in certain cultures led Epstein ([2003] 2007), for example, to prefer the term 'topochrone' as a more appropriate construct for approaching certain non-literary texts. This might be particularly relevant in contexts where the future is either certain or unknowable, whereas space presents significant known or explorable variations. In the discussion of our analysis, we will return to this notion and explain how we think it could be relevant in the study of migrant narratives.

Of course, when we are looking at the discursive spatial self-representations of migrant women, it is clear that various influences are at work. Identity can be seen as a discursive phenomenon, as representations of self and other are co-constructed socially through language and other semiotic resources. But it is also a material phenomenon enacted in time and space, in real settings, and as a consequence of actual events over many years: context and experience determine the identities that individuals take up (McAvoy 2016: 113), and their representations of different spaces are shaped by cultural, social and physical forces. In the words of Preece (2019: 3), 'the identities that people "inhabit" [...] are constrained, among other things, by their access to the types of social spaces and relations (or discursive spaces) in which identities are constructed, constituted, negotiated, accomplished and performed', as well as by the identities that they are 'ascribed' by others, which may position them as outsiders, or as having only limited rights to participation.

Within this, as people 'inhabit' the social spaces available to them, they also take up 'positions' that mark out their own attitude or feelings about these spaces. These 'positions' lack the fixed, routine nature of roles, for example, and instead are dynamic, influenced by evolving discourses and storylines (Harré and Dedaic 2012). Nonetheless, the roles that people have, as well as their personal attributes, characteristics and previous experiences, certainly influence the positions available to them, and that they actually take up. An examination of positioning can bring to light the frames within which people actually carry on their lives, and how they accept or challenge the roles ascribed to them (Harré et al. 2009: 9), shedding light – in our case – on the spatial limitations that they perceive to be relevant. As De Fina explains (2016: 170), an analysis of positioning enables us to capture 'social agents' stances and evaluations of their and others' roles, ideas, actions, etc.' Such an analysis should proceed both from indexical processes (gesture, proxemics, deictics) and from discursive aspects expressly explaining or evaluating spatial and other relations.

In this context, the analysis of social and public spaces inhabited by Muslim African (in our case, Moroccan) immigrant women living in a rural European (in our case, Spanish) area appears to be of special interest. On one hand, the Moroccan immigrant community is one of the fastest growing communities in Europe and it is also the largest foreign community in Spain (Eurostat 2021, Moustaoui, this volume). On the other hand, although women constitute 44 per cent of the Moroccans living in Spain (Observatorio Permanente de la Inmigración 2020) very little is known about their lives and expectations. The status of Moroccan immigrants in various European countries like France, Belgium and the Netherlands (Ennaji 2014), as well as the United States (Gintsburg 2016), has been investigated, but none of these analyses has focused specifically on the women of the Moroccan immigrant community since these studies generally gravitate towards active members of the workforce, usually men, and the more accessible settlers in urban areas. They thus fail to address the kind of migration found in rural areas of countries like Spain, and most particularly, the issue of female experiences of migration, which may well differ radically from those of men.

Some previous research exists focusing on the status and identities of Moroccan women inside Moroccan society (Mernissi 1991; Sadiqi 2016), shedding light on the workings of patriarchal control within both traditional and modernizing Muslim cultures, and exploring the possibilities for resistance. However, so far there is very little research on the experience of Moroccan women in the diaspora, and what there is tends to rely on sociological methods (e.g. Carrasco, Pàmies and Ponferrada 2011).

Previous publications about their situation in Spain concentrate mainly on migrant women's difficulties entering the workplace (Castilla Vázquez 2017), a situation that worsened in the aftermath of the financial crisis (Moreno-Colom and López-Roldán 2018) and is likely to have deteriorated still further after the Covid-19 pandemic. Perhaps because of language barriers, none of the previous studies has attempted to address the female Moroccan population in Spain on its home ground, entering the women's domestic spaces to listen to their own vocalizations of their situations, and their perceived possibilities and constraints.

The present study represents a first step in this direction, using interviews and written narratives from a larger research project on the Moroccan women of the Ribera area along the River Ebro in Navarra, Spain. For the purposes of this chapter, these data will be investigated using an approach centred on how these women's habitus is configured with regard to space and time. This represents an interesting point of departure because, owing to their geographical proximity, Morocco and Spain have complex, long-standing relationships: the Muslim invasion and occupation of Spain in the period of al-Andalus, the Reconquest and the Spanish colonization of northern Morocco, all form part of a complex shared historical background that influences present-day relations between the two countries and their peoples. At the same time, geographical and architectural similarities mean that Moroccans may perceive continuities rather than difference as they continue their journey northwards from the straits of Gibraltar. Our study therefore sets out from the configurations of social space and time within which these women map out their everyday lives, and analyses these to gain deeper insights into these particular experiences of trans-Mediterranean migration.

Sample and method

This chapter is based on narratives and interview data obtained in the course of a larger project dedicated to the identities and situation of Moroccan immigrant women carried out in collaboration with the Regional Government of Navarra (Gintsburg, Fernández-Vallejo and Tayaa 2020). In the course of the project we organized four focus groups in four different rural areas in the south of Navarra (fifty-two women took part in the focus-groups discussions) and conducted forty-two in-depth interviews. The age of participants was 18–70, while the number of years spent in Spain varied between 6 months and 27 years. More than two thirds of the participants originated from the Eastern region (*l-jiha šarqiya*) of the Moroccan Kingdom, but there were also participants from Rabat-Salé-Ammour-Zaer, Chaouia-Ouargha, Tangier-Tetouan, Sus-Masa and Fes-Bulmán. Only a few participants were from an urban background, and the majority originated from rural areas in the above-mentioned regions. The demographic data is displayed in Table 7.1.

The participants took part in four focus groups held in different Spanish villages in the Ribera area and also completed an in-depth interview in which they responded to a set of prompts in Moroccan Arabic designed to elicit spoken or written narrative. Regarding the analysis, our approach was based on the recursive reading and re-reading of the interview and narrative texts, together with consultation among the

Table 7.1 Moroccan women who participated in the study.

Native languages			Education			Employment (low-skills job)	
Arabic (1st language)	Berber (2nd language)	No formal school education	Primary school	Secondary or high school	University degree	Employed	Unemployed
42	4	3	14	17	10	9	33

research team. This enabled us to pinpoint the sections of the responses that appeared to contain references to space and time, to focus on deictics[1] (I, we, here, there) and to identify certain recurring themes that appeared in this context.

Analysis of the interview data

In the following subsections, we set out some of the main spatial configurations identified in the women's narratives and relate these to local-contextual issues and wider cultural themes.

Domestic spaces: Recreating an ideal Moroccan home while living in 'safe' Spain

The social spaces described by these participants tend to be circumscribed to the immediate area inhabited by the woman and her family, and the services available there. The small Spanish towns or villages where the women lived were described in prosaic, unambitious tones as having 'all the necessary services', and as being a 'comfortable neighbourhood' or a place where 'everyone treats me well'. The speaker role adopted is clearly that of a 'humble and unassuming citizen' whose highest expectation is a safe environment where everyday life can be conducted without major difficulties of a social or economic kind.

Safe spaces

A simple examination of the women's responses brought out the importance of the terms 'security' (*amn*) and 'safety' (*amān*), amounting to what we might term a 'safety' motif recurring in the words of almost all the speakers. Thus one woman wrote 'safety exists here, unlike Morocco', while another described the village in Spain as 'a safe environment', and another referred to 'a quiet life with no problems'. Other references are to the relative ease of living in Spain, and the better standard of the housing and towns, with 'all necessary services'. One woman wrote that she would not like to return to her country of origin:

> Morocco doesn't have security and safety. Its future is foggy. Democracy and human rights don't exist there.
>
> (42)
>
> al-Maġrib la amn walla amān wa-l-mustaqbal hunāk ġāmiḍ wa la tūjad la dīmūqrāṭīya wa la ḥuqūq al-insān.

This 'safe' domestic space is not just a place of protection against outside threats. It is also a place where people behave well and are therefore morally safe. The opposite of this is mentioned in the context of adolescent children, particularly boys, who are described as 'drifting away from good behaviour' (43), a spatial representation of their leaving the safe and familiar habitus in a way that is sensed as a threat to the security and integrity of the community.

Spain, Morocco and the reproduction of 'home'

Regarding their specifically Moroccan identity, it was interesting that several women formulated answers that brought out a relationship of similarity between their current surroundings and their places of origin. One woman, who is originally from Guercif, expressed this as a comparison between Tudela and Oujda (Figure 7.1) which then led to a declaration that signals strong affection and acceptance for the people of the Spanish city:

> The city of Tudela is a wonderful city, it is similar to the Moroccan city of Ouijda, I consider all its people to be members of my family. Tudela reminds me of student days in the city of Oujda, as if I came home and feel happy in it
>
> (56)
>
> madīnat Tūdēla hiya madīna rāʔiʕa ušabbihuha dāʔiman bi madīnat Wijda al-maġribīya kulla anāsiha aʕtabiruhu ʕāʔilati. Tūdēla tudakkiruni ayām dirāsati fi madīnat Wijda ʕindama kuntu murtāḥa wa ka-ʔannani mšit ila dāri wa-rtaḥtu fīha

Conversely, another woman, who is a native of Tetouan, brought her hometown in Morocco into a parallel with Spain, linking it first to the Spanish city of Granada (Figure 7.2) and then to the shared tradition of al-Andalus (a general term for the medieval Arabic civilization in Spain and the caliphates spanning southern Spain and much of North Africa over several centuries):

> Very beautiful city, some call it the second Granada. It still bears an imprint of al-Andalus. When a visitor enters it, he is pleased.
>
> (43)
>
> madīnati jidd jamīla, hunāka man yaṭlaqu ʕaleyha Ġarnāṭa at-tāniya ma tazāl yaṭbaʕuha aṭ-ṭābiʕ al-andalusi ḥīnama yadxuluha az-zāʔir yuḥissu bi rāḥa

Circumscribed Transnational Spaces 127

Figure 7.1 Skylines of Oujda (left) and Tudela (right).

Interestingly, the Moroccan 'home' space, with its traditions and customs, is generally placed on an equal level with the Spanish 'outside' space. Thus one woman mapped out a kind of mirror-image vision of the side-by-side existence of cultural spaces, in which she lives alongside her Spanish neighbours while maintaining her own traditions:

> Since I am an immigrant, it is very important for me to maintain my customs and traditions in Spain. I see this as a positive thing when we learn about each other's ways of life: knowing more about them would make our coexistence easier. Or maybe one day he [the Spanish person] will need to travel to my country. I mean at least he will have some knowledge that will be useful for him during his travels and will help him to adjust and coexist with the Moroccan society.
>
> (43)

ka muhājira la budda min al-muḥāfaḍa ʕala ʕādāti wa taqālīdi dāxila Isbānya wa hadihi l-lmasʔala arāha bi ʕayn ījābīya ḥatta yataʕarraf aṭ-ṭarf ʕala-l-axar wa yashal

Figure 7.2 Old town walls in Tetouan (left) and Granada (right).

ʕaleyhi at-taʕāyuš rubbama ḥatamat ʕaleyhi ḍ-ḍurūf li-l-hijra aw as-safar ila baladi (al-isbāni) aqṣud wa bi-t-tāli ʕala-l-aqall ladeyhi maʕlūmāt taxdumuhu atnāʔ safarihi wa tuʕayyinuhu ʕala-l-indimāj wa-t-taʕāyuš maʕa-l-mujtamaʕ al-maġribi.

We may note that in the foregoing explanation the verb forms alternate, so that even though the statements about Moroccan identity are initially delivered in the first person ('I'), there is then a move to 'we' to refer to people in general ('we learn about each other's way of life'). The explanation then lurches to 'they' to refer to 'others' ('knowing more about them would make our coexistence easier'), and then to 'he' (an imagined Spanish person), who learns about these customs so that 'he' can 'adjust to and coexist with' Moroccan society if he needs to venture into the (our) Moroccan space. These abrupt changes of perspective may arise as a consequence of the interview situation, as a result of real or imagined interaction with the interlocutor (see Baynham 2000), but might also index contradictory positioning on the part of the speaker, who seems at times to include members of different groups (everyone, Moroccans) in her 'we' perspective, and at other times to exclude them. Of particular interest in this is the way that she justifies her need to maintain 'her' traditions because she is an immigrant, while the Spanish visitor to Morocco is assumed to have to 'adjust' to Moroccan society.

Along similar lines, another woman explained that she would like to have a place where Spanish and Moroccan women could meet, and 'they' could get to know 'us' better. A third participant expressed the view that Spain was a good country to live in

Figure 7.3 An overview of *salon* in two Moroccan homes in the Ribera.

because 'it has a moderate climate, people from the country (i.e. people of Moroccan origin) and my Moroccan family'.

In all these formulations, the Spanish and Moroccan cultural spaces are envisioned as contiguous and somehow parallel, two equal, cultural areas from which people approach each other. Interaction between the two is envisaged on an equal footing, yet in a way that is curiously vague and theoretical.

Interestingly, we observed that that every Moroccan household in Spain we were invited to visit in the course of our project represented a reconstruction of a typical Moroccan *salon* (living room) reproduced through the use of traditional Moroccan furniture and elements of decor, including religious symbols and tableware (Figure 7.3). This recreation of the Moroccan interior illustrates an appropriation of space on the lines described by de Certeau (1988).

The public arena: Already in Spain or still in Morocco?

Although the women in this sample lived in villages and small towns, their explanations appear to show relatively little interaction with what might be termed the local 'public space', in the sense of visits to public places, interactions with members of the non-Moroccan community, or participation in the workplace. In fact, many of these women tended to spend most of their time at home, only venturing outside for necessary errands, such as shopping or taking children to school, if that. Various issues emerge that appear to act as impediments to social integration, in particular, the hijab, deficient language skills and the issue of gender segregation.

The hijab as barrier – the hijab as protection

On the one hand, the women in this sample all wore the veil or hijab (one actually wore the burqa), and this was understood by several of them as constituting a barrier to entering Spanish spaces – the participants appeared at times to be engaging with a dominant cultural narrative that positions them as 'invisible' (*ġeyr marʔīya*), 'fenced' (*musawwara*) or experiencing 'neglect' (*tamhīš*) (see González Ruiz and Izquierdo Alegría 2014 concerning controversy regarding Islamic dress in Spain). In some cases, this barrier took on considerable importance, leading to a perception that local people could not build any social connection with them, or even make eye contact. Most participants alluded to this situation and seemed to take some degree of exclusion for granted, but did not describe this isolation or rejection in detail. For example, one woman was asked to describe her job, and began by saying 'the hijab has never been a problem for me', thereby reflecting by its contradiction a prevailing social discourse about how the hijab is (of course) generally thought to cause problems in the workplace. A few participants were more vocal about how they felt on this point. One woman put it like this:

> The Spanish society should realize that the hijab worn by woman is part of her religious identity and it doesn't represent a barrier that prevents her from economic or social integration.
>
> (42)
>
> ʕala-l-mujtamaʕ l-isbāni an yadruk anna ḥijāb al-mra huwa min hawiyatiha d-dīnīya wa la yaqif ʕāʔiqan amām indimājiha al-iqtiṣādi walla-l-ijtimāʕi

This statement hardly makes sense if the speaker herself had not experienced the opposite, that is, that the hijab had indeed prevented her from integrating socially or taking paid employment. Another participant expressed her view of this issue as follows:

> My message to a human. I don't say to everyone but to the majority of them. [I would like to ask them] to review their opinion about the Muslim woman, to learn more about her before judging her. Don't look at her with prejudice and don't focus on her hijab. [She is] hidden, yes, but this doesn't mean that her mind stopped working. It would be more correct if you could stop judging her based on the 'surface'. She will be a giving person if only she gets the chance, she will be able to rise and continue in this country towards a better life.

risālati ila-l-insān. la aqūl kulluhum lakin muʕḍamuhum la budda min iʕādat an-naḍr ḥawla l-marʔa l-muslima, taʕarrafu ʕaleyha qabla an taḥkumu wa la tanḍuru ileyha bi ʕayn wāḥida wa la turakkizu ʕala ḥijābiha. Musawwara naʕam. Hāda la yaʕni anna ʕaqlaha mutawaqqif. Maʕna aṣaḥḥ la taḥkumu ʕala ḍ-ḍāhir. Fa hiya muʕṭaʔa ida utīḥat laha l-furṣa qādira ʕala an tarfaʕa wa tazīd bi hāda-l-balad ila-l-aḥsan.

By prefacing this as her 'message to a human', this participant seems to want to mark her statement as public and somehow representative, pointing to the kind of 'semi-theoretical disposition engendered by learned questioning' discussed by Bourdieu (1977: 18). Interestingly, her declarations are organized around the idea of 'the Muslim woman', who is described in the third person ('she', 'her') as though seen from a distance or in sociological terms by the 'you' and 'they' to whom these words are addressed. This suggests that this participant is trying to adopt a distanced or even impartial position, to offer a neutral view of the situation. At the same time, the speaker alludes to the question of the hijab: it is seen as a barrier, but one that can be overcome if people are prepared to go beyond appearances. The implication seems to be that hijab-wearers are being excluded from social spaces that they would like to enter, although ironically the 'fence' and the 'barrier' is something that they themselves wear, rather than a physical barrier impeding entry.

This resonates with the observations made by Mernissi (1991), who argues that that concept of hijab, which is central to the Muslim culture, has a clear spatial connotation being used as a barrier that separates two spaces. But Mernissi emphasizes that linguistically the word 'hijab' can have both a positive meaning – 'protection' and a negative meaning – 'something that blocks/prevents' (Mernissi 1991: 95), revealing an essential ambivalence at the very core of the word itself. Interestingly in the present context, the hijab, as we will see with the language (or lack of thereof), seems to serve the purpose of safeguarding the Moroccan topos that these women continue to maintain despite the many years spent in Spain. The chronos seems to be erased in this account, in a way that is similar to the time negation described by Le Houérou (this volume) among migrants from Ethiopia and the Sudan. The women in this study seem to mirror this ambivalence, conceptualizing the hijab as both a guarantee of safety and a barrier to social engagement, and using it as a way of maintaining an intimate space where they can inhabit a Moroccan 'topochrone'.

Language barriers

Another issue preventing interaction with Spanish society might be termed the 'language problem'. Thus one participant pointed to the low level of Spanish competence among her compatriots, implying that this caused large but unspecified problems:

> It is inevitable that they have a language barrier, although language is necessary for coexistence and communication.

Other participants pointed out that despite having spent in Spain more than ten years, they had not forged any bonds with the Spanish society around them because they still had not mastered the Spanish language, and therefore saw this as a major 'barrier' (ḥājəz). In line with our observations in the previous section, we may infer that this state of 'exclusion' is at least partly 'self-exclusion', in the sense that they opt to inhabit a different topochrone, a situation in which their Spanish neighbours tacitly collude. These barriers may be perceived as confining, but they also protect the women from any possible 'aggression' against their Moroccan topos. For example:

> I can't speak Spanish well, this is the only barrier I have [that prevents me from mixing with Spanish people]
>
> (39)
>
> *ma naʕrafš nəhdər l-isbānīya mzyān hāda huwa l-ḥājəz əl-waḥīd ʕəndi.*

Surprisingly, perhaps, one woman explained this problem as being not just a lack of competence in Spanish. In fact, it seems that some of the women are principally Berber speakers who lacked formal education and thus had poor communication skills in Arabic. This situation seemed to be understood as problematic, and as resulting from a lack of initiative:

> A lot of women need to be woken up. Women don't master either of the two languages – Arabic and Spanish – to the degree they could express their opinions without feeling embarrassed.
>
> (56)
>
> *katīr min an-nisāʔ muḥtājīn ila tawʕīya hunna la tadrayna itqān al-luġatayn – al-ʕarabīya wa-l-isbānīya – li taʕbīr arāʔahunna dūn ḥaraj.*

From a different angle, the women also expressed a desire that their children should receive help with reading and writing in Arabic. One of them said that she would like to see:

> A young child learning reading and writing in Arabic language – this could make easy for him communicating with all his friends in Morocco.
>
> (56)
>
> *al-walad aṣ-ṣaġīr taʕallam al-qirāʔa wa-l-kitāba bi-l-luġa al-ʕarabīya hada yusahhil ʕaleyhi at-taʕāmul maʕa aṣdiqāʔihi fi-l-Maġrib*

By framing this idea as a generalizing narrative, one that is not linked to the particular 'here and now' of Moroccan children in a small Spanish village, this comment reads as curiously 'out of time and space', evoking an ideal topochrone where the child growing up in exile is perfectly integrated into his 'home' culture. While the desire to make sure that child will learn Classical (or possibly Standard) written Arabic is easy to explain based on the direct connotation of Classical Arabic as closely bound up with Muslim religious identity, it is clear for immigrant Moroccan women that knowledge of the language of the Qur'an will not make the process of communication between modern Moroccan children smooth because of the well-known difference between Classical (or Standard) Arabic and Moroccan Arabic. Moreover, since the children growing up in Spain probably do not have lots of friends in Morocco, and would in any case not communicate with them in writing, such a statement takes on a particularly unreal quality, perhaps representing this woman's idealization of the desire to preserve her cultural roots and transmit them to her children, rather than a realistic ambition anchored in her actual experience (see Moustaoui, this volume). Going further, we see how the apparent barriers, both linguistic (poor knowledge of Spanish) and cultural (wearing the hijab), are carefully maintained and even cultivated by these women who see them as protection that prevents the Moroccan habitus (topos) from any possible aggression, rather than as an obstacle.

Gendered spaces

In many of the statements it was clear that the women envisage their ventures outside the home space as taking place mainly in female spaces, thus clearly maintaining the traditional gendered division of both private and public spaces, typical of the sociocultural behaviour of Moroccans in Morocco, conditioned by the Islamic and patriarchal norms that shape this society (Sadiqi 2016). For example, one woman described her social contacts as follows:

> My neighbours are my friends. Both Spanish (feminine form) and Moroccans (feminine form).
>
> (56)
>
> *jīrāni hum aṣdiqāʔi sawāʔ al-isbāniyat aw al-ʕarabīyāt*

Another explains that she 'currently' talks to a (female) social service employee (*muwaḍḍifa ijtimāʕīya*), with the mothers of her children's classmates (*ummahāt al-aṭfāl lli ka yeqraw mʕa bnāti*), and that she previously also talked to her (female) workmates (*zamīlāt al-ʕamal*). No interactions with male neighbours or parents were reported by this particular participant, who emphasized the 'female' identity of all her social contacts.

In this context, there is some evidence in these testimonies of the women themselves perceiving gender barriers as necessary or appropriate:

> There are many differences [between Spain and Morocco]. Relations between a man and a woman. Since I am a Muslim, I respect my religion, I have limits that I should respect.
>
> (42)
>
> *kāyn ixtilāfāt kbīra. taʕāmul ma beyn r-rājul w l-mra bima anni muslima aḥtarim dīni ʕindi ḥudūd yajib an aḥtarimha.*

Similarly, another Moroccan woman insisted that Spain should be offering 'activities for women only' (anšiṭa taxuṣṣ al-mra). One participant even expressed the view that the local community should provide special facilities in which the space was organized according to the principles of gender-segregation:

> There should be sports facilities where a Muslim woman could enjoy them because they are free of gender mixing.
>
> (42)
>
> xāṣṣ yəkūnu amākən ryāḍīya tətmakkan li-l-mra l-muslima tastamtəʕ biha xāliya mən əl-ixtilāṭ

In parallel to this, several of the women expressed views such as that the issue of work or wider integration in society was a problem 'for men', presumably not because it was not a problem for women, but because women did not even attempt to participate in these aspects, nor would it be reasonable to expect this of them.

Notably, this appears not to be the same for all participants. For example, a younger woman expressed the idea that in Morocco, some women are marginalized (implying that this is not desirable, and that this is not the same in Spain):

> There is a certain category of women in Morocco that is a bit left out. It doesn't have the same opportunities that men do.
>
> (28)
>
> hunāka nawʕ muʕayyan min an-nisāʔ fi-l-Maġrib muhammaš qalīlan. Laysat ladeyha furaṣ mitl ar-rajul.

Another came up with the view that women received better treatment in Spain:

> Striking difference when it comes to helping women and children and life is better here from all points of view. [...] everything they have is perfect compared to Morocco.
>
> (56)

Another way of putting this was to say that in Spain people were treated equally, 'regardless of your gender'. Several participants also voiced the perception that children too enjoyed greater social respect in Spain than in their homeland:

> They help the woman and acknowledge children's rights because the woman has its value in the society
>
> huma yəsāʕdūn l-mra w yəʕṭūn ḥuqūq l-ṭifl lianna l-mra ʕəndha qīma fə l- mujtamaʕ

The grouping of women with children can be seen as culturally significant. A number of participants also claimed that they need spaces for themselves and their young children, thus confirming the cultural norms of Morocco, and, in broader sense, in the Muslim world, where the right and obligation to care for the child (ḥaḍāna) are almost always given to women (Sabreen 2017), which means that children, until they reach the age of maturity, almost always inhabit the female spaces.

Finally, for some participants there seemed to be a clear hierarchy of social groups with whom they felt able to communicate. One woman explained that she did not communicate with Spanish men, and talked to Spanish women 'only if that is absolutely necessary' (*fi-l-umūr aḍ-ḍurūriyāt*) because they were not interested in communicating with Arabs. She thus placed Spanish women in an intersectional group that was potentially approachable, yet from which she felt excluded by their lack of interest.

Distance and respect

As we have noted, these women's interaction with local communities was generally envisaged in a rather summary way, with little reference to real involvement in social affairs. At most, they pointed to a kind of mutual respect and tolerance:

> I've been living in this city for more than 16 years. Everyone treats me well. And I, in my turn, treat them with the utmost respect and appreciation.
>
> (56)

aʕīšu fi hadihi-l-madīna aktar min 16 sana. al-kull yuʕālimuni muʕāmala ḥasana. wa ana bi dawri uʕālimuhum bi fāʔiqi t-taqdīr wa-l-iḥtirām

Their accounts of village life were curiously distanced: the following extract is from the narrative of a woman who had lived in a particular village for over fifteen years, and whose two children had grown up there. Her account of the 'fiesta' is that of an observer, an outsider who feels no personal engagement in the 'walking' and 'playful activities' so characteristic of the Spanish fiesta, in which every villager participates, people come from miles around, and anyone with the remotest connection with that village makes the effort to show up for at least part of the time in order to join in the festivities:

> My neighbourhood is in the centre of our village there happen a lot of *los paseos* and playful activities during fiestas.
>
> (47)

ḥayy fi wasṭ el-qarya los paseos fi l-ktīr men el-haraj fi waqt el-ḥaflāt

Visions of integration: Maintaining the Moroccan female space

Although the women generally did not lament their lack of integration, it is clear from most of their writing that they felt different from their Spanish neighbours and that participation in the local society was challenging for them. They all spoke from a position of difference and, to a greater or lesser extent, exclusion. This does not mean, however, that they had not thought about ways in which greater inclusion or participation could be achieved. However, the ideas that they had about this were characterized either by the kind of 'parallel spaces' model observed above or projected into the indefinite future as something that their children might one day achieve.

In line with the first model, one participant considered that a particular social space should be created for Moroccan women where they could communicate 'their voice' to state institutions and so that 'Moroccan women and state institutions could have a direct connection with each other' (43). This strongly echoes the patterns identified above, in which the women took up positions within a specifically female Moroccan space from which they observed the communities around them, and from which they might ultimately envisage interaction with Spanish society on a group to group basis.

When it comes to their visions for the future, we may note that a better degree of integration was envisaged for future generations. However, it is clear from the way that this is sometimes formulated that this involves crossing or overcoming an invisible barrier, or as the following comment puts it, becoming like the 'others':

> I want my children to be the 'others', and help the Spanish people. [...] My dream is to see wonderful blending of Arab and Spanish people, so that peace and safety will be in Spain, Islamic countries and everywhere in the world.
>
> (56)
>
> urīdu min abnāʔi an yakūnu al-axarīn yusāʕidūna al-isbān umnīyati an yakūn indimāj rāʔiʕ beyna l-ʕarab wa-l-isbān an taʕumm as-salām wa-l-ʔamn fi Isbānya wa-d-duwal al-islāmiya wa-l-ʕālam kullihi

On the other hand, there is also considerable evidence here of what might be termed the 'migrants' dilemma', that is, the impossibility of return, however unsatisfactory their current circumstances were. It is striking that, despite the women's obvious pride in their Moroccan identity and their desire to maintain their lifestyle and traditions while living in Spanish surroundings, most of the participants made negative comments about Morocco, commenting that they would not like to go back there, that their children hated going there and that they had no future there.

Discussion

In what follows, we will endeavour to tease out some of the strands that have emerged from this analysis, and to relate them to the framework of space and time, and the 'topochrone' (rather than 'chonotope') that they appear to inhabit. After that, we will comment on some further theoretical aspects concerning the nature of the voices in this study and point to some areas that might be worthy of further enquiry.

Following De Fina (2016: 170), our analysis of the women's positioning has enabled us to capture their stances towards, and evaluations of, their own positions and those of others in the social space available. In their self-representations these women seem to inhabit a curiously constrained topochrone, so that most of their lives are lived out in the domestic sphere and conditioned by a need for safety. Their wariness of social contact with local people is perhaps underpinned not only by an unwillingness to engage with the 'other', but also by a belief that all social interaction should be on an equal cultural footing. One is left with the impression that in these villages two cultures are operating side by side, with a certain degree of mutual observation and occasional interaction: despite their physical proximity, their lives are mainly conducted in hermetic capsules, cultural compartments that guarantee minimum exposure to otherness.

The question then arises as to whether this spatial configuration is characteristically female, a point that we cannot fully address since our study included no men. However, let us discuss briefly how our findings overlap with the bibliography on gendered spaces, and specifically on space and gender in the Arab world. Regarding women and space, there is a long tradition of research on gendered spaces in different cultures. In traditional societies, space is often organized and defined in line with gender roles and expectations, and this has traditionally been considered particularly important in the Muslim world (Baburajan 2020; Bird and Sokolofski 2005; Mernissi 1991). For example, in many Arab countries, just as women are expected to inhabit the home, men are understood to have roles in the marketplace or public arena. Even in modern Western societies, men and women have been found to use physical space differently, giving rise to different patterns of spatial occupation (Bird and Sokolofski 2005). In many cultures, women feel more insecure about entering public spaces and exercise more caution about, say, going out alone at night. In the Arab world, gendered aspects of physical space have been widely analysed. For example, in many countries women are encouraged to wear headscarves, hijabs or even burqas when entering public spaces (Briar 2008), or are expected to be accompanied by male relatives when they go out of the house (Babarujan 2020). In some Islamic cultures, even homes are designed to segregate male from female family members (Babarujan 2020; Osman and Suliman 1996). This means that the public space in many Muslim cultures is generally regarded as male dominated, and may indeed be an 'unsafe' space for women. The gendered patterns of spatial occupation observed in the present accounts bear traces of these underlying cultural patterns, although the women also show awareness of local Spanish behaviours, to which they react with varying degrees of rejection, distaste or attraction, depending on their own inner convictions. In fact, recent bibliography stresses the presence of social change in the Arab world: as more women take up paid employment, participate in higher education, and so on, so the gendered character of public spaces is changing, even in the more traditional Muslim societies in the Middle East and Gulf (Baburajan 2020).

In the case of the Moroccan populations in Spain, it seems that the Moroccan culture is perceived as something to be defended, resulting in a psychological state of siege. Many migrants the world over cling more tightly to their home traditions when living in an alien environment, and these women could simply be a further instantiation of this general phenomenon. However, it is also likely that the (perceived) sharp contrast between Spanish and Moroccan women, in particular, which is perhaps most visible in questions of outward attire and behaviour in the public space, leads to the formation of a specific barrier that is particularly hard to overcome (see Breeze 2013). Ironically, the very garments and habits that the women perceive as protective seem also to imprison them (for further discussion of the women's perceptions of Islamic dress, see also discussion in Hassan 2020). Beyond this, the curiously timeless and non-dynamic quality of the women's accounts tends to suggest that in migration they have come not only to build and preserve their own social space, but that they also perpetuate a very different 'chronos' from their neighbours. Although some of the features of their narratives could be attributed to the specific interview setting, or to a lack of proficiency in the language(s) used, it is still striking that their occasional visions of 'different' ways of being in Spain take on a peculiarly unreal, atemporal quality.

Regarding their discursive performances, we have seen that these women, intentionally or unintentionally, position themselves and others and/or are positioned by them, so that their discourse ultimately shapes the distribution of roles and positions through 'moment-by-moment meanings of speaking and acting' (Harré and Moghaddam 2015: 230). As McVee et al. (2018) note, people's own lived experiences influence the narratives that they choose to construct, or those that they refuse to enter (McVee et al. 2018: 389). The positions that these women take up are, at the moment of writing, probably the ones in which they feel most comfortable, or at least, the ones that they sense that they are expected to occupy in the interview situation. But the rather passive roles assumed by these women should not be regarded as fixed or determining for the Moroccan population as a whole, as change is possible, and the patterns we observe today may well not hold for the younger generation of women passing through mainstream education in Spain, for example. At the same time, other researchers have noted that the kind of positioning observed in this study may vary, even for participants of this social status, depending on which space they are currently occupying in their personal geography. For example, Ennaji (2014: 86) documented how Moroccan women were able to transition regularly from a low status as cleaners in Italy during the winter to a high status as wealthy *emigrées* on their summer trips back to Morocco. Such phenomena, like so many aspects of the migrant experience, are rarely opened to the public view.

Another unexpected aspect of these women's discursive performance was the fact that even though the questions were put to them in Moroccan Arabic, most of them chose to reply in Standard Arabic or, at least because the majority of them have not fully mastered Standard Arabic (see Table 7.1), in some mixture of Standard Arabic and Moroccan Arabic. Linguistically, it seems, again perhaps in response to perceived/imagined expectations on the part of the interviewers, that they attempted to occupy the public space with one of the very few tools available to them – Standard Arabic, the language of the public sphere. Together with this, many of their utterances were also 'public' in the sense that they were speaking less as individuals, more as members or 'representatives' of their community. Sadiqi (2016) argues that in Morocco, rural women who see themselves as members of community tend to talk in the name of their community, while urban women adopt an individualistic tone. Our Moroccan immigrant women, who come from different backgrounds, almost always used the interview space to represent their community rather than their personal opinions. This was, for instance, the case of the 42-year-old woman from Tetouan (who now lives in Castejón) with a university degree and the 56-year-old woman from Guercif (who now lives in Tudela), who also has a degree in Arabic philology from the university of Oujda. Both women preferred not to speak as individuals but, instead, felt it appropriate to speak in the name of the immigrant Moroccans (sometimes both men and women) they represent.

Finally, returning to the themes of space and time, we have seen that space takes a primary, very tangible role in these accounts, while time is very much relegated to the background or rendered intangible. According to Bakhtin ([1980] 2020: 85), 'in literature the primary category in the chronotope is time', but in these lives it is clearly space. For this reason, we chose to adopt Epstein's proposal to use the term *topochrone* to describe and analyse cases where time is not superior or equal to space but, instead, is subordinated to space. The term topochrone is now being introduced in literary studies (Burima 2009), but also proving relevant in anthropology, philosophy and political sciences (Kazakova 2018). The reason behind favouring topochrone over chronotope is related to the need to bring out the role of powerful, sometimes enormous space that has power not only over particular individuals or small groups of people but also over their native accounts. Space is arguably more determining in the lives of migrants than time is (see Le Houérou, this volume). As in Epstein's critique of Soviet civilization (Epstein ([2003] 2007); Gordinsky 2020), the 'chronos' is constantly displaced and swallowed up by the 'topos', since time tends to zero, dwarfed in 'the instantaneousness of revolutionary or eschatological transformation'. We could argue that in traditional Islamic cultures, too, since the future is predetermined (see Gintsburg, Breeze and Baynham, this volume), time loses its essential dynamism, and space remains as the dimension within which degrees of freedom and change are possible. On the other hand, as narrative represents, to at least some degree a reconstruction of lived and, most obviously, seen experiences linked to particular places and spaces (and not to time), it is only reasonable to pay more attention to the determining role of space in migrants' lives. We should therefore consider approaching personal migration narratives, where the crossing of physical barriers and the maintenance of cultural ones appear to play a primary role, from the perspective of the topochrone, rather than the chronotope. In the lives that we have glimpsed here, time is represented as standing still, frozen in the regularity of unchanging routine, undisturbed by ambition or even social interaction outside the family sphere. Space thus takes on a greater role, absorbing time into itself to become the main organizing feature of people's lives. On a Durkheimian account (1982), the external social phenomena that shape social interaction become internalized during the process of socialization and come to shape individuals' inner sense of space and time. In the case of these women, their resocialization as adults into the corners of rural Spanish society available to migrants, and their own compliance with this in the name of 'safety', on the one hand, and consensual Moroccan cultural values, on the other, seems to have left many of them inhabiting a strangely confined space, beyond whose bounds they prefer not to venture. Although these insights would need to be confirmed through further studies using ethnographic approaches (e.g. to gauge to what extent the women's accounts are materialized in the patterns of their everyday lives), this chapter contributes towards a deeper understanding of the migrant topochrone in one specific context and provides pointers for future studies of space and time in migrant narrative.

Note

1 To avoid possible confusion, it is important to clarify that in the Arabic language, especially in its written form, subject/personal pronouns (I, we, you, etc.) are typically used when it is important to emphasize or clarify the roles of agents involved in the sentence. Otherwise, the information on the agent is retrieved the verb form or from the so-called object/possessive pronouns (my, our, your, etc.). Therefore in this chapter we will be routinely referring not to Arabic subject pronouns but rather to the verb forms and, sometimes, to object pronouns.

References

Baburajan, P. K. (2020), 'Gendered Spaces in the Arab World', *Journal of Asian Research*:19–28.
Bakhtin, M. ([1980] 2020), 'Forms of Time and of the Chronotope in the Novel: Notes toward a Historical Poetics', in M. Holquist (ed.), *The Dialogic Imagination: Four Essays. Slavic Series*, trans. E. Caryl and M. Holquist, 85–258, Austin, TX: University of Texas Press.
Bakhtin, M. (1981), *The Dialogic Imagination: Four Essays*, trans. C. Emerson and ed. M. Holquist, Austin, TX: University of Texas Press.
Baynham, M. (2000), 'Narrative as Evidence in Literacy Research', *Linguistics and Education*, 11 (2): 99–117.
Bird, S. R. and L. K. Sokolofski (2005), 'Gendered Socio-Spatial Practices in Public Eating and Drinking Establishments in the Midwest United States', *Gender, Place & Culture: A Journal of Feminist Geography*, 12 (2): 213–30.
Blommaert, J. and A. De Fina (2017), 'Chronotopic Identities: On the Timespace Organization of Who We Are', in A. De Fina, D. Ikizoglu, and J. Wegner (eds), *Diversity and Super-diversity*, 1–14, Washington, DC: Georgetown University Press.
Bourdieu, P. (1977), *Outline of a Theory of Practice*, trans. R. Nice, Cambridge: Cambridge University Press.
Breeze, R. (2013), 'British Media Discourse on the Wearing of Religious Symbols', in K. Wachter and H. van Belle (eds), *Verbal and Visual Rhetoric in a Mediatised World*, 197–212, Leiden: Leiden University Press.
Briar, S. (2008), 'Gendered Spatial Practices and TV in the Arab World', in *Conference Papers-International Communication Association*, 2008 Annual Meeting, Vol. 29, 1.
Burima, M. (2009), 'The Mental Topochrone of Latgale in the Recent Latvian Literature', *Comparative Studies*, 2 (1): 174–84.
Carrasco, S., J. Pàmies, and M. Ponferrada (2011), 'Fronteras Visibles y barreras Ocultas', *Migraciones*, 29: 31–60.
Castilla Vázquez, C. (2017), 'Mujeres en transición: La inmigración femenina africana en España', *Migraciones Internacionales*, 9 (2): 143–71.
De Certeau, M. (1988), *The Practice of Everyday Life*, Berkeley: University of California Press.
De Fina, A. (2016), 'Linguistic Practices and Transnational Identities', in S. Preece (ed.), *Routledge Handbook of Language and Identity*, 163–78, London: Routledge.

Durkheim, E. ([1912] 2003), *Les formes élémentaires de la vie religieuse*, Paris: Presses Universitaires de France.
Durkheim, E. (1982), *Rules of Sociological Method*, New York: Free Press.
Ennaji, M. (2014), *Muslim Moroccan Migrants in Europe: Transnational Migration in Its Multiplicity*, New York: Palgrave Macmillan.
Epstein, M. ([2003] 2007), *Amerussia. Selected Essays*, Moscow: Serebrianye niti.
Eurostat (2021), 'Migration and Migrant Population Statistics'. Available online: https://ec.europa.eu/eurostat/statistics-explained/index.php?title=Migration_and_migrant_population_statistics#Migration_flows:_Immigration_to_the_EU_from_non-member_countries_was_2.7_million_in_2019 (accessed 21 November 2021).
Georgakopoulou, A. (2003), 'Plotting the "Right Place" and the "Right Time"', *Narrative Inquiry*, 13 (2): 413–32.
Gintsburg, S. (2016), 'Moroccan Immigrants in the United States of America: History, Languages and Identities', in F. Moscoso García and A. Moustaoui Sghir (eds), *Identidad y conciencia lingüística: VI congreso de árabe marroquí*, 195–214, Madrid: Ediciones UAM.
Gintsburg, S., A. Fernández Vallejo, and K. Tayaa (2020), *Identidad y expectativas en la comunidad marroquí de Navarra: La perspectiva de las mujeres*, Pamplona: Observatorio de la Realidad Social de Navarra.
González Ruiz, R. and D. Izquierdo Alegría (2014), 'The Debate about the Veil in the Spanish Press. Boosting Strategies and Interactional Metadiscourse in the Editorials of ABC and El País (2002–2010)', in I. Olza, Ó. Loureda, and M. Casado-Velarde (eds), *Language Use in the Public Sphere Methodological Perspectives and Empirical Applications*, 397–444, Bern: Peter Lang.
Gordinsky, N. (2020), 'Den Ort erzählen', in K. Schoor, I. Voloshchuk, and B. Bigun (eds), *Blondzhende Stern. Jüdische Schriftstellerinnen und Schriftsteller aus der Ukraine als Grenzgänger zwischen den Kulturen in Ost und West*, 64–80, Göttingen: Wallstein.
Harré, R. and M. Dedaic (2012), 'Positioning Theory, Narrativity, and Pronounanalysis in Discursive Therapies', in A. Lock and T. Strong (eds), *Discursive Perspectives in Therapeutic Practice*, 45–64, Oxford: Oxford University Press.
Harré, R., F. M. Moghaddam, T. P. Cairnie, D. Rothbart, and S. R. Sabat (2009), 'Recent Advances in Positioning Theory', *Theory & Psychology* 19 (1): 5–31.
Harré, R. and F. M. Moghaddam (2015), 'Positioning Theory and Social Representations', in G. Sammut, E. Andreouli, G. Gaskell, and J. Valsiner (eds), *Cambridge Handbook of Social Representations*, 224–33, Cambridge: Cambridge University Press.
Hassan, S. (2020), *The Representation of Afghan Refugees. Corpus-Assisted and Qualitative Discourse Studies*, PhD Thesis, University of Navarra.
Kazakova, G. (2018), 'Region kak prostransvo-vremya identichnosti. Topochron y chronotop regionalnoy identichnosti', *Kultura Kulturi* 1 (17). Available online: http://cult-cult.ru/region-kak-prostranstvo-vremya-identichnosti-topohron-i-hronotop-regionalinoj-id/ (accessed 21 November 2021).
Lefebvre, H. (2009), *State, Space, World*, Minneapolis: University of Minnesota Press.
McAvoy, J. (2016), 'Discursive Psychology and the Production of Identity in Language Practices', in S. Preece (ed.), *The Routledge Handbook of Language and Identity*, 98–112, London: Routledge.
McVee, M., K. Silvestri, N. Barrett, and K. Haq (2018), 'Positioning Theory', in D. Alvermann, N. Unrau, M. Sailors, and R. Ruddell (eds), *Theoretical Models and Processes of Literacy*, 381–400, London: Routledge.
Mernissi, F. (1991), *The Veil and the Male Elite*, Cambridge, MA: Perseus Books.

Moreno-Colom, S. and P. López-Roldán (2018), 'El impacto de la crisis en las trayectorias laborales de las mujeres inmigrantes en España', *Cuaderno de Relaciones Laborales*, 36 (1): 65–87.
Observatorio Permanente de la Inmigración (2020), Estadística de residentes extranjeros en España. Accessible online: https://www.lamoncloa.gob.es/serviciosdeprensa/notasprensa/inclusion/Paginas/2021/130421-extranjeros.aspx (accessed 21 November 2021).
Osman, K. M. and M. Suliman (1996), 'Spatial and Cultural Dimensions of the Houses of Omdurman, Sudan', in *Human Relations*, 49 (4): 395.
Perrino, S. (2015), 'Chronotopes: Time and Space in Oral Narrative', in A. De Fina and A. Georgakopoulou (eds), *The Handbook of Narrative Analysis*, 140–59, Oxford: Blackwell.
Preece, S. (2019), 'Language and Identity in Applied Linguistics', in S. Preece (ed.), *The Routledge Handbook of Language and Identity*, 1–16, London: Routledge.
Sabreen, M. (2017), 'Custody in Islamic Law: A Law Based on Presumptions', *Islamic Studies* 56 (3–4): 223–44.
Saqiqi, F. (2016), 'Female Perceptions of Islam in Today's Morocco', *Journal of Feminist Scholarship*, 11 (fall): 48–60.

Discussion questions

1. How can the notion(s) of chronotope/topochrone contribute to the research on migrant narratives?
2. What is the major difference between chronotope and topochrone?
3. What are the typical spaces of Moroccan women living in Spain? How are they different from yours?
4. How do these women position themselves in their narratives?
5. Why did we use the term topochrone in order to analyse these narratives and how did it help us to better understand the sense of time in these women's narratives?

8

The Route from West Africa to Europe, the Precariousness of Life in Marie NDiaye's *Three Strong Women*

Odile Heynders

Prologue

Since the 1990s there has been increased migration of sub-Saharan Africans to Europe, mainly consisting of people from Nigeria, Senegal and Ghana (De Haas 2008). Many migrants have tried to get by boat to Italy via Libya, or entered Spain either via the Canary Islands or by crossing the borders between Morocco and the Spanish enclaves Ceuta and Melilla. Migration from West Africa to Europe has a historical context through colonization and confusing border drawing, military involvement, intensive trade, ethnic contests and the exhaustion of resources. Decolonization in the twentieth century has sustained old migratory patterns, such as from North Africa to France, but has also given rise to new ones (Castles et al. 2014: 187–8). When around 1991 southern European countries introduced visas for North Africans, risky boat migration was the result. Due to digitization young generations are now more able and likely to migrate to seek better economic circumstances and labour perspectives (Castles et al. 2014: 196).

Migration is an age-old phenomenon, which is characterized as problematic in current media and policy discourses time and again. Refugees and migrants are approached negatively by the receiving countries, politicians, public opinion and the media who describe them as numbers and statistics. Migrant perspectives are often presented through cliché-heavy lenses (Einasche and Roueché 2019), while attention for personal narratives is lacking (Breeze, Baynham and Gintsburg, this volume). Therefore, migrants are often 'lost in media' (Einasche and Roueché 2019), they have no voice or are only reduced to 'pure testimony' (Trilling 2019: 27), so that we still know very little about their spaces and times. Current transdisciplinary research in migration studies, however, counters the discursive characterization of an invasion, overflow or tsunami of migrants, and underlines the uniqueness of individual migrant narratives and experiences (Alcaraz-Mármol and Soto-Almela 2020; De Haas 2008; Einashe and Roueché 2019).

As anthropologist Ruben Andersson (2014) has argued, migration also is an industry. The 'illegality industry' reveals complex interactions among humans, technology and the environment, as well as a 'values chain' in which migrant illegality is rendered profitable (Andersson 2014: 15). The main motivation for migration today still is a lack of opportunities for a decent living or proper education. Agriculture and fisheries do not provide enough chances, and drought and climate change bring people close to impoverishment. We should note that the migrants are not the poorest people; the ones with access to contact and cash – often young men – set off on the journey to the north while the real poor people stay in the region (De Haas 2008).

This chapter focuses on the route from Senegal through the Western Sahara and Morocco to the Spanish border at Ceuta and Melilla, enclaves on the north coast of Morocco. First, I describe how illegal migration and border crossings from Morocco to Spain are researched and documented by anthropologists, social geographers and journalists. Subsequently, I use Judith Butler's philosophy on precarious life to reflect on the representation and dehumanization of the migrant figure. Butler argues that the demand for images in the media does not lead to the conveyance of a reality. Following up on her thoughts, I make the point that literary fiction, just because it is *not* an immediate representation, provides insights into migrant experiences by evoking an individual narrative and perspective. To elaborate this, I work out a close reading analysis of the third part of the novel, *Three Strong Women* (2009), by French author Marie NDiaye. This novel portrays a young widow who is forced to travel from Senegal to Europe. My main argument is that the literary fiction counters dominant forms of representation of migrants as either victims of war, refugees without agency or people searching for economic progression. The literary fiction confronts the reader with an ambivalent perspective on the precariousness of life, based on the character's constantly changing perceptions and feelings. In the conclusion, I underline the relevance of literature in the context of migration studies as academic research.

The trans-Saharan route

Since 1990, the migration of sub-Saharan Africans has been steadily increasing (Castles et al. 2014: 187). Migrants move to the north to look for work in Libya or elsewhere in North Africa, or to get to Europe, where they often face unemployment, racism and homelessness. Castles et al. point to three misconceptions spread in Western media about African migration: first, the image of a massive exodus of desperate people; second, the myth that all Africans are irregular migrants (while most of them have valid permits); and third, the idea that all migrants are without resources (the really poor people cannot afford to migrate). However, this does not reflect the true spatio-temporal aspect of these migrations. There are various routes via land from West Africa to Europe, which are generally made in several stages, and take anywhere between a few weeks and several years (De Haas 2008). On their way, migrants often settle temporarily in towns to work and save money for the trip, before continuing the journey in open lorries or pick-ups (De Haas 2008).

Many overland travellers go via Agadez in Niger, the historical desert city on the crossroads of age-old trade routes extending deep into West and Central Africa. Since 2016, the EU has been trying to block these routes by establishing 'Migration Partnership Frameworks' meant to stop the smuggling of migrants and to improve the economic and social development of the region. More than 1 billion euros have been paid to stop the illegality industry. The Sahara has thus become the 'south border of Europe' keeping off migration and terrorism (Vermeulen 2018). In a fascinating television documentary on life in Agadez, Dutch journalist Bram Vermeulen revealed how in 2018 smuggling still took place, while most of the European payment had vanished in corruptive networks. Smugglers could not find alternative jobs and picked up their old function of being *guides de caravane*. European bureaucracy had bumped into the boundless freedom of the desert (Vermeulen 2018).

From Agadez most migrants travel to Libya, Algeria and Morocco, and many of them try to continue their way into Europe via the Spanish enclaves Ceuta and Melilla. These old enclaves are based on long-standing bilateral agreements between Morocco and Spain, and as such underline the quintessence of clandestine migration: these are locked off places but also the only opportunity to put foot on European ground in North Africa. The borders around the two territories are manifested as 6-metre parallel wire fences of about 10 km, topped with razor wire, patrolled by the Spanish Guardia Civil, and monitored by video cameras, infrared surveillance, microphone cables and helicopters (Davies 2010). Both Ceuta and Melilla seem to be sealed, but in 2005 *grandes attaques* on the fences were organized, during which hundreds of sub-Saharan Africans tried to get into Spain to claim immigrant status. Hundreds of migrants did succeed in crossing the border, although they were often injured with broken limbs and deep cuts. Some died, while yet others were detained by the Moroccan police and send back to their home regions (Tremlett 2005).

In May 2021, there was another organized attempt to cross the border. About 8000 migrants – among them children aged seven, eight and nine years old – entered Ceuta via the sea. This was made possible by the unresponsiveness of the Moroccan police. Morocco's authorities were in fact using the migrants as a political tool to put pressure on Spain, since Madrid had agreed to allow Brahim Ghali, a Western Sahara independence leader, to be treated for Covid-19 in a Spanish hospital (Kassam 2021). Within a few days 5600 migrants were sent back to Morocco. Migrants thus became the input of a bilateral political game, and the border appeared as a configuration of state authorities, local and regional actors and materialities.

The practices and procedures concerning migration are not only political, security-related (control) and humanitarian (care), but are also economic. This is what anthropologist Ruben Anderson characterizes as the 'illegality industry', which is based on material exchange, local and transnational actors, the geography of offshore enclaves and islands, and precarious supplies of infrastructure and manpower (Anderson 2014: 285). In his ethnographic research, Anderson offers various interrelated perspectives on the border spectacle in Melilla and Ceuta, by interviewing migrants, aid workers, Guardia Civil officers and others. He describes how the 2005 attacks on both enclaves were organized as a military operation since only a critical mass would work to cross the border. The migrants first hid in the hills, the Moroccan auxiliary forces told them when the coast would be clear and received 'some whisky and Nigerian women' (Anderson 2014: 159), and then shortly before dawn, scouts surveyed the terrain after which the first men with ladders and then women followed. Attacks were organized on following days in both enclaves. Migrants, security forces, journalists and aid workers all acted together, with the Spanish Guardia Civil in a double role as 'guardian angels and gate keepers of the external border' (Anderson 2014: 161).

In his fieldwork Anderson interviewed people and described them in their local community and *en route*, using what he indicates as the 'extended field site approach' (Anderson 2014: 284). This approach does not start on either one of the main poles of migration studies – the political scientist's perspective on policies or the ethnographer's perspective on grounded migrants – but focuses on the material, virtual and social interfaces of the illegality system, taking both human and non-human links as actants in a complex network. The illegality industry is big business, and it also is a spectacle and a staging, a 'theater [*sic*] of the absurd' (Anderson 2014: 280).

The anthropological research on the West African routes into Europe can be complemented with journalistic reports, documentaries and photographs on the enclave configurations – see for instance: https://www.gettyimages.nl/fotos/melilla-border. Tinti and Reitano (2018) wrote a mixed reportage, based on first-hand accounts and research, focusing in particular on the figure of the smuggler. They point to the complexity of networks, industries and geographical and ethnic developments, conveying how smugglers are often portrayed as 'exploitative, profit-driven criminals', while they could also be considered as 'service providers' (Tinti and Reitano 2018: 31). Describing the desert highway from Agadez to the North, Peter Tinti underlines that the most lucrative thing to be smuggling is not narcotics or weapons, but people. Smugglers are transporters of people, which becomes clear in Agadez, where West Africa ends and an ocean of sand begins. Every Monday, dozens of convoys leave the city: each vehicle in the convoy packed with twenty-eight to thirty migrants, paying 200–300 dollars a time. The smuggler gets about $750 per trip but must pay various actors such as government officials, militia leaders or Islamist gunmen. Lines between human smuggling and human trafficking are thin. Frequently, migrants are abused and robbed, and women are forced into prostitution and sexual slavery (Tinti and Reitano 2018: 169). Most young smugglers see themselves 'on the raw end of a deal that they never agreed to. Powerful global forces made it on their behalf' ((Tinti and Reitano 2018: 170). Even so, it becomes clear that smuggling is a professional industry based on the transport of migrants and on maintaining the flow for those who make money out of it (Ellis cited in Tinti and Reitano 2018: 48).

While all this empirical information is informative, it still is difficult to imagine what the migrants went through while climbing border fences and trying anxiously to get at the other side (on border experiences, see also Melo-Pfeifer, this volume, and Schmidt, this volume). The moment of dramatic power, violence and vulnerability is not represented in an ethnographic study. However, French literary author Marie NDiaye[1] depicts this purgatorial scene in the third part of her novel *Three Strong Women*, which appeared in France in 2009 (translation into English 2012). In the last part of this novel NDiaye evokes a young woman who was sent to Europe by her husband's family after he passed away. The unschooled woman does not know where she is going, in fact she has no idea at all what is happening to her. In creating this narrative, NDiaye demonstrates how travelling as a female migrant is dangerous, how it is neither planned nor thought through from the beginning, how it is a route full of coincidences, tragedy and hope. NDiaye describes the illegality industry from the particular perspective of a young woman, who has a role but almost no agency in the theatre of the absurd. To investigate NDiaye's portrayal of this young female migrant, I will conduct a close reading of the text and confront the reading with the anthropological findings I discussed above. Before conducting the reading, I will consider the notion of the precariousness of life, as worked out by American philosopher Judith Butler. Precariousness is an interesting lens to look through when analysing the figure of the migrant, a figure that NDiaye portrays as both fragile and strong.

The precariousness of life

Andersson (2014) offered a perspective on migration as a configuration of actors in a network, based on economy. Both the smuggler and the migrant, the Guardia Civil officer and the caretaker, have a role in the circulation of materialities and movements. What is missing from this anthropological description is an ethical stance: could we think of all these people not just as functioning in a network but as human beings sharing a life? How can we come closer to individual experiences and perceptions detached from social and functional categorization? This is what we can find in philosophy, in Judith Butler's thinking on violence and precariousness.

In her essay 'Precarious Life' (2006), Butler reflects on what the humanities stand for and considers the modes of address and moral authority in contemporary society. We come to exist as human beings, Butler explains, 'in the moment of being addressed' and 'something about our existence proves precarious when that address fails' (Butler 2006: 130). The crucial thought that Butler brings to the fore is that human existence becomes uncertain when there is no demand that comes from elsewhere and that articulates obligation. Moral authority is not something that we can give ourselves, it comes to us from elsewhere, unbidden, unexpected and unplanned.

To work out her argument, Butler offers an analysis of Emmanuel Levinas' notion of *face*. Face is not exclusively a human face, not a linguistic utterance, but something that is wordless. 'To respond to the face, to understand its meaning, means to be awake to what is precarious in another life or, rather, the precariousness of life itself' (Butler 2006: 134). Levinas invites us to think about the relationship between representation and humanization: the human being is not identified with what is represented, but neither is she/he identified with the unrepresentable. The paradox is that in the limits or failure of representation the possibility of representation is constituted.

Butler relates this to the media context in which we live today. Those who gain representation, especially self-representation, are considered more humanized, than those who have no chance at all to represent themselves. Paradoxically, the face is also used in the media to effectuate dehumanization, for instance in the case of the representation of the faces of Osama bin Laden, or Yasser Arafat or Saddam Hussein. Faces in the media are often tendentiously framed, and disidentification is then incited through the 'hyperbolic absorption of evil into the face' (Butler 2006: 143). Butler conveys that we could demand a truer image, more images or images that convey the full horror and reality of the suffering. But she also acknowledges that reality 'is not conveyed by what is represented within the image, but through the challenge to representation that reality delivers' (Butler 2006: 146). In the Vietnam War, Butler explains, it was the pictures of children burning and dying from napalm that brought the US public to a sense of shock, outrage and grief. These pictures pointed beyond themselves 'to a life and to a precariousness that they could not show' (Butler 2006: 150). If the humanities have a future as cultural criticism, Butler concludes, it should return us to the human where we do not expect to find it, 'in its frailty and at the limits of its capacity to make sense' (Butler 2006: 151).

The argument on the precariousness of life, and the face representing the unrepresentable, can be related to several migrant cases in current media, for instance, to an iconic photograph published on 2 September 2015 of a toddler lying on the Golden Beach in Akyarlar, Turkey. His mother and brother were found about a hundred metres away on the nearby rocky shore. At around 6 a.m. that day a Turkish photographer took pictures of the boy, named Alan Kurdi, and sent those to her newspaper, *Dogan News Agency*. She also posted the photograph on Twitter. The tweet led to 53,000 tweets per hour. Within twelve hours the photo had reached 20 million screens (Heynders 2018). The boy lying on the sand is faceless, that is, his face is down, we cannot see it. This is what is horrifying in the picture. The photograph came to tell the story of a lower middle-class family, who, like millions of Syrians, were victims of terrorism and geopolitics and forced to flee Damascus in 2012. They then lived under extremely difficult circumstances in Istanbul and later decided to leave Turkey. The father contacted smugglers, and after some unsuccessful attempts, they departed for Greece on the first night of September 2015. It is in the details of the picture, the 'relaxed' shape of the boy as if sleeping, the colourful t-shirt and the small face put down in the sand, that the precariousness of life, an ethical address, becomes clear. The picture points to a life and world that we share.

In much current research in the humanities and social sciences the lives of migrants are described as precarious (Della Porta 2015; Valkeakari 2017), referring to the unstable position migrants have in society. The uncertainty is caused by experiences of displacement and has socio-economic and psychological consequences. Some scholars (Van der Waal 2018; Minnaard 2020) convey that literary narratives on migration engage with precarious subjects and tell 'touching tales' of vulnerability, implying emotionally charged stories of insecurity, loss, pain and fear (Minnaard 2020: 146). I adhere to this line of research, but not without emphasizing that literary fiction does not so much create a vulnerable character, but in the creation (*poiesis*) reflects on representation and unrepresentability, on narrative and (in)completeness. What is important is not that in literature the figure of the migrant is represented as precarious or victim; but that the literary text explores the precariousness of life in relation to the stories and experiences of individual migrants, *and* in relation to the recipients who are addressed and have a responsibility to react. This is what we can recognize in a close reading of NDiaye's text: protagonist Khady Demba has a name and becomes the person carrying that name with self-esteem, as such becoming more than a fragile woman encapsulated in the illegality industry.

Three Strong Women, a close reading analysis

NDiaye's novel *Three Strong Women* is composed as three loosely connected narratives in which female heroines try to establish a life when circumstances are working against them. All three narratives thematize migration topics: return migration, acculturation and taking the trans-Saharan route. The focus of my reading will be on the third narrative, but first I will briefly indicate what the two other stories are about.

In the first part of the novel, we follow thirty-eight-year-old Norah, a Parisian lawyer who visits her old father in Senegal and discovers that he is not the rich, ostentatious man that he used to be. The man who had made his fortune in the tourism industry is now turned 'into a plump old bird that moved clumsily and gave off a strong smell' (NDiaye 2012: 11). In her young life Norah experienced poverty in France – where her mother worked as a hairdresser – and wealth in Africa, where her father owned a bungalow park. Her brother was taken by her father to live with him in Africa, and now appears to be in jail for the strangling of his father's wife – but in fact it was the father who committed the murder. Norah decides to stay in Senegal to defend her brother's case. We could read this as a case of return migration due to specific family circumstances as well as personal decisions. The history of migration described here is that of the father who went for studies to Europe and then returned to Africa, and of the daughter who is a French citizen, but feels connected to West African roots and spheres (see also Coe, this volume, on the West African experience).

The second narrative takes place in the Gironde in the South of France, where Rudy Descas is an inept seller of kitchens, unhappily married to Fanta, a Black woman from Dakar who quit her job as teacher, came to France and gave him a son. In fact, Fanta, as the second strong woman of the novel, does not appear at all in the narrative – she only is present in the thoughts of her suspicious and deeply frustrated husband. He is angry due to the lack of opportunities he has in life, to the fact that he experienced a downfall from being a literature teacher to becoming a seller of kitchens. The intriguing aspect of this story is the absence of Fanta: why is she described as a strong woman? It could be that she has magical qualities and produces the image of a buzzard that several times threatens her husband. Phantasmagorical scenes are interwoven in the narrative of a boring life in the heat of the regional South of France. We could read this as a story of acculturation (Şafak Ayvazoğlu 2021), as a narrative in which aspects of the heritage and the host culture are mixed up. Fanta's physical non-appearance in the story of Descas shows her presence and power. The story of migration here is one of hybrid identities: just as Coe's Ghanaian protagonist (this volume) belongs to Ghana and to the United States, both Fanta and her husband belong to Africa as well as France.

The third, realist part of the novel tells the story of a young woman travelling the route from West Africa to Europe via the Sahara Desert. The plot of this story shocks in its straightforwardness (as Rita Felski 2008 conveyed: shock is one of the four uses of literature, next to enchantment, recognition and social knowledge). Khady Demba is a twenty-five-year-old woman, living with her husband's family after he has passed away. One day, her mother-in-law orders Khady to get her things, and gives her some banknotes and a paper with the address of a cousin in France. Khady is picked up by a smuggler who brings her to a place near the beach where she is supposed to step into a boat. But the boat does not seem to be seaworthy, she jumps out and meets a young man who invites her to join him on the route over land. After travelling in open lorries, they get stuck in a desert city, where Khady must work as a prostitute. Her companion steals her money, and only after more than a year, Khady continues her journey. She ends up in the woods near the fences around the Spanish enclave in Morocco. She joins the attack on the fences to get into Europe, but she fails and dies on the spot. We could read this as a story of the migration route in which the migrant becomes a victim. But it is more than this, since representation – as we saw in Butler – also involves perceptions that are unrepresentable and thus complicate the singular identity of the migrant.

The story, or we could use the terms plot or *histoire* to point at the events in a narrative, is clear in depicting the journey that many West African migrants take. But the plot is not the only piece of insight that we can take out of a literary text. It is in the narrative discourse (arrangement) and in the perspective or focalization that we get more insight into the individual experiences and perceptions of the migrant figure. In the narrative discourse we get to know Demba as a character with ideas, moods and senses; via the narrative perspective or focalizator we are confronted with different perceptions of what is going on and how to evaluate this. In what follows, I will conduct a close reading to elaborate this, connecting the reading to observations on migration, nuancing and supplementing some of the anthropological findings.

The migrant does not always prepare the trip consciously in advance, she just aims to escape a bad life. Both Khady Demba and the young companion that she meets on the beach do not live happy lives. The woman was treated badly by her husband's family, while the young man was abused by his stepmother and sent out of school. They meet shortly after Khady has run away from the boat. After she was pulled up into the vessel, she realized that the bottom was filled with water. She panicked and jumped out, hurting her right calf on the edge of the boat. Later, she finds herself on the beach, looked at by a young man, about twenty years of age named Lamine. He helps her to take care of the wound and shares his intentions: 'he would get to Europe one day or die in the attempt'. It then appears to Khady that 'all he was doing was making her own plan explicit' (250). Until then, she did not have a plan, she was just following orders from others, but now she decides to join Lamine on the route over land. The journey 'would go through the desert and arrive at a certain place where you had to climb to get into Europe' (253). Lamine dreams of studying and becoming an engineer. When he tells her this, Khady does not know what it means.

Migration can be dangerous. The female migrant en route *is vulnerable and often gets involved in the sex industry.* Khady and Lamine travel in an open lorry through the desert, the young man helps her out in sitting safely on top of the packs and bundles. After a day and night on the road, the lorry stops at a frontier, passengers must form a queue, while soldiers take their money. When the amount is not enough, one soldier slashes the sole of Lamine's shoes and hurts his feet. Khady then pays for Lamine. They travel further to another desert city, a town 'invaded by sand, with low sand-coloured houses and with streets and gardens covered in sand' (261). From there they cannot continue. When they are out of money but in need of food, they go to a cheap eating place in which they are served, after which Khady is forced by the female owner to work as a prostitute. She spends her days lying on a foam mattress on the hard floor, 'her body in a permanent state of suffering' (265). Lamine visits her to sleep next to her in the night. Khady earns a bit of money, given to her by the woman of the shop. One morning she finds all the money gone, and Lamine has disappeared as well. Khady stays for a long time (more than a year, but her time measurement is vague) in this situation, with 'exhaustion as the natural condition of her organism' (271). Finally, she has money to continue the journey.

Finding self-esteem on the route. Khady was married for three years, during which she was obsessed with procreation. Not getting pregnant had caused 'barely perceptible but fatal blows to her precarious self-assurance: it had all prepared her to find it not abnormal to be humiliated' (221). Living with in-laws who despised her, she became 'a poor, self-effacing creature (…) mechanically dragging her feet with indifference, and, she believed, hardly suffering at all' (221). The third-person narration is effective here as an outside perspective on the young woman, who does not claim a position and place for herself, and who constantly slides into 'a kind of mental stupor' which stops her from understanding what is going on around her (222). This woman is 'strictly irreplaceable, even though her parents had abandoned her, and her grandmother had only taken her in because there had not been a choice' (223). The point of view here is crucial. This is how Khady sees herself, she is the focalizator, but it also is the at-a-distance perspective of an omniscient narrator portraying a young woman as self-effacing and impassive, but as well as someone who is discovering her identity.

Khady is sent away by her relatives without knowing where she is going. As a woman with no education, she does not know what happens to her when she leaves the house and is picked up by a man dressed in Western clothes and gleaming sunglasses. He asks her to follow him but does not pay attention to her. Walking through the city, in a batik cloth and on plastic flip-flops, gives Khady a new sensitivity, breaking through the indifference. The narrator underlines this new affectivity with emphasizing her name: 'Hello Khady, she said to herself' (232). The smuggler – who she sees in various identities as her companion, shepherd, jailor or guardian angel – brings her to a group of people laden with packages sitting at the end of a boulevard. Later he pushes her in the back of a car occupied with people. They arrive at a square in which many vehicles are parked and 'a crowd of men and women was moving between the cars haggling over fares' (239). When the evening falls, the man brings her to a courtyard packed with people, and there Khady realizes the contingency of what is happening: between 'herself and the other people there was one simple connection: they all found themselves huddled together in the same place at the same time' (241). Before leaving her, the man asks for money, and Khady pays him.

Migration is an illegality industry. All the details of the journey show how people are interconnected, being transported from one smuggler to another. The narrative demonstrates how in every migrant as individual human being certain perceptions or moods are evoked. During the journey Khady becomes stronger, less apathetic. After jumping out of the boat, she realizes 'that she had just done something that *she* had resolved to do, once she had decided – very quickly – how vitally important it was for her to leave the boat' (247). Never before had she made a decision on her own. The title of the novel, *Three Strong Women*, underlines how female migrants have difficult lives, can be vulnerable and hurt, but are not just victims without agency. NDiaye describes the realistic circumstances of the illegality business in a nuanced and convincing way, without turning the protagonist into a weak person.

Companionship, loss and the resilience of a human being. When deciding to join Lamine on the route over land, Khady is convinced that she is 'in control of the precarious, unstable equipage that was her existence' (251). Life offers new opportunities. We could characterize the relationship between Khady and Lamine as friendship – until he takes her money and disappears. Khady, still forced to perform as a sex worker, does not let herself be blown away by the disappointment, and here, of course, we recognize her strength.

> Truth to tell, she would not regret anything, plunged in the reality of an atrocious present which she could see clearly, to which she would apply thinking that was replete both with pragmatism and with pride (she would never have pointless feelings of shame, she would never forget the value of the human being she was: Khady Demba, honest and true), a reality which above all she considered transitory, she was convinced that this period of suffering would have an end, and that she would certainly not be rewarded (she could not believe she was owed anything for having suffered) but would simply move on to something else.
> (259/60)

Again, the point of view is effective. Khady is the focalizator, seeing herself, but we also hear the voice of an omniscient narrator telling the story of a courageous young woman. What this fragment makes clear is that the protagonist, the female migrant as a young woman, suffers under very horrible circumstances. But she addresses us in her resilience and pragmatism, in her hope that conditions will change. When Khady sees herself in a mirror when she finally continues her journey, she barely recognizes herself in this image with a grey face, reddish hair, dry skin and a skeletal body. But even then she still sees herself as Khady Demba 'unique and indispensable', while exhaustion has become 'the natural condition of her organism' (271). The narrator depicts the details of a harsh life and underlines how even then self-confidence is possible. Although the migrants 'form an undifferentiated mass. They were all young, like her' (245), they are individual human beings as well; they have names, identities, feelings and hope.

Precarious life. NDiaye depicts the young woman in her unique situation, subtly demonstrating how she is transforming, how she realizes that her life is changing all the time, but that she still is 'the same person with a unique, coherent destiny' (231). When Khady follows the smuggler from her home to the beach, she forgets 'the uncertainty of her situation, or rather its precariousness no longer appeared so serious' (231). The conditions are hazardous, Khady's existence is fragile, but what is at stake in this narrative is not the demonstration of the vulnerability of the female migrant, I would argue, but the precariousness of life in a Butlerian sense. The readers, French, European and global, who are confronted with the story, 'have to interrogate the emergence and vanishing of the human at the limits of what we can know, what we can hear, what we can see, what we can sense' (Butler 2006: 151). The narrative prompts us, affectively, to understand, question and engage.

Migration is dangerous; many people lose their lives. We follow Khady when she finally climbs the fence:

> She tried to go higher and remembered that a boy had told her that you must never, never stop climbing until you have reached the top, but the barbed wire was tearing the skin off her hands and feet and she could now hear herself screaming and could feel her blood running along her shoulders and down her arms. She kept telling herself never to stop climbing, never, repeating the same words over and over again without any longer understanding them, then giving up, letting go, falling slowly backwards, and thinking then that the essence of Khady Demba – less than a breath, scarcely a puff of air – would surely never touch the ground, would float eternal, inestimable, too evanescent ever to be made to crash in the cold, blinding glare of the floodlights. She was still thinking "It's me, Khady Demba" the moment her skull hit the ground.
>
> (276)

At the moment of death, the narrative perspective helps us to imagine and understand what happens to the migrant who perishes. We see through the character's eyes and language, we acknowledge her experiences, but we also see through the author's eyes and language, realizing how a human existence ends. Identifying with Khady, we are encouraged to reflect on what NDiaye tells us: how vulnerability and resilience, freedom and injustice, violence and mourning, Africa and Europe are and will be interconnected.

All three narratives in *Three Strong Women* end with a very short 'Counterpoint', which offers another perspective on the story. After Khady's passing away, we read how Lamine works in several jobs to make money, and 'every time euros passed from a foreigner's hand to his own, he thought of the girl' (276/7). He has made it into Europe. On some days he sends his 'thanks to her' (277). Survival implies shame and thankfulness. That is the counter message with which NDiaye ends her story.

Conclusion

Most migration studies do not include *aesthetic* writing and thinking in the research, rooted as it is in imagination and the invention of a fictional world. The literary novel is considered the opposite of objective description, empirical analysis and academic reasoning, and as such not acknowledged as relevant activity in scientific investigation. But as this chapter argues, it is in aesthetic writing that representation, perception, affects and contra-perspectives can be found. It is in aesthetic writing that readers are stimulated to start thinking about contrasting and subversive conceptions and observations, which will ultimately lead to new insight and critical perspectives on established research.

NDiaye does not offer literature as a testimonial or therapeutic form of writing. She writes fictions of migration, imagining and re/framing migrant experiences. Migration in her literary work is a phenomenon of the precariousness of life, in a Butlerian sense, inviting the reader to reflect and engage on more than just the story of individual women. We could add here another philosophical stance: Gilles Deleuze's idea of writing as becoming: 'in writing, one becomes-woman, becomes-animal or vegetable, becomes-molecule to the point of becoming-imperceptible' (Deleuze 1998: 1). To become is not to attain a form, to identify or imitate, but to find the zone of proximity. For Deleuze literature is *symptomatological* in the gauging of the process of life as nonorganic and impersonal power. Literature confronts us with affects and percepts, not with concepts as philosophical terms. Literature is about *haecceitas,* moments of the world, in which we can understand what living in *this time and place* is about.

The aim of connecting NDiaye's literary fiction to the anthropological and ethnographical findings was not to prove how one discipline or perspective or the other is more (scientifically or artistically) relevant, but to underline the complementarity of various ways of thinking and doing research. If in anthropology and journalism we learn about the networks of the illegality industry, in literature we learn about narrativity as devoted to the understanding of personal identity (Brooks 2011: 5). This is crucial in a modern world in which identity is threatened by anonymity, and in which people, in particular migrants, have become numbers and statistics. The self is a construction; there always is a past self about which the present self has an idea, but it is impossible to decide upon a valid distinction between the self known and the self as knower (Brooks 2011: 8). This is what NDiaye explores in her three women characters, acknowledging that identity and self-knowledge are developing and transforming constantly as they cross time and space. The literary fiction confronts the reader with an ambivalent perspective on migration, based on the character's ongoing changing perceptions and feelings. What literature does, as American-Bosnian writer Alexander Hemon explains, is 'allow for individual narrative enfranchisement. The very proposition of storytelling is that life is a multitude of details, an irreplaceable combination of experiences which can be contained in their totality only in narration' (Hemon and Mohamed 2019: 70).

The power of literature also is that it can describe death. In the moment of the death of the young woman migrant, life is an impersonal and nonorganic power that goes beyond her lived experience (Deleuze 1998: xiv). We read about the fragile woman falling down, her head hitting the ground at the moment at which she still realizes who she is: 'It's me, Khady Demba'. NDiaye does not write a realistic report on the 2005 attacks on the enclaves, she writes fiction as *symptomatological* diagnosis: as an analysis of an experience of migration as process of life, inviting us to think about what migrants are going through and why: what gives us the right to seal off Europe for a young woman like Khady Demba.

Note

1   Born in Pithiviers in France in 1967, Marie NDiaye spent her childhood with her French mother (her father was from Senegal). She studied linguistics at the Sorbonne. She has written around twenty novels, plays, short stories and non-fiction. She was awarded the prestigious Prix Goncourt for *Three Strong Women*. She lives partly in the Gironde region and partly in Berlin.

References

Alcaraz-Mármol, G. and J. Soto-Almela (2020), 'Refugees' Dehumanization in the Spanish Media: A Corpus-assisted Study within the Semantic Preference Framework', *Applied Linguistics Review*, 20. Available online: http://dx.doi.org/10.1515/applirev-2019-0069 (accessed 21 October 2021).

Anderson, R. (2014), *Illegality, Inc. Clandestine Migration and the Business of Bordering Europe*, Oakland: University of California Press.

Brooks, P. (2011), *Enigmas of Identity*, Princeton and Oxford: Princeton University Press.

Butler, J. (2006), *Precarious Life. The Powers of Mourning and Violence*, London and New York: Verso.

Castles, S., H. De Haas, and M. J. Miller (2014), *The Age of Migration, International Population Movements in the Modern World*, 5th edition, London: Palgrave Macmillan.

Davies, N. (2010), 'Melilla: Europe's Dirty Secret', *The Guardian*, 17 April 2010. Available online: https://www.theguardian.com/world/2010/apr/17/melilla-migrants-eu-spain-morocco (accessed 21 October 2021).

De Haas, H. (2008), *Irregular Migration from West Africa to the Maghreb and the European Union, an Overview of Recent Trends*, International Organization for Migration Geneva. Available online: https://heindehaas.files.wordpress.com/2015/05/2008-irregular-migration-from-WestAfrica-to-the-maghreb-and-the-eu-iom.pdf (accessed 21 October 2021).

Della Porta, D. et al. eds (2015), *The New Social Division: Making and Unmaking Precariousness*, Basingstoke: Palgrave Macmillan.

Deleuze, G. (1998), *Essays Critical and Clinical*, trans. D. W. Smith and M. A. Greco, London and New York: Verso.

Felski, R. (2008), *Uses of Literature*, Oxford: Blackwell.

Einasche, I. and T. Rouché (2019), *Lost in Media. Migrant Perspectives and the Public Sphere*, Amsterdam: Valiz.

Hamon, A. and N. Mohamed (2019), 'Agency and Displacement. Aleksandar Hemon in Conversation with Nadifa Mohamed', in I. Einashe and T. Rouché (eds), *Lost in Media. Migrant Perspectives and the Public Sphere*, 65–84, Amsterdam: Valiz.

Heynders, O. (2018), 'We Didn't Know? Alan Kurdi, Life Writing and the State of the World', *Diggit Magazine*, 4 October 2018. Available online: https://www.diggitmagazine.com/column/alan-kurdi-and-state-world (accessed 21 October 2021).

Kassam, A. (2021), 'Ceuta Influx Highlights Fragility of EU's Approach to Migration', *The Guardian*, 20 May 2021.

Minnaard, L. (2020), 'Lampedusa in Europe; or Touching Tales of Vulnerability', in M. Boletsi, J. Houwen, and L. Minnaard (eds), *Languages of Resistance, Transformation, and Futurity in Mediterranean* Crisis – Scapes – From Crisis to Critique, 145–63, Cham: Palgrave Macmillan.

NDiaye, M. ([2009] 2012), *Three Strong Women*, trans. J. Fletcher, Quercus and London: Maclehose Press.

Şafak Ayvazoğlu, A. (2021), *Acculturation of Syrian Refugees in Turkey and the Netherlands*, PhD Diss., Tilburg University.

Tinti, P. and T. Reitano (2018), *Migrant, Refugee, Smuggler, Saviour*, London: Hurst and Company.

Tremlett, G. (2005), 'African Migrants Die in Quest for New Life', *The Guardian*, 30 September 2005. Available online: https://www.theguardian.com/world/2005/sep/30/spain.gilestremlett (accessed 21 October 2021).

Trilling, D. (2019), 'Uncomfortable Facts. The Migrant Crisis in the European Media', in I. Einasche and T. Rouché (eds), *Lost in Media. Migrant Perspectives and the Public Sphere*, 21–37, Amsterdam: Valiz.

Valkeakari, T. (2017), *Precarious Passages: The Diasporic Imagination in Contemporary Black Anglophone Fiction*, Gainesville: University Press Florida.

Van Der Waal, M. (2018), 'Making Precarious Lives Visible: Imagining Europe's Marginalized "Others"', in K. Czerska-Shaw, M. Galent, and B. Gierat-Bieroń (eds), *Visions and Revisions of Europe*, 129–41, Göttimgen: Universitätsverlag.

Links

Documentary: Vermeulen, B. (2018). *De Trek, Episode 1 The Smokkelaar* [The Smuggler] https://www.vpro.nl/programmas/de-trek/kijk/afleveringen/smokkelaar.html.
Getty Images: https://www.gettyimages.nl/fotos/melilla-border.

Discussion questions

1. How and why have Sahara and Agadez become the 'south border of Europe'?
2. How does the notion 'precarious life' enable us to look critically at digital representations of migrants and their experiences?
3. How can a close reading of literary narratives featuring the topic migration improve our understanding of migrants' experiences?
4. Through the close reading of *Three Strong Women*, what do we learn about the life trajectories of the migrants who follow the trans-Saharan route?
5. Do you know any other literary narratives that address the topic of migrants' experiences?

9

Tar or Honey? Space and Time of Moroccan Migration in a Video Sketch Comedy 'al-Kāmīra lakum'

Mike Baynham and Sarali Gintsburg

Introduction

Migration is a dominant twenty-first-century theme, and its impact on cultural production of different sorts, songs, stories, films and here comedy performance, is hardly surprising, especially in a country like Morocco with its long tradition of migration. Ennaji (2014: 81) argues that Morocco has a deeply rooted culture of migration, such that young children, including girls, while growing up, already feel the pressure to emigrate. Sociolinguistic research on migration stories (e.g. Baynham and De Fina 2005) has focused on oral tellings of the processes of dislocation/displacement involved. Here we focus on the ways that narratives in filmed oral literary production tell the different facets of the migration story, though, as we shall see, many features of performed oral narrative described in the sociolinguistic studies are also present.

The theme of migration has attracted creative responses of many kinds, including novels: Ben Jelloun's *Partir*, for example, takes up the theme of economically and socially frustrated Moroccan youth who feel their only option is to leave, as does Taia's *L'Armée du Salut*. Frustration of opportunity and desire to leave can also be encountered in popular songs, like that of the French Algerian rai singer Reda Taliani (Reda the Italian), which frames the first scene in the performance we analyse[1]:

ya l-bābūr ya **mōn amūr**
xarrəjni məl la misère
fə blādi rāni maḥgūr
ʕīt ʕīt **tout j'en ai marre**
Ah the boat, ah **my love**,
Take me out of **this misery**,
In my country I live in disgrace,
I'm tired, tired, **I've had enough**

Taliani's song expresses the frustration and aspiration of un/underemployed and frustrated youth, whose sole desire is to leave:

> En route pour l'eldorado
> Tellement plein, c'est quoi? *Dīru*, le sac à dos
> Partir loin, sans les cousins
> On my way to the Eldorado,
> The boat is already full, so what? Will go with a backpack,
> [All I want is] to go faraway, and leave my cousins behind.

As well as the desire to get away from economic and social misery, such songs express a picaresque spirit of adventure, to leave in search of an Eldorado – a pattern that can be traced back a long way, to well before the current migration crisis. So, although these literary and cultural products directly reflect the conflicts and tensions of the present, we can see them drawing on oral literary and cultural continuities.

This chapter will analyse one such product, a fifteen-minute episode from a comedy show, featuring the topic of migration. Before presenting the show, we will briefly discuss some characteristics of the literary canons in Morocco and the Arab world, as well as the chronotopic approach we will use to analyse the spatio/temporal aspect of the narrative.

On the specificity of literary canons in Moroccan verbal art

General trends

Morocco is usually regarded by researchers as a peripheral culture on the margins of the Arab world and, together with the rest of the cultures in the Greater Maghreb, is regularly presented as a curious case and exception from the general rule. However, both oral and written varieties of Moroccan literature bear a number of characteristics typical of Arabic literature in general. One of these is the seeming incoherence of a given text when evaluated against Western norms: in this tradition, various events and protagonists participating in these events often appear to be at odds with each other. This trait has been observed by a number of researchers in, for instance, the *maqamas* (Dolinina 2017), as well as in *One Thousand and One Nights* (Encyclopaedia of Islam Vol I 1986: 358). In the case of *One Thousand and One Nights* this composition is often referred to as a 'frame-work story' (362), as we shall see below.

This seemingly illogical and 'broken' structure in Maghrebi narrative is typical of oral genres, or genres that have been initially oral, where the narrator (or storyteller) had an important role to play as performer. The narrator would often submerge into the fabric of their own narrative to the degree that they would inevitably become one of the central characters of their own stories. However this can also be understood as narrative where, instead of organization on principles of logic and causality, the story is organized on principles of chance and coincidence. This narrative organization based on chance, luck or randomness can be connected with the picaresque:

> a literary genre/tradition with a history going back to the late European Middle Ages, though with antecedents in Roman literature and indeed in Classical Arabic

literature......A trickster hero, living on his wits makes his way through life, confronting and overcoming a series of challenges... there are some interesting connections to be made between this literary genre and that of the trickster in folklore, most notably in Turkish/Iranian Mullah Nasreddin stories and in North African Jeha stories.

(Baynham 2015: 81)

Taliani's song embodies just this picaresque response to economic and social misery.

A typical literary feature of these traditions is framing: stories nest within a story (framework story), where a narrator tells stories about another narrator, so that the literary text becomes extremely complex in terms of both space and time. This, in some cases, has led to emergence of a curious duo: the first protagonist, or the narrator, would become a traveller, and the second protagonist would become a wandering vagabond, or trickster. This trend is especially manifested in the *maqama* (*maqāma*), in a special subgenre known as *kudya* (*kudiya*), or mendicancy. Specific attention has been paid to the 'spaceless' nature of the *maqama*: as Hämeen-Anttila (2008: 34) puts it, 'the chameleon-like hero of the *maqama* is constantly on the move' because he is 'a man of no place, or all places'. Scenes in the *maqama* would constantly move from town to town and from land to land, following the narrator and the trickster. At times, as in the case we consider, the narrator and/or the trickster is a woman: for instance, Shahrazad in *One Thousand and One Nights*, who skilfully manages to save her own life by tricking Shahryar into listening to her endless stories until he decides to spare her life.

Morocco

We know that the genre of *maqama* reached al-Andalus and North Africa (Encyclopaedia of Islam 1991 Vol VI: 110). In Morocco, the *maqama* intertwined with various local traditions (Amin and Carlson 2012: 26; Jay 2018). One of them is *halqa* (*həlqa*), where the narrator performs partly improvised, partly memorized stories. The *halqa* ('ring' in Arabic), meaning both the space where the performance takes place and the performance itself, usually takes place on market squares, or in tents specifically pitched for this occasion. The role of the traditional storyteller, *hlayqi* (*ḥlāyqi*), combines a set of archetypical characters, the most prominent again being the trickster (Jay 2018).

One of the well-known places where professional storytellers perform is Jemaa el-Fna in Marrakech. In recent decades, the tradition of *halqa* started to rapidly disappear; so in search of entertainment, *hlayqi* audiences are making a mass exodus to digital spaces: YouTube, Vimeo and Dailymotion. Interestingly, traditionally *hlayqis* were themselves wandering actors, always, displaced, on the move, similar to the *maqamas*' narrators, so the wondrous nature of their stories is similar to the ones in the *maqamas*. This apparent spatio-temporal inconsistency, typical of traditional Arab and Moroccan oral genres, should therefore be treated not as evidence of incoherence or poor artistic skills, as emphasized by some researchers mentioned above, but rather as a key characteristic of the picaresque chronotope.

Halqa is therefore a complex construct involving several actors: the storyteller, his/her cameos and the audience, the actors connecting to each other through a network of spatio-temporal connections.

Space and time in narrative: On chronotopes and topochrones

'Every story is a travel story – a spatial practice.' (De Certeau 1988: 115)

The chronotope (Bakhtin 1981) has long been a theme in literary theory, but more recently has become significant in sociolinguistics, including the study of migration narratives. The extension of the chronotope from literary theory to the space/time constitution of the social world, mentioned programmatically in Bakhtin's work but undeveloped, was taken up by Agha (2007) and by others such as Perrino (2015) or Blommaert and De Fina (2017). Agha emphasizes a third dimension crucial to the Bakhtinian chronotope, that of personhood. Blommaert and De Fina (2017) emphasize identity in a similar way. Baynham (2003), De Fina (2003), Georgakopoulou (2003) and others have argued that, while time has an important place in contemporary narrative theory, the significance of space has been neglected. This perspective resonates with the Aristotelian perspective, where time is treated as secondary to movement. In his *Physics* (Vol IV) Aristotle explains that time (*chronos*) is nowhere equal to movement, instead, it exists to measure movement.[2]

Chronos always moves in one direction, that is, from past to future. According to Aristotle the only moment when time can be 'touched' is *now*, which serves as indivisible boundary between past and future. *Now*, however, is a subjective concept. Aristotle did not use the word *space*, probably to avoid vagueness and ambiguity: he preferred the term place (*topos*), defined as a motionless boundary of a thing. Following this logic, any event would necessarily be an interaction between *topos* or *topoi* and *chronos*.

Bakhtin suggests that any plot represents a combination of two variables (time and place). Researchers on the chronotope in oral narrative (e.g. Perrino 2015) suggest that a narrative typically contains at least two chronotopes (the story chronotope and the storytelling chronotope).[3] These are aligned by the narrator in the telling or retelling. Research on digital narratives pushes us even further: in the narration the concept of *topos* (place or movement from place to place) is primary, as Aristotle suggests, while chronos (time) is secondary and only serves to mark and measure this movement. Time is not essential, not the gist of the story. This is especially true when watching or sharing online digital narratives (YouTube), as is the case in this chapter: the mere fact that it is possible to return to the same video uploaded to YouTube as many times as we want disturbs and reorders the relationship between the story chronotope and the chronotope of its telling.

This re-emphasis of the importance of space over time is picked up in the work of Epstein, who argues that the privileging of time over space should be reversed. Reversing Bakhtin's term *chronotope*, he introduced the term *topochrone* to describe cultures/spaces where time appears to be subordinated to place or space: in Epstein's terms (2007: 78)

> *chronos* is consistently displaced and swallowed up by *topos*. *Chronos* tends toward zero, toward the suddenness of miracle, toward the instantaneousness of revolutionary or eschatological transformation; *topos*, correspondingly, tends toward infinity, striving to encompass an enormous land mass, and even the earth itself.

Epstein's topochrone describes the Soviet and, subsequently, Russian culture, saturated with the comprehension of living on enormous lands, where time becomes invisible. This observation invites comparison of the Russian *topos* with the topos of the internet: myriads of channels (*topoi*) coexist with each other, together creating digital space. Servers and clouds let us watch and listen to them at any time. *Chronos* therefore becomes reversible and secondary, while *topos*, or *topoi* forming an enormous virtual space, become primary. In this chapter we share Epstein's emphasis on topos over chronos, although not systematically adopting his term 'topochrone', most especially when we come to consider the dynamics of storytelling on the internet.[4]

Introducing the video (the *halqa*)

This chapter analyses an episode of a television series online understood here as a digital *halqa*. As suggested above, since the audience of traditional *hlayqis* is rapidly moving to digital spaces, *hlayqis* are also going digital. In addition, *hlayqi* is becoming a reputable profession, especially if a *halqa* becomes hosted by a TV channel. Such is the case of the show titled *al-Kāmīra lakum* (the Camera is yours), a comic show hosted by al-Aoula public TV channel. The title *al-Kāmīra lakum*, a play on words and built on the expression *al-kalima lakum* 'have your say', suggests an opportunity for ordinary people to tell their stories on camera, though of course all these 'ordinary people' are played by Hanane el-Fadili. The show ran for one season (2015–16) with several dozen episodes produced and staged by Hanane, a professional Moroccan actress and comedian, and her brother Adil el-Fadili, a producer. Each episode, lasting for about fifteen minutes, has a title, usually a popular proverb or saying. The theme of the title relates to the episode, which is divided into three or four parts. The fact that it is only Hanane who is involved in performing, skilfully impersonating men and women from all walks of life and all ages, using her talent as a comedian with modest props, mostly clothes and some sort of backdrop, enables us to compare each episode to a digital *halqa*, where the performer, who similarly uses only minimal props to connect to their audience digitally, receives feedback via likes and time-delayed comments. The episodes prepared by Hanane become a series, both a television series and a series of performances such as are regularly offered by *hlayqis* to their audiences.[5]

Until recently, Moroccan theatre offered only limited access for women as actresses and playwrights and directors: indeed it was via the genre of *halqa* that women started to gain wider access to the public sphere of theatre. Among them was Fatema

Chebchoub (1952–2006), a hereditary storyteller and performer but also actress, scholar and playwright (Jay 2018). Chebchoub innovatively combined the traditional canons of the *halqa* with contemporary, Western-inspired theatre trends, allowing her to give Moroccan women an audible voice in public spaces and freely express feminist ideas. These possibilities inspired a number of younger Moroccan actresses, among them the already mentioned Hanane el-Fadili, who, following the pattern created by Chebchoub, re-produces in her artistic creations the tradition of *halqa*, where the actress combines in her performances the functions of trickster, healer and comedian (Jay 2018).

The *halqa* we chose for this chapter is entitled *qatrān blādi wulla ʕasal əl-buldān* – 'The tar of my home country or the honey of foreign lands', a popular pan Maghrebi proverb often related to the topic of emigration. As the title indicates, the *halqa* features the topic of emigration from Morocco and consists of three parts: in part one a young Moroccan man in his twenties dreams about emigrating to Italy, part two involves a Moroccan woman who emigrated to France a long time ago and now only visits Morocco on holidays and part three presents an old Berber woman, whose son (and we may infer that she is the mother of the young man from the first part) has supposedly emigrated to Italy. The backdrop for the three parts remains the same: an easily recognizable port in northern Morocco, where many Moroccans start their migration journey.

Framing the *halqa*

As we have pointed out above, the *halqa* genre is noted for its complex framing and cross-chronotopic reference, so we will start by discussing the framing and three-part structure of this *halqa*. The framing is in part derived from the text but also involves the knowledge the viewer brings to the viewing. It includes the episode we are considering as part of the whole series entitled *al-Kāmīra lakum,* with the implication of giving ordinary people a moment in front of the camera to tell their story. The knowledgeable viewer will be aware that all these 'ordinary' people are played by Hanane. As we have shown Hanane is a high-profile female performer, in a tradition of politically challenging and outspoken feminist comedy. So the viewer will come to a Hanane video with further expectations. The *halqa* is also framed by its proverb title. Is it better to leave or stay, to be satisfied with *la misère* at home or seek honey in an uncertain journey in search of Eldorado? The proverb title encapsulates the dilemma and life choice of migration which the comedy explores.

As the video opens we are at the quayside in the port of Tangier, cameras signalling outside broadcasting. An elegantly dressed woman (Hanane) seated in a deckchair welcomes us politely to the show in Standard Arabic. The knowledgeable viewer will realize that there are surprises in store. The port setting itself provides a framing for the sketch, a liminal space, specialized in leaving and arriving. As the introduction fades into the first cameo, we see Hanane transformed into a young man in casual hiphop dress, sitting on a bollard and crooning the lines from Taliani's song discussed above. Taliani's song is another framing of the narrative that is to unfold, responding as it were to the sentiment expressed in the title/proverb.

It is interesting to consider how the transitions between the introduction and the three cameos are achieved visually and musically: the concluding image unravels and rewinds at high speed for a few seconds then switches to the start of the new cameo to emerge from the blur, rather like a succession of magic tricks, the magic lying in part in Hanane's transformations from disaffected youth plotting his escape, to a well-padded mother of eight returning from France on holiday, to the mother, apparently, of the youth in the first cameo.

The *Halqa* – Part one: *xarrəjni məl* la misère

The scene opens with the young man crooning the words of Taliani's song then, looking straight at the camera, addressing the audience in an intimately direct way to complain of the misery of his life. Importantly, he aligns himself, drawing on the resources of generic narrative (Baynham 2006) with a whole group of young men in the same situation:

> w kēyn wāḥəd əl-fiʔa waḥəd eṭ-ṭabaqa dyāl š-šabāb ktār bḥāli **dīprīsyō** w-tfīq mʕa ṣ-ṣabāḥ tsanna n-nhār yəṭīr bāš bāš yəji l-līl w-l-līl ja tsannā yəṭīr bāš yəji n-nhār… **ainsi de suite et ainsi de suite**… rā f škəl.

> There is a group, a numerous class of young men like me, who are **depressed**: they wake up in the morning and [can't] wait for the day to fly away, so, so that the night could come. When the night comes, they wait for the day to come… **ainsi de suite et ainsi de suite**… This is hard!

He describes his attempts to realize his dream and effect his escape by securing the affections of an older European woman. He has decided on an Italian:

> ana l-ḥulm dyāli huwa nəmši l-Ṭalyān ā nəmši l-Ṭalyān..bəzzāf də-n-nās ki-ygūlu ʕalāš Ṭalyān ʕalāš Ṭalyān..Ṭalyān fī ṣ-ṣarf a ṣaḥbi w-zād waḥəd lli ka-yəhbaṭ f tirītwār dyāl Ṭalyān ka-təlqa wlād əl-blād fhemti ka-yəməddū lek īdd əl-musāʕada.. ha ha fatt hna kunt hna w-nti dəbbərti ʕala **sījōrna**

> My dream is to go to Italy, yep, to go to Italy.. lots of people tell me: Why Italy? Why Italy? Italy has money, my friends, plus if you 'fall' on the Italian territory, you will meet people from your country, you know what I mean, and then they will help you… here, here, move here, and you will get your papers fixed.

Here we have a hypothetical, future-oriented narrative, what would be termed a 'projection' by Georgakopoulou (2007: 47–9), with the characteristic shift into performance via unframed direct speech (*ha ha fatt hna kunt hna* – here, here, move here) as the guys he imagines he will meet up with (*wlād əl-blād* – people from your country) offer help. Again we have the picaresque event structure, echoing the migration story described in Baynham (2016): the speaker falls onto Italian territory, and happens upon guys from his country who help him.

He has bought a teach yourself Italian book, *Italian in 24 Hours*, though in six months has not got beyond *buon giorno*, then drifts into a fantasy of watching Italian films and seeming to recognize his own family in the actors. He continues to imagine the small coin in his pocket turning into an 100 dirham note so he can send it to his mother[6]:

> rā dāk š-ši ġīr alla... tṣuwwrū kūn ja qarš 100 dərham b jībi kūn nəmši būsṭa ka-nṣəyfəṭ lə l-wālida ġīr bāš thiss əl-wālida b dāk l-əhsās zaʕma rā ʕinnda l-wild tāʕna rā huwa fə ṭ-Ṭalyān w-rā ka-yəṣeyfeṭ līhum... fhəmti?
>
> I swear by God... imagine – if a *qirsh* that I have in my pocket happened to be equal 100 dirhams, I would have gone to the post office and sent it to my mother, so that my mother could have that feeling of 'our son, he lives in Italy' and sends them [money]... do you understand?

In this hypothetical narrative we have a characteristic blending of rapid perspective shifting between '**our** son he lives in Italy', in the voice of the mother, and 'sends **them**', in the voice of the narrator. Other typical features of such performed oral narratives are his explicitly addressing the audience, so as to elicit solidarity: *fhəmti*? (Do you understand?)

At the conclusion of this fantasy sequence, he slips back into present misery, seemingly addressing those who have the power to change the fortunes of disenfranchised youth: do something for us since we are just sitting here.

> ṣʕība l-qaḍīya zaʕma... mkarfasīn dyāl s-ṣahh zaʕma hna bġīna w-ka-nəmšiw w-ndīru ši hāja.. w-l-muhimm kun glisna hna yədīru bīna hāja mzyāna w-hād š-ši lli kēyn
>
> this is a difficult problem... we are in a terrible situation, that is we would like to go [somewhere] and do something.. well, since we are sitting here, do something nice for us, this is what I mean

In another scene shift, he describes his day working hard in a cyber cafe to attract an older woman who might provide both his meal and his ticket out of **la misère** to Italy.

> dāba nhār kullu w-xūkum ʕāṣər f sībēr kāfē xəddām ʕla š-šāṭ š-šāṭ
>
> Now, all day long your brother spends in a cyber cafe, working [hard], chatting, that is

So the means of realizing the dream is through forming a relationship with a wealthy older person who can take you out of misery, a pattern that echoes Abdellah Taia's novel *L'Armée du Salut* and Ben Jelloun's *Partir*. Like the characters in *L'Armée du Salut* and *Partir*, Hanane's young man on the quay-side in Tangier dreams of leaving, and a relationship is the bridge that can make this happen. So he works hard in the internet cafe and connects with Barbara, an apparently (at least in his eyes) elderly Italian woman. Concealing his distaste, he woos her and invites her to Morocco.

sāʕa gult lha bə l-burūda ha gult lha nti āji zaʕma ana bāġi ġīr nzənnadha ana fhəmti ndīr mʕaha l-ʕilāqa w-ndabbər ʕla l-fīza hā lukāt hnāya gult lha aji nəddūk a xti l Mūlāy Yəʕqūb nti hāniya... jāt z-zaʕra ddīnaha Mūlāy Yəʕqūb ʕajəbha Mūlāy Yəʕqūb... ka-nədxul ka-nəlqāha xəddāma ʕla l-kāsākəs ka-təʕrəf ka-tləggəm l-kusksū w-gāʕ gāt lak ʕərafti aš ġa-ndīru ġa-ngəlsu hna... gult lha nti wāš tsassīṭi ġa-nglis hna ana wāš ana msayfəṭ ʕaleyk bāš ddīni ntiya... wulla ma fhamtš aš bġīti ddīri gāt lak wālu ngəlsu hna... ġādi mʕa dūzāra mʕa dūzāra aš ġa-ndīru ktāb ʕaliya l-wāqəʕ... ya rabbi huwa yəšūf mən ḥāli w-yəšūf mən š-šabāb lli ka-yəsufrīw hna māši sahla hna gāʕ

Suddenly, I told her indifferently 'come here', I mean, I wanted to inflame her, do you understand, I was [hoping] to get my visa done if she were here [and so] I told her: 'come here, my sister, we'll take you to Moulay Yacoub, you relax... the red-haired came, we took her to Moulay Yacoub, she liked Moulay Yacoub... and so [one day] I see her working on couscous, eating couscous and she says: 'you know what we will do? Let's live here', I told her: 'are you out of your mind – I should live here? I've sent for you so that you could take me out [of here].. or what? I didn't get what is that you are going to do?' she said: 'Nope, we are staying here'. Argument after argument... What can we do? [God] has planned this for me... Lord, please help me and help the young men who are suffering here, here it's not easy at all

The scheming comes to nothing. He takes Barbara to the tourism and pilgrimage destination Moulay Yacoub. She likes it so much she wants to stay, defeating the escape plan. Mutual recriminations ensue. He returns from the particular case to the generic 'Lord, please help me and help the young men who are suffering here, here it's not easy at all' (*ya rabbi huwa yəšūf mən ḥāli w-yəšūf mən š-šabāb lli ka-yəsufrīw hna māši sahla hna gāʕ*). At the end of the sketch, the young man is again miserably crooning the lines that opened it, the circularity perhaps ironically indexing both the circularity of the social and economic trap in which he and so many other young people are caught and the circularity of the *halqa*. This young man sitting on the quayside is part of what is known as *harraga (ḥarrāga)*, where Maghrebi clandestines (from the verb *ḥrəg* – to burn) are people who are ready to burn not only their documents, in case they have them, but everything associated with their previous life, social contacts, families and friends. The practice of *harga* is closely associated with crossing the straits on *pateras* (rafts), and can be heroically construed as an echo of historical events such as Tareq Ibn Ziyad ordering his men to burn their boats as they land to conquer Spain.

Part two: J'suis belle?

Now Hanane magically transitions into a well-padded Moroccan matriarch, mother of eight and long-time resident in France. She speaks a variety of French that is distinctively Moroccan, as described by Giacomi, Stoffel and Veronique (2000), mixed with Moroccan Arabic. Her main concern as a mother is to ensure her children remain connected with Moroccan culture and do not absorb chiefly American culture:

> les enfants *défendés,* j'ai dis *défendés* parler français à la maison – 'parle français avec la *mitrēz,* parle français avec tes copains, la maison tu parles arabe! Voilà *répondī* en arabe, c'est tout hein?' Moi *défendé* les enfants: 'écoute music de 50 cents ou écoute la music *dī* Eminem *awla* écoute la music *dī* 113'... oui *défendé.* J'ai dis: écoute...... écoute moi très bien, t'écoute Senhaji, t'écoute Daoudi, t'écoute Jedwane, écoute Najat Aâtabou, écoute la musique *marocān* (marocaine), c'est tout.

> my children are forbidden ... I mean forbidden to speak French at home – speak French with the teacher, speak French with your mates... at home you speak Arabic! That's it, reply in Arabic, that's all ok? I forbade my children to listen to the music of 50 cents, listen to the music of Eminem, *or* listen to the music of 113. I tell them: listen to me, you listen to Senhaji, you listen to Daoudi, you listen to Jedwane... you listen to Moroccan music, that's all.

However, she identifies herself as from an earlier generation of migrants, when the migration processes were more regulated and organized, with treaties and agreements between countries such as Morocco and France with a former colonial history and active recruitment in Morocco for specific industries:

> **Nous, on est parti à l'époque des immigrations** *šwīya kānet* **klāz** *d-dunya u-kān...* **on était pas nombreux.**

> **We left in the days, when the immigration** *didn't pick up, there was a bit of class then* **and... we were not many.**

She disapproves strongly of the current chaotic and unregulated migrations:

> maintenant quand tu vois *š-šubbān,* tu vois les gens hein? Rīsquē, rīsquē ça.. faire comme ça, dans la mer et la plage, c'est pas bien, il faut pas faire ça, attendez mariage, attendez quelque chose, de.. de bien hein? C'est pas, c'est pas comme ça, les gens n'est partent... Moi je suis pas d'accord, je pas du tout d'accord.

> Now, when you see *these young folks*, you see these people, huh? To risk, risk... to act just like that is not good, [throwing yourself] into the sea, into the beach, is not good, you shouldn't do that, wait for marriage, wait for something, something good, huh? ... I disagree with this, I totally disagree.

She goes on to tell a story of a girl she knows who is so desperate to get to France that she climbs into a washing machine in the coach travelling to Europe, but the wash cycle was triggered:

> La pauvre, elle a foutue dans le car, comme le car était bien rempli, elle a mise dans une machine à laver.. les gens, c'est même pas que j'raconte la misère, la misère: quelqu'un appuie sur le bouton *da* marche et la fille *məskīna* tournait, tournait, passait par l'essorage, par le lavage, par le rinçage et elle été arrivée

à la douane française tout essorée, le douanier demande: "Madame d'ou vous *sortē*?" et elle lui dit "monsieur dans une machine à laver" et il le dit *retournez y* elle n'as pas bien *répondē*. *Ma ʕarfat š tjāwbu ma..u-kūn kunt ana kunt nqūl lu:* "monsieur *retournez* vous, toi-même *tī*, toi pour que tu t'apprends!

Poor thing, she stuffed herself into the coach, as the car was really full she put herself in a washing machine... people, I can't even tell you the misery, the misery: someone pushes the start button and the girl *poor thing* **was turning, turning, going through spinning, washing, rinsing and she arrived at the customs all spun out, the customs officer asks: "where have you come from Madame?" and she said to him "Monsieur in the washing machine" and he said to her well go back there and she didn't reply nicely. She didn't know how to reply properly [to him]**, *but if it was me I would have said to him*: **"Monsieur go back [there] yourself, you, yes you, so you can learn!"**

Having expressed her shock at this story, she returns complacently to her own children who she has brought up properly:

u-lakin l-ḥamdilla, ddīna wlādna u-rabbīnāhum... **on leur a donné une bonne éducation**, *dāba* **quand tu viens au Maroc, hein** – **c'est** *l-fəšṭa a*, **c'est** *l-ʕawnīyāt* **hein, c'est** *n-našāṭ*... **Je les ramène pour voire** *s-sādāt*, **je les ramène pour voir le vrai Maroc, qu'ont.. sont pas déphasés.. je veux pas des enfants déphasés moi, je veux des enfants qui savent d'où ils viennent, parce que quand tu sais d'où tu viens et que tu es, tu sais où tu vas.**

But thank God we brought up our children and educated them... **we gave them a good education** *now* **when you come to Morocco ok – it's** *fiesta*, **it's** *water springs* **it's** *active lifestyle*... **I bring them back to see....I bring them back to see the real Morocco, so they... they aren't out of touch... me I don't want out of touch children, I want children who know where they come from, because when you know where you come from and who you are, you know where you are going.**

When she goes back with them on holiday it seems she is revisiting a tourist Morocco, 'le vrai Maroc' as one might hear it described in the tourist brochures: her life is in France and Morocco is now a holiday destination.

She has a message for all the émigrés: we are happy here, but bring us a cassette of Moroccan music if you are coming:

Alors, je dit à tout les émigrés: 'bonjour nous somme très contents et *passē* **nous un cassette** *hein*, **si c'est possible, on n'vous pas**... *ndāxlu ʕaleykum.. ḥna ġādīn... a u-gāl lak -ḍḍeyf ḍeyfak šta u-ṣeyf... kāṣēṭ*, **quelle** *kō* **chose** – *Dāwdi wulla Sṭāṭi wulla Jədwāni*

So I say to all the emigres: 'hello we are very happy and *bring* **us a cassette ok, if possible. We are not**... We are asking you, we are... there is a saying, guest is [always] your guest, [both] in winter and summer.. **a cassette, anything** – of Daoudi, or Stati, or Jedouani.'

Something seems to trigger here, perhaps some memory of youth. She tosses her hair.

on adore la music, on adore, on est très.. très..j'suis *bēl* (belle)?

We love music, we love, we very much.. very.. am I beautiful?

As if she is looking at herself in the mirror or remembering that she is being filmed, she draws herself up, her eyes flash and she asks the camera: *J'suis belle?* (Am I beautiful?)

Part three: Yummu ʕAbdərraḥīmu

The last cameo in the *halqa* is the old mother (*yummu*), most probably Berber, identifiable from her tattooed chin. She is wearing a jellaba, and a loosely tied headscarf allows us to notice her grey hair. The repetitive speaking style of the mother suggests an oral poem or a song: every small part of the story is followed by a refrain: 'Abderrahim, the tall and handsome, with arched eyebrows and bright eyes' (*wīldi ʕAbdərraḥimu ṭ-ṭwīl z-zīn w-l-ḥəjbu məgrūnīn w-ʕaynīnu mbəllgīn*). Very soon we infer that this character could be the mother of the young Moroccan fellow from part one: it turns out that her child wanted to go to Italy so that the poor mother had to sell everything she had to help him realize that dream. We also learn that her son is addicted to smoking, a detail which resonates with the personality of the young Moroccan man from part one. The mother thinks that her poor child is now having a miserable life working for some spoiled Italian woman, though in part one, the son dreamed of this. Generally speaking, the speech of the old mother, leaving aside the irony behind the story, reminds us a lot of the popular *chaabi* songs from the 1970 to 1990, where the topic of immigration started to become an issue in Moroccan society, as exemplified in this song by the famous Moroccan popular singer and poet Mohammed Laaroussi (Gintsburg 2005):

māl wildi gyābu ṭawwal	What happened to my son, his absence has been so long!
w-ʕalāš fina ma yəsawwal	Why doesn't he ask about us?
fə l-ġurba mḍat iyāmu	His days passed in a foreign land,
w-l-qalb aley yəthawwal	And the heart feels fear for him
ma ktib ma baʕat risāla	He didn't write, didn't send a letter
w-la qāl kīf əl-ḥāla	And he didn't say how he is faring

Suddenly, the mother assumes generically the role of a representative of all mothers whose children have disappeared somewhere between Morocco and Western countries, and switches to address *l-məsūlīn ya n-nās ya ṣ-ṣuḥāba ya n-nās əntum ʕārfīn al-qānūn*, asking them to do something to stop this constant flow of young Moroccans from the country. Interestingly, this corresponds with the strategy used by the young man in the first sketch, possibly Abderrahim, who aligns his misery with that of all the other young people using a generic narrative.

Towards the end of the story, the mother breaks the frame to send her greetings to her missing son on camera. It is not clear until the very last phrase whether she is simply narrating this to a friend, when, suddenly, she says:

slāmi līk ka-nsəlləm ʕaleyk w-ka-tsəlləm ʕaleyk bint xāltak ya ʕAbdərraḥim ya gūlūha ya qūlūha fi 'l-kāmīra lakum'

Your mother has been missing you [ever since], greetings to you, I send my greetings to you and your cousin also sends her greetings to you, oh, Abderrahim, tell it, tell it right to al-*Kāmīra lakum*.

At the beginning of the phrase we think that probably the poor mother is asking someone to write a letter to her, but when the last words are said, we immediately realize that it is Hanane again who is talking, closing the *halqa*.

Discussion

Moroccan migration as a chronotope

In the introductory sequence of the video, Hanane as a practised TV presenter welcomes the audience politely: *sīdna s-salāmu ʕaleykum*. The polite, plural pronoun *kum* echoes the one selected in the title of the series *al-kāmīra lakum*, indicating that the programme is there to give ordinary audience members a chance to tell their stories, in a sense honouring the audience. However, as in all the best stories, things are not what they seem. The humour and magic lie in the fact that Hanane is the one who transforms, jinn-like, into all these 'ordinary' characters, male and female, young and old. The programme is a kind of hybrid of the TV programme genre and the genre of the *halqa*. The proverb title of this particular programme (*Tar or Honey*) sets the scene, pithily indexing, as proverbs do, both the dilemma and the chronotope of migration. As Agha (2007: 322) points out: 'the concept of chronotope is of vanishingly little interest when extracted from a frame of contrast.' So what is the cross-chronotopic contrast, the dilemma here? It is precisely to stay or to go. Each of the episodes portrays a different facet, a different protagonist in the migration story: the frustrated and desperate young man, plotting his escape; the French Moroccan matriarch, between two worlds, desperate to ensure that her children, immersed in Western, specifically American culture, imbibe Moroccan culture; the elderly mother, as we may perhaps assume, of the young man in the first scene, caught between missing her much loved son and thinking of the money and presents he will bring back. Hanane seems to be speaking directly, confidentially to the camera, as if to another person. Her storytelling style conforms uncannily to the much studied style of conversational narrative, unsurprising perhaps as she is a consummate mimic.

The young man in the first scene seems to represent the chaotic determination of the *harga*, also bringing in a rather older trope of striking up a relationship with an older European woman hoping for a visa and papers. This is a well-trodden path. So each story, while located in the present, seems to invoke earlier versions of the Moroccan migration chronotope. The French Moroccan matriarch specifically harks back to an earlier more orderly migration chronotope, with country-to-country agreements, and recruitment to work in specific industries. She is horrified by the *harga*. The story she tells of the young woman who travels to Paris in a washing machine perhaps alludes to the rinsing which the *harga* risk in their dangerous crossings. The third story of the mother left behind, mourning her son, while at the same time dreaming of his return with money and presents, again demonstrates a chronotopic ambivalence, which is in fact characteristic of the whole programme. So Hanane synthesizes a whole history of migration, indexed by the proverb, up to and including the current chronos and topos of the *harga*, echoing in their leaky boats the reckless and heroic journeying of Tariq Ibn Ziyad. The very name *harga* after all contains this history within it, as we saw above.

Halqa 'Tar or Honey' as a chronotopic event

The *halqa* studied in this chapter represents yet another artistic realization of the chronotope of Moroccan migration produced according to Arabic (Moroccan) literary and performative canons. The performer, in this case Hanane, acts as the 'impresario' of the chronotope, telling different stories related to the topic of migration. Time and space are in the hands of an archetypical trickster – and we mentioned earlier that in the Moroccan culture of storytelling, the figure of *hlayqi* is traditionally associated with the figure of a trickster – who juggles them. Morocco, which is pictured with the liminal image of the quayside, represents the *topos*, while the heart of the stories unfolding before our eyes, the dynamics, the change, the act of leaving behind and getting somewhere represents the migration *chronotope*. But the *topos* expands enormously, spatially encompassing the Moroccan coast, associated with the migration background of all three stories, but also Italy, France, presumably, a Berber village in Morocco, Algeria, as well as Italy and even the transnational appeal of the United States.

All three cameos played by the trickster-performer in the *halqa* are in some ways visibly stuck in the *topos* – none of the characters played by Hanane, even the case of the mother who actually migrated to France, it can be argued, have actually left the coast, none of them has got anywhere – the young man from the first part keeps spending his days in cybercafés and day dreaming, so life stands still, nothing ever happens and young people like our character 'wake up in the morning and [can't] wait for the day to fly away, so, so that the night could come. When the night comes, they wait for the day to come… **ainsi de suite et ainsi de suite**' (*tfīq mʕa ṣ-ṣabāḥ tsanna n-nhār yəṭīr bāš bāš yəji l-līl w-l-līl ja tsannā yəṭīr bāš yəji n-nhār*… **ainsi de suite et ainsi de suite**).

The matriarch from the second part of the *halqa*, who now lives in France and delivers her story in French, appears to be someone who was able to complete the mission. However, mentally she continues to live in Morocco, perhaps the Morocco of her youth, indexed by her strong Moroccan accent,[7] her cultural preferences and her fears that her children might turn out to be more French than Moroccan. The children, as she puts it, have received a very progressive education and they are open to the world – (**l'éducation très développée – ouverture le monde**) but at the same time she tries to align them to her remembered Morocco, they are not allowed to speak French at home or listen to non-Moroccan music. Instead, she instructs them to listen to the Moroccan *chaabi* music, popular when she was young.

The mother from the third part, seemingly not involved in the story of migration because she is not planning to go anywhere, is nevertheless also drawn into it, perhaps, against her will: her son wanted to go to Italy and so she had to sell everything she had so that he could go. Those who remain are also actors in the migration chronotope. As suggested above, this chronotope involves both going and staying. Migration research has been very focused on those who go, but those who stay behind with regrets but also hopes of bounty when the migrant returns are also players in the migration story. The mother has been waiting for her son ever since, asking everyone she meets if they met her son somewhere:

s-salām ana yūmmu ʕAbdərraḥīmu ʕarəftu ʕAbdərraḥimu ma ʕarəftu š ʕAbdərraḥimu a wīldi ʕAbdərraḥimu ṭ-ṭwīl z-zīn w-l-ḥəjbu məgrūnīn w-ʕaynīnu mbəllgīn a tšūfu howa tšūfūni anāya yəšbuh līya wlīdi.

Greetings, I am Abderrahim's mother, you know Abderrahim? You don't know Abderrahim? No way! Abderrahim, the tall and handsome, [with] the arched eyebrows and bright eyes, yes, [if you like to know] what he looks like, look at me, my son looks similar to me.

Online dimension of 'Tar or Honey' as a chronotopic event

The relative insignificance of time compared to the importance of space becomes even more obvious when we consider the fact that Hanane's performance does not happen live as is the case with the traditional *halqa*. Instead, the episode, pre-recorded and premiered in 2016, was uploaded to the official channel of *Al-Awla* on YouTube, and is instantly available to anyone who clicks 'play'. Anyone with access to YouTube can watch the performance an indefinite number of times, which would be impossible if the performance took place in real space/time. The settled chronotopic alignment in face-to-face performance is further disrupted in virtual space through the ability to share texts/memes/performances across platforms, with the consequence that an online performance can be shared, watched, simultaneously or not, by audiences in different space/times round the world. The phenomenon of the sharing and circulation of online material across platforms is termed by Jenkins (2006) and de Souza (2022 forthcoming) as transmediatization. The performance event can be put on pause, rewound or fast-forwarded, shared, as if time did not exist any more.

Additionally, performance, and especially performance of the storytelling type, implies live interaction with the audience: without feedback from the audience, it would not exist (Gintsburg, Galván Moreno and Finnegan 2021). Hanane's performances, although clothed in the contemporary media genre of the television programme, are clearly influenced by the traditional *halqa*. They follow, perhaps intuitively, the traditional pattern: she interacts with the audience as if this were a live performance. All three cameos use body language, such as pointing, all three ask the audience dialogic questions. The young man from part one asks: 'you know what I'm saying?' (*fhəmti aš bġīt ngūl?*), or just 'do you understand?' (*fhəmti?*). The French Moroccan mother from part two uses interrogative interjections (**hein**?), while the Moroccan mother from part three keeps asking the audience if they happen to know her son. The feedback of the audience, however, typically taking place immediately during the traditional *halqa*, is now delayed in time, continuing long after the performance. The comments section below the video contains comments dated by years 2019–2021, including comments that could be very appropriate for live performance: 'Hanane is always the best' (*Hanane dima top*), 'Honestly, bravo!' (*bə ṣ-ṣirāḥa brāfu*), 'I can't stop laughing' (***j'arrête pas de rigoler***). Five years after the *halqa* was recorded, Hanane keeps getting digital feedback for her digital performance. Performance remains, time freezes.

Conclusion

Morocco is a country profoundly marked by migration. In this chapter we have shown how popular culture genres (proverbs, songs, storytelling and performance) in Morocco and the greater Maghreb engage with the theme of migration. We have focused in particular on a comedy performance by Hanane el-Fadili, understood as a transposition of the *halqa* performance into digital space. We have analysed the implications of this with an analysis of the migration chronotope, paying particular attention to the privileging of space over time in our analysis. Hanane's performances showcase different facets of the migration chronotope in the different protagonists: the young man desperate to leave, the matriarch who left and must deal with the conflicts that leaving brings, the mother who misses her son yet waits for his return with gifts. As such the performance illuminates the key dilemma or cross-chronotopic contrast that configures the imaginative space between staying and going.

Notes

1 In this chapter French and translation of French is in **bold**. Moroccan Arabic and its translation are transcribed as *italic*. Moroccan Arabic-influenced pronunciation of French is in *bold italic*.
2 Aristotle also used the concept *kairos*, a turning point or decisive moment in time, but in this chapter we will build our discussion on *chronos*, the linear version of time, where we always have past, present and future.
3 In the example from *One Thousand and One Nights*, the chronotope of telling is that of Shahrazad telling stories to Shahryar to save her life, the other chronotopes being of the stories she tells him.
4 Interestingly, the notion of chronotope was first introduced by Aleksey Ukhtomsky (1875–1942), a famous Russian physiologist, who intuitively formulated it as 'connectedness of spatial and temporal relationships' (2002). Bakhtin borrowed this term from Ukhtomsky and gave its temporal component more importance.

5   The Arabic word for 'episode' is also *halqa*, which again demonstrates another continuity of oral genres from live to recorded and then digital modes in the Moroccan and, in a more general context, Arab culture.
6   Sending back money and gifts is another characteristic element of the migration chronotope.
7   Today, on Facebook there are several pages dedicated to contemporary Moroccan comedy, and some pages, dedicated to and run by Moroccans, living aboard. This episode was posted on several pages, and it was the accent of the French Moroccan mother that provoked numerous jokes by upper-middle class Moroccans living in both Morocco and France. For instance, see this page: HYPERLINK 'https://www.facebook.com/Maroc-Morocco-%D8%A7%D9%84%D9%85%D8%BA%D8%B1%D8%A8-304633419710709/videos/les-immigr%C3%A9s-hanane-fadili/532503400257042/'https://www.facebook.com/Maroc-Morocco-المغرب-304633419710709/videos/les-immigrés-hanane-fadili/532503400257042/.

References

"الكاميرا لكم - قطران بلادي ولا عسل البلدان https://www.youtube.com/watch?v=9vxoYPKz7WU" - YouTube.
Agha, A. (2007), 'Recombinant Selves in Mass Mediated Spacetime', *Language and Communication*, 27: 320–35.
Amin, K. and M. Carlson (2012), *The Theatres of Morocco, Algeria and Tunisia: Performance Traditions of the Maghreb*, New York: Palgrave Macmillan.
Aristotle, *Physics* Book IV (1941), trans. R. P. Hardie and R. K. Gaye, in R. McKeon (ed.), *The Basic Works of Aristotle*, New York: Random House.
Bakhtin, M. (1981), *The Dialogic Imagination: Four Essays by M.M*, Austin: University of Texas Press.
Baynham, M. (2003), 'Narratives in Space and Time: Beyond "Backdrop" Accounts of Narrative Orientation', *Narrative Inquiry*, 13 (2): 347–66.
Baynham, M. (2006), 'Performing Self, Family and Community in Moroccan Narratives of Migration and Settlement', in A. De Fina, D. Schiffrin and M. Bamberg (eds), *Discourse and Identity*, 352–76, Cambridge: Cambridge University Press.
Baynham, M. (2015), 'Identity: Brought about or Brought along? Narrative as a Privileged Site for Researching Intercultural Identities', in F. Dervin and K. Risager (eds). *Researching Identity and Interculturality*, London: Routledge.
Baynham, M. and A. De Fina (eds) (2005), *Dislocations/Relocations: Narratives of Displacement*, Manchester: St Jerome Publishing.
Ben Jelloun, T. (2006), *Partir*, Paris: Gallimard.
Blommaert, J. and A. De Fina (2017), 'Chronotopic Identities: On the Timespace Organization of Who We Are', in A. De Fina, D. Ikizoglu and J. Wegner (eds), *Diversity and Super-diversity*, 1–14, Washington, DC: Georgetown University Press.
De Certeau, M. (1988), *The Practice of Everyday Life*, Berkeley: University of California Press.
De Fina, A. (2003), 'Crossing Borders: Time, Space and Disorientation in Narrative', *Narrative Inquiry*, 13 (2): 367–91.
De Souza, J. (2022 forthcoming), Transmediatization of the Covid-19 Crisis in Brazil: Communication across Media Spaces and the Emergence of (Bio-/Geo-)political Repertoires of (Re-)interpretation, *Humanities and Social Sciences Communications*.

Dolinina, A. (2017), *Makami: srednevekovaya arabskaya novella* (*Maqamas: the Medieval Arab Novella*), St Petersburg: Peterburgskoye Vostokovedeniye.
Ennaji, M. (2014), *Muslim Moroccan Migrants in Europe: Transnational Migration in Its Multiplicity*, New York: Palgrave.
Epstein, M. ([2003] 2007), *Amerussia. Selected Essays*, Moscow: Serebrianye niti.
Georgakopoulou, A. (2003), 'Plotting the "Right Place" and the "Right Time"', *Narrative Inquiry*, 13 (2): 413–32.
Georgakopoulou, A. (2007), *Small Stories, Interaction and Identities*, Amsterdam: John Benjamins.
Giacomi, A., H. Stoffel and G. D. Veronique (2000), *Appropriation du français par des marocains arabophones à Marseille: Bilan d'une recherche*, Aix-en-Provençe: Publications de l'Université de Provence.
Gintsburg, S. (2005), 'Seven Folk Songs from the Region of the Jbāla (Northern Morocco)', *Acta Orientalia*, 66: 73–107.
Gintsburg, S., L. Galván Moreno and R. Finnegan (2021), 'Voice in a Narrative: A Trialogue with Ruth Finnegan', *Frontiers of Narrative Studies*, 7 (1): 1–20.
Hämeen-Anttila, J. (2008), 'Building an Identity: Place as an Image of Self in Classical Arabic Literature', *Quaderni di Studi Arabi Nuova Serie*, 3: 25–38.
Jay, C. (2018), *Performing Change? Contemporary Performance Practices in Morocco*, PhD diss, SOAS, University of London.
Jenkins, H. (2006), *Convergence Culture: Where Old and New Media Collide*, New York: New York University Press.
Perrino, S. (2015), 'Chronotopes: Time and Space in Oral Narrative', in A. De Fina and A. Georgakopoulou (eds), *The Handbook of Narrative Analysis*, 140–59, Oxford: Blackwell.
Taïa, A. (2008), *L'Armée du Salut*, Paris: Seuil.
Ukhtomsky, A. (2002), *Dominanta. Selected Essays* (1887–1939), St Petersburg: Piter.

Discussion questions

1. What is the main specificity of the canons in the Arab and Moroccan literary traditions discussed in this chapter?
2. How is the notion of chronotope used in sociolinguistics?
3. What are some major views on chronotope in contemporary oral narrative studies?
4. Why is the term topochrone also being used?
5. What do the three cameos from 'Tar or Honey' express about the topic of migration?
6. How can Hanane el-Fadili's show *al-Kāmīra lakum* and, in particular the episode 'Tar or Honey', be analysed as a chronotopic event?
7. What is the main chronotope of 'Tar or Honey'?

10

Once a Dancer, Always a Dancer: The Story of Ahmad Joudeh

Jan Jaap de Ruiter

Introduction

At the end of the second semi-final of the Eurovision Song Contest, held in Rotterdam in May 2021,[1] the Syrian dancer Ahmad Joudeh (born in 1990) gave an impressive performance. Joudeh developed as a dancer in his hometown of Damascus and later on joined the Dutch National Ballet in Amsterdam, the Netherlands. His remarkable story is the subject of this chapter. The key question is how Ahmad Joudeh dealt with the displacement in time and place he underwent and what story or stories he created in order to live with this displacement. Another question is if Arab culture and Islam have influenced him in his stories and if so, how.

The chapter is divided as follows. This introduction is followed by a section ('The Syrian revolution') containing a short description of the Syrian revolution that broke out in 2011 and which quickly developed into a civil war that has not ended until today. The next section ('Stories shape people's lives') discusses the importance of stories shaping people into who they are, and it goes into the question what happens to people if circumstances of whatever nature cause them to change place in a certain period of their lives. Section 'Displacement in Arab culture and Islam' treats aspects of Arab culture and Islam that may relate to the story of Ahmed Joudeh. Section 'Questions and procedures' presents the questions asked and procedures followed in order to answer them. Section 'Who is Ahmad Joudeh?' describes, in brief, Ahmad Joudeh's life. Section 'The stories that shape Ahmad Joudeh' is the essence of the chapter, presenting relevant stories in Ahmad Joudeh's life and analysing them in the light of the questions asked. Section 'Ahmad Joudeh, a story of displacement?' wraps up the findings and discusses them.

The Syrian revolution

At the end of 2010/the beginning of 2011, the world was surprised by massive risings among the peoples of North Africa and the Middle East against their leaders, referred to as the 'Arab Spring' (Haas and Lesch 2016). It started in the small country of

Tunisia, spread to Egypt and Libya and then to Yemen and Bahrain. In Tunisia and Egypt Presidents Ben Ali and Moubarak stepped down. In Libya, Colonel Muammar Gaddafi was killed. The rebellion in Bahrain was suppressed and the people's rising in Yemen led to a bloody war; President Saleh was killed as well. In Syria people rose against the Assad regime, which had been in power in the country since 1970 (see Van Dam 2017 for an excellent overview of recent events in Syria). Syria is governed by the Ba'ath Party, just as Iraq under Saddam Hussein used to be. The Ba'ath Party formally stands for a secular ideology, which is quite unique in the Arab Islamic world where state and religion are hardly separated. Still, ideology notwithstanding, once the Ba'ath supporters came to be in charge of the country this soon if not immediately led to a dictatorship where the Shiite Alawi community, numbering only around 17 per cent of Syria's population, would hold firmly onto power.[2] Present President Bashar al-Assad (b. 1965), son of former President Hafez al-Assad (1930–2000), is from an Alawi background and has been president since 2000, when his father died. The Syrian regime reacted immediately to signs of unrest and responded with violence to the peaceful demonstrations that started in March 2011 in the southern city of Daraa. Soon enough the country was plunged into a complex civil war. The major parties in this were the regime, the secular opposition, the different Kurdish factions living in the north of the country, the Islamist terrorist movements, al-Qaeda and the Islamic State in particular, and other, smaller, groups (cf. Van Dam 2017). The country was to be the stage for a proxy war as well. The regime is backed by Shiite Hezbollah forces from Lebanon, and by Iran and Russia, whereas the Syrian secular opposition was supported by Western powers like the United States, France and Turkey. The Kurds are supported by Kurds from Turkey, Iraq and the United States. The Islamic State was secretly supported by Qatar and received illegal funds from individuals and associations. The country became a mess and is still a mess today.

The war did not leave Syria's capital untouched. On the contrary, it suffered severely from the violent fights between the regime and all kinds of opposition groups, from secular opposition to Islamic State jihadists. For a considerable amount of time, opposition groups held various pockets in the suburbs of Damascus and the areas surrounding the city. A case in point is the suburb of Eastern Ghouta where fierce fighting took place leading to its nearly total destruction, so that in the end it had to surrender to the regime. It was also the place where the regime used chemical gas against its population in August 2013. In the course of time opposition pockets in the country lost the fight against the regime or were forced to surrender, surrounded as they were by the regime, because of a lack of means to fight, or simply to live. In the end there is still the northwestern province of Idlib, bordering Turkey, where fighters from the various pockets were transported and where many refugees still reside today. According to UNHCR statistics, there are 6.7 million internally displaced persons in Syria and 6.6 million Syrian refugees worldwide,[3] 5.6 million of them hosted by countries near Syria, Turkey, Lebanon and Jordan in particular. The Syrian civil war led to an unprecedented stream of refugees to Europe in 2015 (see Melo-Pfeifer, this volume). It was German Chancellor Angela Merkel who welcomed many of them, stating 'Wir schaffen das' ('We will manage this').

Stories shape people's lives

'People's efforts to understand their experiences often take the form of constructing narratives (stories) out of them' (Baumeister and Newman 1994: 676). This simple truth applies to all people in all times. If we want to know more on who people are and what shaped them, stories tell us a lot. It goes without saying that stories are dependent on place and time. They take place in certain places and in certain times. They accompany people for the rest of their lives wherever they live or in whatever times they live. It is interesting to see how stories, or narratives, accompany people, how they influence them in their behaviour and how they fine-tune their identities.

Questions on the role of stories become more interesting when human beings undergo dramatic changes in their lives, affecting their walks of life intensively. Cases in point are refugees, people who are forced to leave their country because of war breaking out, oppression, famine or similar issues (cf. Maryns 2005). They did not intend to leave, but in order to survive they found themselves forced to. The often violent and disturbing, if not traumatic, circumstances in which they saw themselves forced to leave are expressed in stories they construct to give sense and meaning – if possible – to what they are experiencing. They may hide these stories deep in their bosoms, but they carry them with them every day. The stories cannot change their core identities, but they can considerably add to who they are and influence their personalities.

Baynham (2015: 123) states that 'Every story is a travel story' and 'Nowhere is this more obvious than in migration stories, where displacement and mobility in time/space constitute the narrative action.' If we want to analyse 'stories that are centrally about mobility and displacement – where mobility in space effectively is the story' – we need to 'problematize... this narrative orientation' (2015: 120). We may wonder what the intriguing aspects of stories of displacement are. Why do they fascinate us? Why is the story of a migrant or refugee so much more intriguing than that of a person who has lived his or her entire life in one place and, in a way, in one time? The obvious answer is of course that we find these stories of displacement intriguing because they are the stories of people who sometimes voluntarily, but more often involuntarily, leave their homes on their way to an uncertain future, leaving behind everything that they took for granted. The Greek philosopher Aristotle in his *Poetics* stressed the importance of stories and storytelling (Tierno 2002). People learn from them, they can identify with the protagonists, they feel comforted by the suffering of the characters in the story; they dream away with their dreams; they feel the pain when dreams do not come true and they feel cleansed once the story has been told, the so-called catharsis. Stories shape human beings, shape their characters and have done so ever since humankind started creating stories, fathers and mothers telling them to children and grandchildren. Today is no exception to that historical thread. There are more stories available than ever on the internet. All people use social media to tell their stories. And even in their modern shape they still have those old Aristotelian functions they had from the beginning on.

Baynham (2011) presents formats for how to analyse stories or narratives. The linguistic ethnographic approach he describes is the one most suited to the present case.

Baynham refers in this context to earlier work of, among others, Blommaert (2001), Labov (1972), Bauman (1986) and Hymes (1996) whose 'approaches... emphasize narrative as monologue, employing... structural functional analytic resources to make sense of their patterning' (1996: 73). 'The difference is that, for Labov, narratives were elicited in interview contexts, while for Bauman and Hymes, performance was captured in the domains and settings of daily life' (1996: 73). Capturing performance in the domains and settings of daily life applies to the present case as well. The data that are available to us come from the numerous interviews Joudeh gave and the documentaries on him. That means that we have no direct data from the man himself. We contacted his management for an interview, but it never reacted. Still, the data set is abundant and in what follows we will try to construct the story of Joudeh, asking ourselves the questions that are treated in section 'Questions and procedures'.

Displacement in Arab culture and Islam

Stories of displacement exist at all times and in all places. Focusing on the Arab cultural background of Ahmad Joudeh, one sees that this culture is characterized by a strong poetic and prosaic tradition of storytelling. Most famous is the era just before the advent of Islam and the coming of the prophet Mohammad (570–632), the so-called *Jahiliyya*, the 'time of ignorance'. From that time date the *Muʿallaqāt* ('The Hanging Poems'), 'a collection of pre-Islamic Arabic poems, generally numbered at seven stems' (Lecomte 1993: 254). These poetic collections basically tell the story of the vicissitudes of the old Arab Bedouin tribes, on, among other themes, their displacement in the desert to find water and fresh greens in the oases for their herds of camels, sheep and goats. The poems bewail the silence and loneliness of the places where the tribes stayed some time before moving on. The poems tell of the traces the tribes and their flocks left behind, of the wind that erased the tracks in the sand, of the fires that died out and that left the stones charred black. These Arab Bedouins led a hard and frugal life as there was little material wealth. The desert would not allow it. What they did have was their language in which they composed and recited poems, handed down from generation to generation in the evenings, by the fire. The Bedouins moved from place to place. They formed a case of displacement through place and time, but their poetry was the constant. In pre-Islamic times, Arab tribes held poetry festivals and the poems that were considered the best ones were hung at the *Kaʿaba*, which still functions as a holy object in Islam. The *Muʿallaqāt* are still taught in religious institutions as the language of what ultimately was to become the language of the Qur'an (Chaudary 2017; De Ruiter 2004). That is also a reason why the *Muʿallaqāt* were and still are highly valued by the later Arab literary traditions to this day. Arabic poetry is, as it were, timeless and it still enjoys a high status with Arabs. Poetry evenings are still organized in all Arab countries and they enjoy an enormous audience (Arberry 1965).

Talking about religion, it is relevant to discuss the meaning Islam gives to the term 'displacement', it being the dominant religion in the region. Formally speaking the ruling Ba'ath regime is based on a secular ideology but practice shows that no ruler ever presents himself as non-religious. Syrian society as well is 'leavened' with religion and the daily language is full of expressions referring to God, such as *inshallah* ('If

God wants it'; see De Ruiter and Farrag 2021). 'Islam... is the "seal of the prophecy", manifested in the Qur'an, which aims to "perfect the religion"' says Jomier in the *Encyclopaedia of Islam* (1978: 173). According to the first part of a much-quoted *hadith* (tradition), the best of all things is Islam. 'The Koran defines Islam as religion, but not as *a* religion' (Jomier 1978: 174; author's italics). Islam, many Muslims claim, is universal by nature; Islam is not dependent on place and time. Everywhere and in every place, they claim, Islam is the same – an understanding that perhaps reflects the other side of the general sense of predetermination found in Islam and many parts of the Arab world (Breeze, Baynham and Gintsburg, this volume). Whether this is actually true or not is not relevant to us; it is the idea that counts and the mindset that goes with it.

Culture and religion are two concepts that are in fact inseparable. Every religion developed a culture and in cultures religions sprang up. This link between the two is a theme in the work of Canadian theorist of religion Cantwell Smith. He devoted himself to the study of comparative religions and worked out the concept of 'religious pluralism'. In his *The Meaning and End of Religion* (Cantwell Smith 1964) he states that what we understand by religions today consisted in the first place of an 'accumulation of traditions'. Or in his words (as quoted by Hashas 2021: 8):

> By 'cumulative tradition' I mean the entire mass of overt objective data that constitute the historical deposit, as it were, of the past religious life of the community in question: temples, scriptures, theological systems, dance patterns, legal and other social institutions, conventions, moral codes, myths and so on; anything that can be and is transmitted from one person, one generation, to another, and that an historian can observe.
>
> (Cantwell Smith 1964: 140)

And in fact, religions today still consist of this 'accumulation of traditions'. This concept goes well with what I described above on Arabic poetry and its link to Islam. They are closely intertwined, and the one can hardly function without the other. Interestingly, Cantwell Smith in the quote refers to 'dance patterns' as a tradition in religion as well. And dancing is indeed an aspect of Islam. In mystical Sufi brotherhoods and sisterhoods, dancing is one of the means to try to get in touch with the spiritual world, to get closer to God. The dancing dervishes always appeal to people's imagination. In his entry on dervishes in the *Encyclopedia of Islam* MacDonald (1965) states that 'the (Sufi dancing) ritual always lays stress on the emotional religious life and tends to produce hypnotic phenomena (auto and otherwise) and fits of ecstasy' (1965: 164). 'It is plain that a *ḏikr* (Sufi dance session) brings with it a certain heightened religious exaltation and a pleasant dreaminess' (1965: 164). Sufism is not undisputed in Islam. Orthodox and fundamentalist circles reject it as they consider the dancing of the dervishes as an unlawful attempt to create a union with God. God's oneness is one of the basic tenets of Islam and 'melting' with him harms this oneness and is in some cases considered a capital offence. Nevertheless, the Muslim world is swarming with Sufi brotherhoods and sisterhoods, and Syria is no exception to that (MacDonald 1965).

In what follows, Joudeh's dancing narrative will be connected to Arab culture and Islam.

Questions and procedures

Dancer Ahmad Joudeh's life is intriguing. Formally speaking, he is not a refugee, as he was invited to come to the Netherlands as a dancer. In the documentary on him, he said that at the time he insisted on coming as a student and not as a refugee (documentary *Dance or Die* 2018).[4] Still, if he had stayed in Syria, he would have had to join the army. That was something he categorically did not want. He might have become a refugee then after all. I collected, with the help of my assistant, as much information on Joudeh as possible, from what he himself has said in interviews and videos or written in articles. In doing so, I tried to answer the question what stories Joudeh created in order to deal with the displacement in time and place he experienced. Furthermore, I tried to connect his stories to Arab culture and Islam, asking the question if and how they influenced Joudeh in making his stories. In his autobiography (Joudeh 2021) Ahmad Joudeh tells the story of his life, describing it from the start of it in Syria until his career as ballet dancer in the Netherlands. The book does not entirely convince, in that sense that, although Joudeh is mentioned as writer, it does not seem improbable that the book is heavily edited by professional ghostwriters. Its English is of an impeccable level. Furthermore, the book contains literal conversations that took place, for example, between his parents or between him and his good friend Saeed. It is known that it is virtually impossible to recount exactly the conversations a person ever had, years after they took place (cf. Smith and Watson 2010: 7): 'In autobiographical narratives, imaginative acts of remembering always intersect with such rhetorical acts as assertion, justification, conviction, and interrogation.' For these reasons I do not quote from his memoir, my second argument being that the interviews he gave and the documentary on him, less edited by nature than a memoir, procured more than enough material to construct his stories.

Who is Ahmad Joudeh?

Ahmad Joudeh, aka 'the Syrian Billy Elliot', was born on 4 April 1990 in Yarmouk, a Palestinian refugee camp in Damascus, the capital of Syria.[5] This camp housed Palestinians who had fled Palestine in 1948 when the state of Israel was established, and their offspring. Palestinians were offered shelter but did not get Syrian nationality. That therefore goes for Ahmad's stateless Palestinian father as well. His father is a musician by profession. His Syrian mother is a teacher. Ahmad is the oldest in a family of three children. He has a younger brother, who is a visual artist, and a younger sister, an athlete. His parents divorced in 2011. Joudeh had a passion for dance from an early age. When he grew older, this passion created friction with his father, who sometimes even made it physically impossible for him to dance, threatening to break his legs. From 2006 to 2015, Joudeh attended courses at the Enana Dance Theater in Damascus; from 2009 to 2016 he was affiliated with the Higher Institute for Dramatic Arts in Damascus. In 2014, Ahmad participated in the Arabic version of the television dance talent show *So You Think You Can Dance*,[6] in which he got to the semi-finals.

The Syrian civil war changed the stages he was living in. The family house was destroyed and two uncles and three cousins of his were killed in that same war. After witnessing the killing of children, Ahmad set up dancing classes for children orphaned by the war. He went to work for *SOS Children's Village Syria* in order to distract them from the horrors of war.⁷ His dancing activities made him the target of threats from extremists. His response was that he had a tattoo set on his neck with the text, in Sanskrit, 'Dance or Die'. He has continued organizing dance workshops for children until today. In 2016, Dutch television paid attention to Ahmad's dancing and his efforts for children in Syria. This led to international attention and invitations to come to various countries to dance. In the same year he accepted an invitation to join the Dutch National Ballet.

In 2018, Roozbeh Kaboly made the documentary *Dance or Die* about Ahmad's life (see note 4). This documentary won an Emmy Award in the category *Arts Programming* in November 2019. In the same documentary we see Ahmad's meeting and cautious reconciliation with his father in a refugee camp in Berlin. In 2019, Joudeh was named an International Friend by *SOS Children's Villages International*. Meanwhile he acquired Dutch nationality in 2021. During the Eurovision Song Contest 2021 in May he performed the interval act during the second semi-final, together with BMX player Dez Maarsen. His mother still lives in Syria with his brother and sister. His father lives in a refugee camp in Germany.

The stories that shape Ahmad Joudeh

On the occasion of his performance for the Eurovision Song Contest 2021 in Rotterdam, Ahmad Joudeh said: 'This will be the most important performance of my career. My mission in life is to tell my story, because my story relates to many people who need a voice.'⁸ Ahmad Joudeh states that his mission in life is to tell his story, a story for the benefit of people who need a voice. What then is this story?

When it comes to the issue of – physical – place, it is, in a way, a paradox that Joudeh was born placeless, as his former civic status in Syria was 'stateless', like that of his father, who was Palestinian by birth. As indicated above, Palestinians who fled from the newborn state of Israel in 1948 found refuge in Syria but the hospitality of the neighbouring country was limited to a place in a camp, without a new nationality. Palestinian refugees in the whole Arab world hardly ever obtain another passport, in order to maintain pressure on Israel for their eventual return home. Joudeh expresses his feelings on statelessness as follows:

> I don't know. Actually, I have no connection to a home, you know? I'm a dancer and dance is my passport. But when it comes to the official papers, I have no passport. I'm a stateless refugee, so I have no home. I have no place to go back home, to build a life.⁹

There is no home; there is no place to go back to. Therefore, dancing, he says, is his passport. Joudeh did in the end obtain Dutch nationality and he was very much aware of this highlight in his life, when he said on the occasion of his performance in the Eurovision Song Contest in Rotterdam in 2021: 'It means everything to me to perform here and represent the Netherlands. I also represent all refugees and people without nationality around the world.'[10] Joudeh was twenty-one years old when the revolution in Syria broke out. As described above, this revolution, which started with peaceful demonstrations, soon turned into a bloody war the consequences of which Ahmad would soon experience: 'It's terrible to walk down the street knowing you could be hit by a bomb, mortar or missile at any moment. Yet fear does not come from outside, it is a feeling that takes hold inside you. A feeling of sadness.'[11] He tells of the dulling effect of war and violence on man's spirits:

> I have lost five relatives and have seen my uncle murdered. After we buried him, I went to school. I was late for class, the principal asked why. I said, 'Sorry, I was burying my uncle, to which he replied, 'If you bury your mother, you may be late.' That's Syria. There is no heart, no more emotion. People live like in a morgue. They see the dead, but they think: we too will die soon, just like them.
>
> (see note 11)

It is tempting to assume that Ahmad Joudeh is a refugee. But that is not the case. His appearance in Arab talent shows and his YouTube dance videos generated fame in the world and led to him being invited to come to the West. He never wanted to leave Syria as a refugee. In an interview with the Dutch newspaper *Het Parool* (see note 11) he was asked the following question:

> 'You have a small part in Coppelia (a dance show that Joudeh was invited to perform in). Can you imagine that people will think you only got this opportunity because of your background?' Joudeh replied: 'Yes, that's why I said from the start that I would only come if I got a visa as a student, not as a refugee.' The interviewer replied: 'That's quite a risk. What if they couldn't offer you that?' 'Then I would have stayed, believe me. I've been a refugee all my life through no fault of mine. And being a refugee once is enough.'
>
> (see note 11)

In this last sentence, Joudeh refers to his statelessness in Syria. The hypocrisy of the Syrian state is that it calls the stateless young men to conscription as well and it may be clear that that is something that Joudeh would want to avoid, as the army is known for its rudeness and a ballet dancer would certainly be regarded as unmasculine: 'In Arab culture, dance and especially ballet are at odds with the image of masculinity. Men are sporty and aggressive, ballet is for girls or "pussies". Men apparently feel threatened in their masculinity.' [12]

This passion of his for dancing led to an enormous conflict with his father:

> That went really far; my father did everything possible to prevent me from going to ballet class. He even called the principal of the school and asked him not to hire me. Otherwise he would ask the government to send him to prison. Nevertheless, the director refused to cooperate. He said, 'If Ahmad wants to come, he is welcome.' Whenever my father found out that I had gone to ballet class, I was beaten; once he purposely injured my legs so that I simply would not be able to dance.
>
> (see note 12)

In the end Ahmad realized that he could not avoid conscription any more, which is one among other reasons that made him accept the invitation to come and dance in the Netherlands:

> In March 2017 I should be in military service. I managed to stretch that endlessly by studying for a year longer, but that was no longer possible. (*Dance for Peace*, no date). It is the first time in my entire life that I have been treated with respect when entering a new country. The arrival was overwhelming. A very welcoming committee was waiting for me. Someone put their arms around me and only then could I cry.
>
> (see note 12)

Once in the Netherlands, Ahmad settled in Amsterdam and continued his formation as a ballet dancer with the Dutch National Ballet. He did not stop his work for the benefit of children and set up an organization for the enhancement of dancing among children. In 2019, he was appointed as an *International Friend* by SOS Children's Villages International.

Ahmad's displacement from Syria to the Netherlands led to a serious change in his life, something he confirmed in the documentary *Dance or Die*:

> This transition between coming from the Arab world to Europe took me like almost six hours by plane or whatever. All the whole journey in six hours I changed all my life (...) In Syria I was not myself. But here in Europe I am totally myself now. It feels great.

In Europe Ahmad can do what he wants, and he can perform as he wishes without being afraid of persons wanting to kill him or as a BBC journalist states in the documentary: 'Dance or die; his motto tattooed on his neck just in case he was beheaded by ISIL. He wanted it to be the last thing they saw before he died.'

Still, Joudeh was confronted with other threats as well. He says in the documentary that dancing as a boy in Syria is quickly associated with being gay and therefore reprehensible:

> For my family you know it is a traditional Arab family and dancing it was shameful. Something to be really ashamed of.
>
> (*Dance or Die*)

> In Syria, people think that if a man wants to become a ballet dancer, he must be gay, and that is punishable by law. Moreover, you harm the honour of the family if you want to become a dancer. That's why my mother took me secretly to the Enana Dance Theater the first year.
>
> (see note 11)

In the documentary Joudeh does not refer to his sexual identity, but once in the Netherlands he started using his refugee and dancing experience and qualities for the sake of the LHBTQ+ community. He featured, for example, in a promotion video for the 2018 Exhibition Pride & Prejudice in Amsterdam.[13] In the video, Joudeh stressed the tension of being a refugee and the freedom to be a dancer:

> Being a refugee is the most difficult thing in the world because you have a limited daily life and you are not really free. But being an artist is the way that you can create your freedom wherever you are.

He mentioned this same freedom in the documentary as well:

> I feel so free while I am dancing. Wherever and whenever and it is always the same feeling since the beginning. In the ballet class, on stage, in the theatre, in the garage, the Yarmouk camp, in Palmyra. Everywhere it used to be the same feeling for me.

In analysing the preceding two quotes from Joudeh, it seems as if the feelings of displacement vanish when it comes to his dancing. Key quotes in this sense are the following:

> When I dance, I am in another dimension and I forget all my worries. I am convinced that it has guided me through the horrors of the war. I remember a mortar impact in the dance school while I was training. People ran away, but I was still standing at the bar doing my exercises. Dancing has changed my life. It made me feel confident, powerful and less anxious.
> (*SOS Children's Villages*, spring 2020)

> It's a wonderful feeling: that I can be myself. I believe that dance can change lives. I myself am living proof. If I can get from the ruins in Syria to the stage of Dutch National Ballet, then dance must be something important.
> (see note 11)

Ahmad was born as a dancer and nothing in the world has changed this. His story of displacement is indeed a story of dramatic changes in place and time, but not in his deepest inner self, the dancer that he was and is and the joy and consolation he wants to bring to his audience, and in fact, to the world. That, basically, is his story.

Ahmad Joudeh, a story of displacement?

Not all migrants and refugees have a story similar to Ahmad's. All of them in their stories undergo changes in time and place; they also feel displaced and disoriented in their new countries (see Le Houérou, Zaripov and Gintsburg and Breeze, this volume). They certainly have things to hold on to: their memories, the loved ones that came along with them. And maybe they find employment that resembles the employment they had in the home country. But they might have to go without the universal values of something like dancing. Dancing, one might say, is of all times and of all cultures. This is a cliché and therefore also very true. And it certainly is true that the function of stories, expressed by dancing as well, as formulated by Aristotle, applies to all forms of dancing all over the world too. Dancing takes dancers and audience into another hemisphere. Dancing tells stories of its own and dancers evoke universal feelings of grief, joy and astonishment. As Ruth Finnegan notes, 'why should we think that language is somehow the top art? ... Why not dance?' (Gintsburg, Galván Moreno and Finnegan 2021: 10). Not all dancers are aware of this, but Ahmad Joudeh is. He is one of those rare cases of a person who got displaced, but whose inner self did not.

One may wonder if Joudeh's case may be related to Arab art culture. Arab poetry, as explained above, was one of the few arts Arab Bedouins in the desert had at their disposal to dream away from the stern circumstances in life. Their poetry focused on the places they had to leave, expressing their grief at having to leave, but the poetry gave consolation as well and it did so irrespective of time and place. There is a tradition in Arab poetry that has always been transcending time and place, and we can assume that this mindset has influenced other artistic expressions as well. The idea is that Arab art and culture are, at least in the eyes of the beholders, eternal and universal. This goes very well with the other idea that the religion of most Arabs, Islam, is considered eternal and universal as well. And when it comes to dancing, we notice that Islam has this dervish dancing tradition. And from that perspective it is more than interesting to note that Joudeh performed a dance in a Dutch landscape dressed as a dervish, with the characteristic white skirt. He recorded this short dance on his site as a reaction to the Covid-19 pandemic that struck the world in 2020-1.[14] The theme of the dance was: 'Love and Prayer under Pandemic – Our Best Days Are Yet to Come.' And there is another video of him dancing as a dervish on his site. So here we see a direct link between Joudeh and the Sufi tradition of Islam, both in text and in presentation. Therefore, it seems defensible to state that the eternal and universal values of dancing that he has been experiencing since his early childhood may very well be inspired by the general mindset in the Arab world of the superiority of Islam in all its – dancing – diversity and of the timeless Arabic language and culture.

It may be clear from several of Ahmad Joudeh's quotes that for him dancing is his *raison d'être* and that for him dances can be performed everywhere and in every place. Ahmad has danced among the debris and under the threat of fire in Damascus and he has danced on the stage of the Eurovision Song Contest with over 100 million people watching him. Dancing for him is unconnected to time and place – he derives his identity from dancing and has done so from his earliest years on. It is dancing that made him survive the horrors of war, killings and violence and with his dancing he spreads joy and moments of oblivion for the people who watch him and for the children he entertains with his dancing skills. Physical displacement has definitely taken place in his life, he changed places, he lives in another era, but a spiritual displacement never seems to have taken place. He is a case of a physically displaced person who has remained the same, irrespective of time and place. His dancing made him survive and enjoy life 'there' and 'here' simultaneously.

So, how can we explain the absence of the notion of displacement in Joudeh's dancing? He experiences dancing as a universal act, taking place irrespective of time and place. Maybe Islamic culture can once more give an answer to that question. In

Islam depicting God and human beings, like in Jewish culture, is not allowed. The reason behind this prohibition is the idea that no image can ever present God in all His mightiness, presence and omnipresence, and for that matter making pictures of human beings is not allowed either: each picture is necessarily a degradation of who God is and who human beings are. 'Most Islamic scholars, like Ibn Arabi (1165–1240) and Al-Ghazali (1058–1111), believe that God, in His essence, is the transcendental unity who is majestic and beyond any human comprehension.'[15] It is therefore for a reason that many Islamic theological texts end with the expression *Allāhu ʾa ʿlam* (God knows best). In the building containing the shrine of Sidi Mahrez shrine in Tunis one can read this text on the wall (Figure 10.1): *Mahma taṣawwarta bi-bālika fallāhu lā yušbih dalika* (Whatever you imagine God to be, He does not resemble that).

God, when it comes to it, remains a mystery. But the other side of the coin is that there is this Islamic conviction that God is the perfect 'knower'. God in Islam has ninety-nine names referring to all kinds of qualities. The nineteenth name is *al-ʿalīm* (The Knower) and the twenty-sixth name is *al-samīʿ* (The Hearer): he knows his believers and listens to them, and it is partly for that reason that human beings resort to religion in order to find protection and consolation with an all-knowing God. Ahmad Joudeh's religion is dancing; through it he can be who he is and through it he can reach his admirers and his audience. It is this universal function of art and literature that Joudeh understands perfectly. He mourns the ruins of a country devastated by war, just as the *Hanging Poems* mourn the quiet and loneliness of the places where

Figure 10.1 Inscription on the shrine of Sidi Mahrez.

the Bedouins once vividly lingered. At the same time, he gives consolation, a spiritual space in which to process grief and traumas. With his dancing he conveys joy and perhaps fulfilment, and he is able to do so anywhere and anytime, as if it were the universal message of Islam. Analysing his narrative from this perspective we cannot but label Ahmad Joudeh a 'homo universalis', not as a great thinker or scholar, but as a great universal artist who understands that people do not understand why human suffering takes place, why God allows all that misery. He understands that this is a universal question and that, at the same time, human consolation, in his case through the art of dancing, is universal as well. It is his passion for dancing that made him this universal artist and his cultural and religious background may just have stimulated him to see dancing the way he sees it.

Notes

1   My sincere thanks go to Leonie van Esch for helping me collecting data for this chapter and to my friend and colleague Mohammed Hashas for his valuable remarks on an earlier version of this chapter.
2   Izady, Michael, *Syria: Ethnic Shift, 2010–mid 2018*. https://gulf2000.columbia.edu.
3   https://www.unhcr.org/syria-emergency.html.
4   https://www.npostart.nl/het-uur-van-de-wolf/25-06-2018/VPWON_1293620.
5   Information on Ahmed comes from his website: http://www.ahmadjoudeh.com/; Roozby Kaboly's documentary *Dance or Die*: https://www.npostart.nl/het-uur-van-de-wolf/25-06-2018/VPWON_1293620.
6   http://www.ahmadjoudeh.com/438210662.
7   https://www.sos-syria.org/.
8   https://songfestival.nl/nieuws/bijzondere-interval-act-balletdanser-ahmad-joudeh-en-bmx-er-dez-maarsen-tijdens-h.
9   *Deutsche Welle*, 29 April 2019. https://www.dw.com/en/dance-is-my-passport-syrian-ballet-dancer-ahmad-joudeh-on-dancing-as-home/a-48502423.
10 *AT5*, 20 May 2021. https://www.at5.nl/artikelen/209072/danser-ahmad-joudeh-treedt-op-tijdens-het-songfestival-ik-ben-zo-excited.
11 https://www.parool.nl/nieuws/syrische-ahmad-joudeh-bij-het-nationale-ballet-dans-kan-levens-veranderen~bcbdc947/.
12 https://www.danceforpeace.nl/ahmad-joudeh.
13 https://www.facebook.com/watch/?v=119914745543578.
14 http://www.ahmadjoudeh.com/.
15 https://isv.org.au/the-relationship-between-knowing-ones-self-and-knowing-god/.

References

Arberry, A. J. (1965), *Arabic Poetry: A Primer for Students*, Cambridge: Cambridge University Press.
Bauman, R. (1986), *Story, Performance and Event: Contextual Studies or Oral Narrative*, New York: Cambridge University Press.

Baumeister, R. and L. S. Newman (1994), 'How Stories Make Sense of Personal Experiences: Motives that Shape Autobiographical Narratives', *Personality and Social Psychology Bulletin*, 20 (6): 676–90.

Baynham, M. (2011), 'Narrative Analysis', in K. Hyland and B. Paltridge (eds), *The Continuum Companion to Discourse Analysis*, 68–84, London-New York: Continuum.

Baynham, M. (2015), 'Narrative and Space and Time', in A. De Fina and A. Georgakopoulou (eds), *The Handbook of Narrative Analysis, First Edition*, 119–39, Chichester: John Wiley & Sons.

Blommaert, J. (2001), 'Investigating Narrative Inequality: African Asylum Seekers' Stories in Belgium', *Discourse & Society*, 12 (4): 413–49.

Cantwell Smith, W. (1964), *The Meaning and End of Religion*, New York: The New American Library of World Literature.

Chaudhary, A. (2017), 'Why the Holy Qur'an Was Revealed in the Arabic Language', *Inviting Reflections*, 4 February. Available online: https://www.linkedin.com/pulse/95-why-holy-quran-revealed-arabic-language-series-chaudhary/ (accessed 22 November 2021).

De Ruiter, J. J. (2004), 'Quel arabe pour communiquer? Passé et présent', in Frédéric Bauden (ed.), *Ultra mare: mélanges de langue arabe et d'islamologie offerts à Aubert Martin*, 29–39, Louvain, Paris and Dudley: Peeters.

De Ruiter, J. J. and M. Farrag (2021), 'Allah, Allah, Allah: The Role of God in the Arab Version of *The Voice*', *Religions*, 12 (6): 412. https://doi.org/10.3390/rel12060412.

Gintsburg, S., L. Galván Moreno, and R. Finnegan (2021), 'Voice in a Narrative: A Trialogue with Ruth Finnegan', *Frontiers of Narrative Studies*, 7 (1): 1–20. https://doi.org/10.1515/fns-2021-0001.

Haas, M. and D. Lesch (2016), *The Arab Spring: The Hope and Reality of the Uprisings*, New York-London: Routledge.

Hashas, M. (2021), 'Pluralism in Islamic Contexts – Ethics, Politics and Modern Challenges', *Philosophy and Politics – Critical Explorations*, 16 (Springer).

Hymes, D. (1996), *Ethnography, Linguistics, Narrative Inequality: Toward an Understanding of Voice*, London-Bristol: Taylor and Francis.

Jomier, J. (1978), 'Islam', in *The Encyclopaedia of Islam*, Volume IV, 171–7, Leiden: Brill.

Joudeh, A. (2021), *Dance or Die: From Stateless Refugee to International Ballet Star. A Memoir*, Watertown, MA: Charlesbridge Publishing.

Labov, W. (1972), *Sociolinguistic Patters*, Philadelphia: University of Pennsylvania Press.

Lecomte, G. (1993), 'Al-Muʿallaqat', in *The Encyclopaedia of Islam*, Volume VII, 254–5, Leiden: Brill.

MacDonald, D. B. (1965), 'Darwish', in *The Encyclopaedia of Islam*, Volume II, 164–5, Leiden: Brill.

Maryns, K. (2005), 'Displacement in Asylum Seekers' Narratives', in M. Baynham and A. De Fina (eds), *Dislocations/Relocations: Narratives of Displacement*, 174–93, Manchester: St Jerome Publishing.

Smith, S. and J. Watson (2010), *Reading Autobiography: A Guide for Interpreting Life Narratives*, Minneapolis: University of Minnesota Press.

Tierno, M. (2002), *Aristotles Poetics for Screenwriters: Storytelling Secrets from the Greatest Mind in Western Civilization*, New York: Hyperion.

Van Dam, N. (2017), *Destroying a Nation: The Civil War in Syria*, London and New York: I.B. Tauris.

Discussion questions

1. Reading the story of Ahmad Joudeh, and the role Arab art and Islam played in his life, how do you consider Arab art and Islam?
2. Do you think that Western artists, dancers or singers, could go through a similar history as Joudeh's?
3. Do you find it credible that Joudeh states that dancing presents real freedom to him?
4. What does poetry mean to you? Does it bring consolation to you too? Do you write poems yourself?
5. Do you think that religion and culture can be separated? If you do, why? If you do not, why not?
6. Do you think the Middle East will ever be a place of freedom such as Joudeh experiences in the West?
7. Do you think Western Europe is indeed a place of real freedom?

Digital Narratives of Syrian Political Dissidence in the Diaspora: Chronotopes of the Syrian Revolution and Transnational Grassroots Activism

Francesco L. Sinatora

Introduction

The years following the 2011 Arab Spring have witnessed unprecedented flows of migration from Syria to Europe. Many of these migrants are dissidents whose narratives have remained marginal in the global discourse about the Syrian conflict and the refugee crisis. In this chapter, I shed light on the digital narratives of three Syrian political activists in the European diaspora, building on current sociolinguistic literature on language, migration and social media communication (Androutsopoulos and Staehr 2018; Blommaert and Rampton 2011; Canagarajah 2017). Accordingly, I subscribe to an idea of language as 'resources' that are constantly mobilized in increasingly digital and transnational contexts to construct identities revolving around multimodal repertoires (Blommaert 2010). I draw on the notion of *chronotope* to account for the spatio-temporal, ideologically mediated dynamics underlying their digital repertoires. This term, a compound word of Greek origin meaning 'time-space', was introduced by Russian scholar Mikhail Bakhtin (1981) to capture the way in which novelistic spatio-temporal constructs (such as 'the castle') serve as quintessential distinctive markers of different literary genres, informing the trajectory of the narrative and its characters.

Bakhtin's insight that time and space are inseparable units through which humans construe and position themselves in relation to the social context was taken up by linguistic anthropologists and sociolinguists, who argued that chronotopes underlie identity performance in everyday social interaction (see Blommaert and De Fina 2017). These scholars also showed how language choices (such as the use of dialectal and standard forms), dictated by linguistic ideologies, interact with different time-space settings. A growing strand of scholarship has demonstrated that chronotopes are a particularly useful tool to analyse processes of identity construction in contexts of globalization (e.g. De Fina et al. 2019; Karimzad and Catedral 2018; Lyons and Tagg 2019).

In this study, I embrace Blommaert's definition of chronotopes as 'invokable histories' with 'powerful normative language-ideological dimensions' (Blommaert 2015: 112). To paraphrase Blommaert's words, chronotopes are particular spatio-temporal, or historical contexts in which certain linguistic forms are deemed to be more appropriate than others in the performance of determined identities. These contexts can be revived, or *invoked* (Blommaert 2015) linguistically and multimodally to shape and regulate present social situations and discourses.

The main chronotope observed in the digital discourse of Syrian revolutionaries in exile is that of the 2011 Syrian uprising, which represented a pivotal moment in the lives of these individuals. During this time, many of them changed the linguistic repertoire on their personal Facebook pages from a mixture of English and Arabic to Arabic only in order to reposition themselves as dissidents (see Sinatora 2019). In the past ten years, this new chronotopic repertoire, consisting of a mixture of Modern Standard Arabic and Syrian dialects, has allowed activists to perform their political identities and negotiate alignments. In this chapter, I show how the chronotope of the Syrian revolution is evoked linguistically and multimodally in the Syrian activists' digital network through the recontextualization of regional and global images of grassroots activism.

The data presented in this study is part of a larger ethnography of Syrian revolutionaries' digital discourse since 2010. These migrants left Syria for Jordan in 2012, and subsequently relocated to France and Austria, where they currently live. Despite their increased international mobility and their expanded multilingual repertoire, their predominantly political online practices have remained in Arabic. From an analysis of social media texts through diglossia, indexicality (Bassiouney 2017) and multimodality (Kress and van Leeuwen 2006), complemented with interviews with the authors (see Androutsopoulos 2008), it emerged that their linguistic choices and discourses are motivated and constrained by a need to anchor their political identities in the chronotope of the Syrian conflict and by their chronotopic positioning as anti-Assad dissidents. The exclusive use of Arabic has become the subject of metalinguistic reflection due to the increased desire of these migrants to universalize their political cause and to make their struggle accessible and visible to their European Facebook friends.

A prominent strategy underlying Syrian political dissidents' practices consists of the recontextualization of institutional discourse (e.g. current political news), as well as of digitally mediatized images of grassroots protest in the Arab world and beyond in their social media platforms (Sinatora 2021). Through the recirculation of satirical posts, as well as posts related to global sociopolitical events, Syrian revolutionaries in the diaspora have rekindled and foregrounded their anti-Assad secular identities, which emerged in the historical context of the 2011 Arab Spring, and have reframed them in the context of current global sociopolitical events. This chapter further valorizes everyday linguistic digital practices as a central component of Syrian political activists' life in the European diaspora. These texts, I argue, constitute the backbone of bottom-up narratives, whose reconstruction requires spatio-temporal contextualization as a central analytical focus. An analysis of this spatio-temporal, or chronotopic, recontextualization sheds light on how these migrants have relied on social media to reframe the discourse about the Syrian conflict from a local to a universal fight against people's oppression. In so doing, they presented the 2011 uprising as a grassroots, transnational, human struggle, comparing their upheaval to that of other oppressed populations in the Arab world and beyond.

Syrian political dissidents' digital narratives are not visible in current globally mass-mediatized representations about recent migration from Syria, which are predominantly populated by the images of refugees living in camps or risking their lives to reach Europe via land or sea. Nonetheless, they constitute an important aspect of migration and exile in the era of social media. Unlike the dominant representations of migrants as refugees produced by Western mass media, digital narratives are forms of self-representation, through which political opponents in the diaspora control the discourse surrounding the Syrian conflict. The analysis of migrants' own digital narratives sheds light on their subjectivity, as well as on their deployment of social media activism as a tool of empowerment (also see Chapter 11, this volume).

Language and transnational migration in the digital era

The current trend of globalization, characterized, among other things, by unprecedented flows of migration and by the advent of social media, has led to a higher sociolinguistic awareness of language as mobile resources (Blommaert 2010). The affordances of contemporary digital communication, such as immediacy, the permanence of the script, as well as the circulation of multimodal and multilingual content (see Androutsopoulos 2015; Blommaert and Rampton 2011), have led to profound changes in migrants' and non-migrants' imagination and experience by engendering new space and time dynamics underlying the construction of contemporary transnational identities.

A burgeoning strand of enquiry in sociolinguistics and linguistic anthropology has captured these spatio-temporal dynamics through the Bakhtinian conceptual lens of *chronotopes* (e.g. De Fina et al. 2019; Karimzad and Catedral 2018; Kroon and Swanenberg 2019; Perrino 2015), namely space-time dimensions through which (mass-)mediated representations of social phenomena, such as voice and identities, are construed and thereby different aspects of sociality are engendered (Agha 2007). In addition to the application of *chronotope* to migrants' and non-migrants' digital communication with relation to the construction of (non)modern identities (e.g. Koven and Simões Marques 2015), this notion has been influential in the analysis of language and discourses of political activism (e.g. Taylor-Leech 2020) and digital protest (Sinatora 2019). The historical dimension of space-time representations explained in the introduction, and brought to bear by a number of studies in linguistic anthropology (Blommaert 2015; Woolard 2013), is particularly relevant in this line of scholarship.

In Sinatora (2021), I showed how Syrian political dissidents in Europe use linguistic hybridity and multimodality to invoke the historical context of the 2011 civil uprising in their social media interactions and to position themselves as secular Assad opponents. I shed light on how social media affordances add a retrospective function to chronotopes, exploiting the *here-and-now* of digital communication to constantly rekindle historical identities. The insertion of fragments of digital protests in the Syrian digital network to revive the historical context of the Syrian revolution, I argued, can be described as 'chronotopic recontextualization'. This strategy, which can be observed in the action of sharing photos, memes or dissidents' personal daily experiences, will be illustrated through the examples below. Through the affordances of social media, Syrian revolutionaries reframed the discourse of the Syrian uprising by juxtaposing two chronotopes, that of contemporary regional and global grassroots activism with that of the 2011 revolts.

A study of digitally enhanced chronotopes is particularly critical in the case of political, ideologized contexts of migration, such as that of Syrian dissidents in the diaspora. Through their chronotopic work on social media, Syrian activists have both legitimized themselves as 'real Syrians', despite their physical displacement, as well as worked against the Syrian government's discourse that painted them as foreign infiltrators, and as backward, and misogynist religious extremists. Documentation of their chronotopic practices can shed light on this bottom-up counter-narrative, adding complexity to a dominant, Western dichotomic representation of migrants as terrorists, on the one hand, and as victims, on the other. Before I illustrate the pervasive presence of spatio-temporal anchoring in Syrian activists' digital practices, I will briefly outline some salient historical phases of the Syrian conflict in relation to Syrian revolutionaries' repositioning towards it.

The Syrian conflict and post-2011 grassroots political activism

When anti-Assad demonstrations started in March 2011, following a wave of sociopolitical upheaval across the Arab world known as the Arab Spring, some protestors concomitantly reorganized their linguistic practices on social media to emerge in the political discourse about the uprising and to reject the Syrian government media delegitimization of their *sawra* (revolution, in informal Arabic) as sedition stirred up by radical Sunni Islamists. Changing their Facebook repertoire from a hybrid mixture of English, Modern Standard and Damascene Arabic to one of Modern Standard Arabic, Damascene and humorous creative forms which mocked the regional dialect of Syrian president Bashar al-Assad, they repositioned themselves chronotopically towards the Syrian conflict, redefining what linguistic resources would be appropriate to foreground anti-Assad dissident identities in a post-2011 digital community of revolutionaries (Sinatora 2019). MSA is the official language of Syria. It denotes formal situations and is used performatively in Arabic as resource to take authoritative stances (Bassiouney 2017). Dialects are associated with private and informal situations. Syrian revolutionaries' use of these linguistic varieties is also related to the context of Syria's cultural, linguistic, religious and ethnic complexity, which has been at the centre of political projects and divisions.

With the rise to power of Hafiz al-Assad in 1971, the Alawites, a religious minority from the coast of Syria, increasingly consolidated their power at the expense of the hitherto urban-dominant Sunni elite (see Salamandra 2004). The political agenda of

Hafiz al-Assad's ruling Ba'ath party was informed by a pan-Arabist ideology, which proposed overcoming sociocultural differences through the construction of a Syrian Arab national identity. MSA played a central role in this cultural and sociopolitical project. In addition to sustaining the government's postcolonial narrative, its predominance in the public sphere is also motivated by the Syrian Ba'athist government's Arabization policy, which privileged MSA over dialects, minority and foreign languages (see Miller 2003). The urban Damascene variety, on the other hand, has acquired a political meaning in opposition to both MSA as the language of Ba'athist Arabization, and to Hafiz and Bashar al-Assad's coastal dialect. A way in which this political distinction has been emphasized linguistically is through the sound *qāf*, pronounced as a voiceless uvular plosive in MSA and in al-Assad's dialect, and as a *hamza* (glottal stop) in the Damascene vernacular.

Syrian revolutionaries in exile are secular male and female artists, intellectuals and journalists, in their thirties and forties, with different ethnic, confessional and geographic backgrounds. Some of them were already politicized before the 2011 uprising and were active in the Syrian Communist Party, a historical rival of the ruling Ba'ath party. The latter has been in power since 1963, under Alawite presidents Hafiz al-Assad's (1970–2000) and his son Bashar al-Assad (2000–present). Despite the consolidation of the Alawite community's political power and the repression of the Muslim Brotherhood during Hafiz al-Assad's tenure (Hinnebusch 2016), the Syrian government portrayed itself as a secular, supraconfessional force capable of keeping the country united under the aegis of Arab nationalist ideology. This narrative, supported by the allegiance of some conservative Sunni scholars, which in part deteriorated during Bashar al-Assad's tenure (Pierret 2014), has been challenged by Syrian secular dissidents.

When the protests erupted in 2011, Bashar al-Assad exploited the bugbear of Sunni extremism to delegitimize demonstrators, pointing out the cultural backwardness and misogyny of radical Sunni groups as opposed to the ostensible secular and progressive stance of his government. Since the 2011 Syrian uprising, Assad opponents contested government propaganda through their Facebook pages. They used creative linguistic forms and made orthographic choices (such as the spelling of the uvular sound *qāf* to mock the Alawite dialect) to satirize the inconsistencies of the Ba'athist government anti-sectarian policy, alluding to its links with Lebanese Shiite militia Hezbollah and Shiite Iran. In so doing, they deconstructed Bashar al-Assad's government's narrative of 'multicultural accommodation' which portrayed Syria as a country in which multiple religions and ethnicities peacefully coexisted in a way that was 'rendered *cultural* and thereby unthreatening in the official discourse' (Wedeen 2013: 843, note 6).

The dissidents' migration trajectory and their digital practices are intrinsically connected with political dynamics since the 2011 protests. By the end of 2011, with the civic uprising turning into a civil war, many of them started fleeing to neighbouring countries, including Lebanon, Turkey and Jordan. Between 2012 and 2017 the conflict escalated into a civil war first and a proxy war later, which saw the involvement of regional and international forces, including Turkey, Russia, the United States, Kurdish forces and radical Islamic combatants (Salafi, al-Qaeda-affiliated fighters and ISIS) financed by Gulf families and organizations from Kuwait, Qatar and Saudi Arabia.

During this phase, some Syrian secular Assad opponents who participated actively in the 2011 uprising proposed aligning with al-Qaeda-affiliated group al-Nusra. According to them, it was the only local force capable of defeating the government's army militarily. This stance was criticized by other revolutionaries on social media. In 2015, many of the activists I met in Jordan migrated to Europe, where they have continued their political activism through the organization of protests and cultural events, all documented on their digital platforms, as well as through their digital practices. The latter include status updates, sharing fellow dissidents' posts, liking and commenting on them, as well as participating in social media campaigns and petitions. Their Facebook activism is a bottom-up, grassroots dialogue and ongoing work of historical reconstruction surrounding the social and political motivations which led to the Syrian uprising.

Syrian dissidents in the diaspora and digital activism, methods and data

The role of digital media in the Arab Spring has informed a vast array of studies on social and political mobilization (e.g. Eltantawy and Wiest 2011; Tufekci and Wilson 2012). More recently, scholars have emphasized the need to study the new trends of activism emerging in the context of the refugee crisis, focusing on the political impact of this wave of migration in the Arab world and beyond (Khoury 2017; Lynch and Brand 2017). In this study, I subscribe to a strand of sociolinguistic scholarship that envisions activists' digital practices as 'actions' toward social change through ethnographic, longitudinal and multimodal analysis (Al Zidjaly 2019b). Through these practices, individuals construct complex identities underlying the emergence of new ways of sociality (Al Zidjaly 2019a). These identities transcend purported online-offline separation and are intertwined with personal styles and 'thick' social categorizations (Blommaert 2018), such as education and gender. The circulation of similar digital content suggests a shared awareness of the vertical, sociopolitical context and its sociolinguistic rules, on the one hand, as well as a shared awareness of the horizontal, digital norms of the politicized digital environment in which they operate, on the other (see Esposito and Sinatora 2021).

The data selected for this chapter is drawn from a larger longitudinal corpus of Syrian dissidents' Facebook status updates between 2010 and 2021 and is analysed through the lens of linguistic hybridity, understood as the indexical mixing of symbolic snippets of different registers (see Sinatora 2020). In the chronotope of Syrian revolutionaries' digital repertoire, these registers include Damascus Arabic, indexically associated with the Syrian uprising and with local authenticity, the Alawite register, associated with the repressive police practices under Ba'athist rule, and Modern Standard Arabic, used both in association with its index of authority (Bassiouney 2017), and in association with the Ba'athist government, which privileged MSA over the dialects in its policy of Arabization (see Miller 2003). The Alawite registers and MSA are often used as strategies of satire. What emerges from the examples is that the recent trend of digital recontextualization of transnational protest has led to a further stage of metalinguistic reflection, that is to say an increased awareness of the impact of their linguistic choices both at the horizontal and at the vertical level of contextualization. This emerges at the end of the analysis from the realization, on the part of one of the activists, that the current transnational scope of protest requires the use of linguistic forms which are accessible to wider, local and global audiences: in other words, new rules of sociolinguistic engagement.

Layla, Samer and Khalid

The examples below are drawn from the digital practices of three dissidents, identified here through the pseudonyms of Layla, Samer and Khalid, between 2015 and 2021. Although Layla, Samer and Khalid are Sunni Arabs from Damascus and Homs, Christian and Damascene Kurdish revolutionaries are also part of this digital network. Their identification as secular political activists overrides their ethnic and confessional backgrounds. The latter, however, can be deduced from their real names associated with their social media accounts. I started following some of their social media profiles in 2012 and met them in Jordan in the summers of 2014 and 2015, where I conducted interviews and participant observation at Syrian cultural events and at a Syrian dissident radio station (see Sinatora 2020). Following their online activities allowed me to observe wider community practices and interactions, such as liking, sharing and commenting on other activists' posts.

Layla, Samer and Khalid worked at the same radio station in Amman. Samer is a prolific playwright who continues his literary activity in Arabic in France. Interestingly, in the background information of his Facebook page he indicates that he still resides in Damascus, Syria, an element which contributes to the construction of his chronotopic identity of Syrian political migrant. Khalid is a famous actor who repositioned himself publicly as an Assad opponent in 2011. Layla has a background in journalism and was active in different divisions of the Syrian communist party before 2011. Layla has a strong and assertive personality, which emerges both in her offline and online interactions through the frequent mixture of Damascene vernacular and Modern Standard Arabic. For example, an idiosyncratic expression I observed her using numerous times in her radio show, in her online interactions with other dissidents, as well as in my interviews with her, is *bass wa-lākin*, meaning 'but' respectively in Syrian Arabic and in MSA. She often uttered this phrase to assert her political views, using MSA to legitimize her stance. In the aftermath of the Syrian uprising, Layla was arrested for participating in protests. She then volunteered as a nurse with the Free Syrian Army, and eventually escaped to Jordan in 2012. In Amman, she co-wrote and co-hosted several radio programmes, in which she provided critical commentary of contemporary political events in Syria, shedding light on the role of female activists in the uprising. For several years, her Facebook profile photo has been an illustration of her brother, who is detained in Assad's prisons. This avatar has allowed her both to illustrate the issue of missing political prisoners and to foreground her identity as an Assad opponent.

Syrian political migrants' views and experiences are multifarious, and the authors of the posts and comments analysed below are not representative of this complexity. Nevertheless, Layla, Samer and Khalid's frequent social media posts widely circulate among different audiences of Syrian dissidents in the diaspora, including less politically active ones. Their texts exemplify the central role of everyday digital practices in the migrants' political performance.

Through the following examples, I show how these three activists capitalize on the affordances of digital media, including linguistic hybridity and multimodality, in order to invoke the 2011 uprising historical context, thereby discrediting official discourses and positioning themselves as Syrian Assad opponents in the diaspora. In my previous research (Sinatora 2019, 2020), I applied the concept of chronotopes to Syrian dissidents' digital practices in different historical phases of the Syrian conflict to illustrate the relationship between their linguistic choices and their politically informed work of sociohistorical construction. I focused on three phases: the beginning of the uprising in 2011, the 'radical Islamic turn' between 2012 and 2015 and the global war on radical Islamic terrorism in 2017. It was shown how, in 2015 and in 2017, some dissidents used Arabic linguistic resources to position themselves, in their social media interactions with other fellow activists, as anti-Assad peaceful protestors and secular revolutionaries, evoking the 2011 historical phase of the Syrian uprising in the context of rising Islamic radicalism. In the following examples, I shed light on a more recent trend, characterized by a growth of digitally mediated transnational grassroots activism. The overarching questions guiding the analysis are: How do these Assad opponents position themselves linguistically and multimodally towards this historical phase? How has this repositioning affected their discourses about the Syrian conflict and the revolution?

Transnational grassroots activism and the chronotope of the Syrian uprising

The 2019–21 period witnessed different waves of anti-government rallies across the Arab world. Protestors demonstrated against corruption and social inequalities exacerbated by years of conflict and instability in the region. These protests were largely peaceful and, in addition to criticizing the failure of Arab governments to implement structural reforms, they rejected the sectarian divisions underlying some of their political systems (Muasher 2019). Women's involvement in these protests was given particular visibility by traditional and digital media, as well as by academic literature (see Esposito and Sinatora 2021; Stephan and Charrad 2020). In addition to the 2019 demonstrations, several rallies took place in 2021 against the Israeli occupation and the attack on Gaza. These recent uprisings occurred in a wider, sociopolitical context characterized by the rise of global grassroots movements, such as the MeToo protest against patriarchy and misogyny, as well as by the American Black Lives Matter movement, which was able to make its voice heard globally in

2020. Their discourses have been taken up by Arab grassroots movements, which highlight the commonality between their demands and those of the feminist and anti-racist movements. For example, the slogan Palestinian Lives Matter was coined after Black Lives Matter to show that the oppression of the Palestinian people is comparable to the injustice endured by African Americans.

The circulation of images of protest on social media has arguably contributed to this uptake. In the following examples I show how, through the recontextualization of the 2019 and 2021 revolts, Syrian dissidents in the diaspora have universalized the discourse about the Syrian uprising, highlighting the similarity between their demands and those of other oppressed people around the world. I will also show how their transnational existence, as well as their frequent interactions with other Syrian dissidents around the world, has contributed to this shift in discourse.

In the Figure 11.1 post, Layla shared a photo which circulated widely across social media platforms of Syrians in the diaspora, including Facebook, Twitter and Instagram. The photo shows two men in Syria holding a protest sign in support of the Egyptian protests against President Al-Sisi's government. The sign evokes the chronotope of the 2011 Arab Spring intertextually through the word *yasquṭ* (downfall), which echoes the famous slogan *iš-ša'b yurīd 'isqāṭ an-niẓām* (the people want the fall of the regime), and the word *ḥurriya* (freedom). It also includes the hashtag #enoughofyoualsisi, which trended on Twitter in September 2019, and the slogan 'Friday of rage', which evokes the Friday protests in Egypt and Syria during the 2011 uprisings.

In the caption, in the Syrian vernacular, Layla recontextualizes the meaning of the photo in order to criticize current Syrian institutional opposition. She evokes the chronotope of the 2011 Syrian revolution, highlighting the contribution of the Syrian revolutionaries ('we') to the current waves of world protests. Sarcastically, she counterposes the revolutionaries, implicitly intended as the 'real dissidents', to the Syrian Constitutional Committee, which is an UN-backed project of reconciliation between the Syrian opposition and the Syrian government. The commenter agrees with Layla, humorously evoking another historical dimension which characterized the Syrian conflict, namely the discourse surrounding civil society. Whereas until 2011 Syrian civil society was controlled by the government, and its role was restricted to apolitical, charity work, the number of civil society organizations rose at the beginning of the uprising (Khalaf 2015). These groups, however, became economically dependent on regional and international actors and their agendas (Al Achi 2020). The commenter presumably alluded to this lack of independence to ironically emphasize his alignment with Layla's positioning of the Egyptian and the Syrian revolutions as transnational, grassroots protests against all forms of institutionalized political formations.

In the following examples, Samer capitalizes on the affordances of Facebook to chronotopically recontextualize images of feminist protest from the 2019 anti-government demonstrations in Lebanon and Sudan in the context of the Syrian uprising. The iconic illustration of women in protest through stylized images was observed in the framework of feminist digital activism in the MENA region (see

Figure 11.1 Layla's post, 21 September 2019. Photo author unknown.

Caption translation: We are the people that endorsed all the revolutions in the world, and yet we're still waiting for a constitutional committee formed by a third stream, an internal opposition, and independent assholes to determine our future

Photo translation: Long live Egypt from Syria Down with Al-Sisi's government. Down with the military rule #freedom – isthedemand – of the peoples #enoughofyoualsisi Fridayofrage

Comment translation: And dirty civil society [winking face with tongue emoji]

Esposito and Sinatora 2021). Indeed, these images emerged in the chronotope of fourth-wave Arab feminism (Tazi and Oumlil 2020), a mobilization rooted in the Arab Spring and which relies 'on an intersectional understanding of nation, patriarchy, and Islam as both resources for mobilization and grounds for revolution and reforms' (Stephan and Charrad 2020: 5). The first image (Figure 11.2), inspired by a shot taken by photographer Lana H. Haroun, is that of the 'Sudanese kandakka', or 'Nubian queen', the iconic pop name attributed to Alaa Salah, a young Sudanese woman who became the symbol of the anti-government demonstrations in Khartoum in April 2019. This iconized image, which reads in Arabic 'women's voice is a revolution', went viral worldwide. It also appeared in a mural in Syria by Abu Malik al-Shami, also known as Syria Banksy, and shows a striking resemblance with the photo of a Syrian woman holding a protest sign on the top of a car in anti-government protests in Syria in 2018 (see Esposito and Sinatora 2021). Samer captioned this image with the word *sawra* (revolution), linking the chronotope of the 2019 Sudan revolution to that of the 2011 Syrian uprising. The comment accentuates this chronotopic recontextualization by reiterating that the 'women's voices are the most beautiful revolution'.

Figure 11.2 Samer's post, 10 April 2019.

The next example (Figure 11.3) is a post shared by Samer in the context of the 2019 anti-government protests in Lebanon. The image, produced by Rami Kanso, is one of a series of illustrations that iconized the figure of a girl, dubbed the 'kick queen', who became famous for a viral video footage of her kicking an armed male security guard during the demonstrations. The image reads 'we will kick their asses', in which 'we' stands for women and demonstrators, whereas 'they' represents the government apparatus. It was reported that the security guard works for former Druze Education Minister Akram Chehayeb, whose party took a stance in support of the Syrian uprising against Bashar al-Assad in 2011, despite supporting the Syrian government and its allies in the past. Although the woman's action against the bodyguard epitomizes the fight against the sectarian system governing Lebanon since the end of the civil war, which was a central issue characterizing the 2019 protests, it soon became symbol of feminist power against patriarchy, likely following the example of the 'Nubian Queen'. Kanso's illustration, which circulated widely particularly in feminist digital environments, was

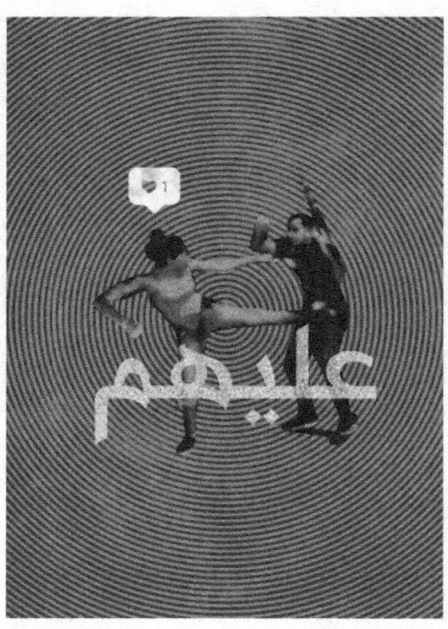

Figure 11.3 Samer's post, 18 October 2019.

recontextualized by Samer in the Syrian dissidents' chronotope through the caption *aš-ša'ab ḍidd al-milīšyāt* (the people against the militias). Like Layla, Samer's Facebook status updates are exclusively in Arabic. When I asked him, in a follow-up conversation on Facebook Messenger, about the relationship between the Lebanese protests and the Syrian revolution, he explained:

> There is a fundamental relationship between the 2019 protests in Lebanon and the protest in Syria, as the people in Syria and Lebanon fight against the same rulers. These rulers are allied against the freedom of the Syrian and the Lebanese peoples, and they spend their efforts to prevent democracy from entering Syria and Lebanon… so the decision of marginalizing the state and supporting the militias that attack the demonstrators and kill them was clear in Syria and it's repeating itself in Lebanon. In Syria the regime used hundreds of thousands of militia agents to kill Syrians and occupy their cities. These agents came from Afghanistan, Pakistan, Iraq, Lebanon. They came and they're still in Syria to destroy the Syrian revolution. And this issue is repeating itself in Lebanon […]. The militias that are oppressing the demonstrators in Lebanon are affiliated with Hezbollah. They oppress women, fight liberties, and place religious protection on the citizens who follow them. The same thing is happening in the cities controlled by the militias in Syria and of course it's the same in Iraq.
>
> [author's translation from Arabic]

The bodyguard kicked by a female demonstrator in 2019 is not a Hezbollah agent, but one hired by the Lebanese Druze Progressive Socialist Party. By circulating the kick queen meme on his Facebook page, and by captioning it as a rebellion of 'people against [Shiite] militias', Samer drew on the chronotope of the Lebanese and feminist protests to foreground his anti-Assad chronotopic positioning. In so doing, he also deconstructed the government's delegitimization of protestors as backward misogynists, thereby characterizing the Syrian revolution as a fight against oppressive patriarchy.

The strategy of iconicization of protest, pervasive in Arab grassroots digital environments (see Esposito and Sinatora 2021), can also be observed in the photo in Figure 11.4, which also circulated in the Syrian dissidents digital transnational network. The photo, by Omar Haj Kadour/AFP, captures a wall painting of George Floyd, the African-American man whose killing became symbol of police brutality in the United States. The painting was done on the ruins of a bombed building in Idlib, theatre of some of the most violent clashes between the Syrian government and the rebel militias. By recontextualizing George Floyd's iconicized image in the framework of the Syrian conflict, Syrian dissidents chronotopically compared the fight against police oppression to that against the Syrian regime.

In a public post by a Syrian migrant currently living in London, the photo of the mural of George Floyd in Idlib was further recontextualized and juxtaposed to one which appeared on the Israeli separation wall (Figure 11.5). By presenting these two images simultaneously, the author framed the Syrian, the African-American and the Palestinian issues as one transnational struggle.

Figure 11.4 Mural of George Floyd in Idlib, photo by Omar Haj Kadour/AFP.

Figure 11.5 Post on George Floyd's murals in Idlib and Ramallah.

Caption translation: George Floyd on two Levantine walls in Idlib and Ramallah.

In the context of the 2021 pro-Palestinian protests, which followed a raid by the Israeli police on al-Aqsa mosque, several posts circulated in the Syrian dissidents' digital network, in which the 2011 chronotope of the Syrian uprising is linguistically and multimodally juxtaposed to that of the Palestinian revolt. The Palestinian issue is historically connected with the Syrian political context. More than many other Arab countries, Syria has integrated Palestinian refugees in Syrian society since 1948, granting them virtually equal citizenship and socio-economic rights (Brand 1988). Brand noted that, although Syria recognized Palestinians as a separate national identity, the Baʻathist totalitarian ideology has prevented the emergence of independent Palestinian political entities. The Syrian Baʻathist government has also long prided itself for backing Palestinian resistance, consistent with its pan-Arab, anti-Western imperialist project. The juxtaposition between the Syrian upheaval and the struggle for Palestinian liberation has been present in Syrian revolutionaries' digital discourse since the beginning of the

Figure 11.6 Khalid, 11 April 2021. Protest at al-Aqsa.

Caption translation: Our people in glorious Palestine – you couldn't have expressed it more clearly

Comment translation: Free people of the world

uprising, whereby the Syrian government has been compared to a foreign occupier (Sinatora 2020). The digital circulation of pro-Palestinian protests has arguably reinforced this comparison. The post in Figure 11.6 embeds the photograph of a Syrian anti-Assad rally in front of al-Aqsa mosque. The inclusion of the Syrian revolution flag and of the Dome of the Rock in the same image symbolizes Syrian dissidents' perception of the Syrian and the Palestinian protests as part of the same discourse of self-determination.

Through the idiomatic Levantine expression *kafféto u-wafféto* (you couldn't have been expressed more clearly), the post author emphasizes the popular character of the Palestinian and the Syrian protests. The commenter further highlights the transnational character of this protest movement by denominating the demonstrators as 'free people of this world'. The term *'aḥrār* was adopted by Syrian dissidents at the beginning of the 2011 uprising as an ingroup appellative to denote all those who repositioned themselves as anti-Assad protestors.

In another post (Figure 11.7), the same author brings together the two chronotopes of the Syrian and the Palestinian revolts by identifying himself symbolically as a person from Homs – an anti-Assad stronghold since the beginning of the Syrian uprising –

Figure 11.7 Khalid, 11 May 2021. Homsi from Jerusalem.

Digital Narratives of Syrian Political Dissidence in the Diaspora

and, at the same time, as a Jerusalemite. The commenters to the post reiterate the same sentences with slight variations to stress the commonality between the Palestinian and the Syrian and Arab fight.

By juxtaposing the chronotope of the Syrian revolution with that of Palestinian independence, Syrian dissidents capitalized on the digital circulation of current transnational protests to foreground their political fight. In so doing, they deconstructed the Syrian government's appropriation of the Palestinian cause, framing the Syrian conflict as a grassroots transnational struggle for liberation.

It was shown in the previous examples how several Syrians migrants have exclusively used Arabic in their social media pages to anchor their political identities in the 2011 chronotope of the Syrian uprising. In a recent Facebook post, however, Layla urged her fellow activists to use their 'adoptive' languages (Figure 11.8).

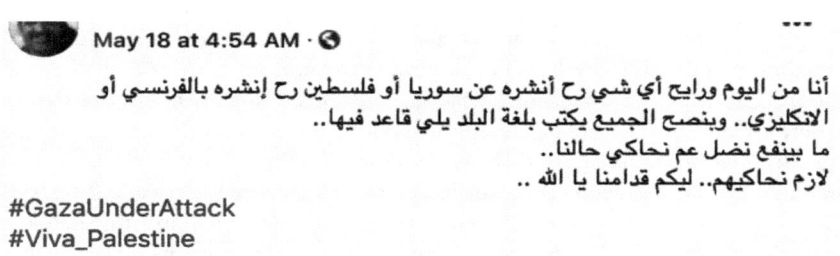

Figure 11.8 Layla, 18 May 2021, post urging use of adoptive languages.

Post translation: From today on, every time I will post something about Syria or Palestine I will post it in French or in English. I advise everyone to write in the language of the country in which they live. It's useless to keep addressing each other. We need to talk to them. C'mon, let's look to the future
#GazaUnderAttack
#Viva_Palestine

Figure 11.9 Layla, 20 May 2021, post in French.

Translation: Why would the French government ban pro-Palestine demonstrations, and at the same time authorize, on French soil, the vote for Bashar al-Assad in this farce called 'elections'?

In Figure 11.9, Layla follows through with her intention to reach out to an international audience by publishing her social media post in French.

Although Layla has lived in France for six years, her political digital practices have always remained in Arabic. Her recent exhortation to compose social media posts about Syria and Palestine in European languages demonstrates a new level of sociolinguistic awareness, which, in my view, has been accelerated by the new chronotopic conditions, whereby Layla sees her digital sociopolitical engagement increasingly as part of a transnational grassroots struggle.

Conclusions

This chapter sheds light on the digital narratives of a group of Syrian revolutionaries in the European diaspora through the conceptual lens of chronotopes, namely spatio-temporal anchors underlying linguistic choices and discourses. An analysis of digital, spatio-temporal recontextualizations is particularly relevant in an ideologically and politically fraught diasporic environment, such as that of Assad opponents, in which issues of legitimization, coherence and authenticity are vital to the performance of their political identities. With a focus on the recent chronotope of grassroots transnational activism on social media, the present analysis showed how three Syrian dissidents living in France recontextualized images and texts of digital grassroots protest to rekindle the chronotope of the Syrian uprising. Echoing transregional, Arab and global social media feminist movements, they further discredited the Syrian government's official narrative, emphasizing the intersectional character of their revolution. In other words, by recontextualizing transnational grassroots protests in their social media platforms linguistically and multimodally, Syrian activists have changed the discourse of the Syrian revolution from a local to a universal one, comparing their struggle to that faced by other oppressed populations around the world.

The main question guiding the analysis concerned the type of linguistic and multimodal resources used by Syrian political activists in their digital platforms. It was observed that, despite their increased mobility and their expanded multilingual repertoire, these migrants have continued to use Arabic resources in their daily digital practices. Their linguistic choices, I argued, have been intrinsically related to their chronotopic positioning as anti-Assad dissidents throughout the different phases of the Syrian conflict. This chronotopic anchoring has allowed them to sustain and negotiate their political positionings despite their physical displacement from the homeland. The current engagement with the digitally mediatized chronotope of transnational grassroots activism, however, has led to the emergence of an unprecedented metalinguistic reflection. It was shown how a dissident, Layla, problematized the exclusive use of Arabic, exhorting her friends to use the languages of the countries they live in to engage the local population. Further longitudinal, sociolinguistic, empirical analysis is needed to monitor the impact of this sociolinguistic trend on their political discourse.

In addition to their linguistic choices, it was shown how images of protest occupied a central role in the Syrian activists' digital chronotopic recontextualization. By sharing the photo of George Floyd's murals in Palestine and Syria, photos of Syrian revolutionaries participating in anti-Sisi protests in Syria and in pro-Palestinian rallies in Jerusalem, as well as memes of Arab feminist protest, they juxtaposed the chronotope of grassroots protest to that of the Syrian uprising. In so doing, they further emphasized how these two space-time frameworks can nurture each other, creating a space for a global dialogue against systems of oppression worldwide.

This study has wider implications in terms of language and migration. Recent sociolinguistic literature has increasingly challenged the vision of migrants' multilingualism as an obstacle to integration, showing how migrants, through their digital practices, are in fact *integrated* in different transnational communities (Blommaert 2018). Layla's exhortation to use French and English, followed by her use of French, was not motivated by her need to 'integrate' herself in the French culture. Rather, it was triggered by a need to narrate her local, Syrian dissident experience to the French audience. One could say that her attempt is to 'integrate' her French-speaking audience in her Syrian and transnational political experience. Whereas, on the one hand, one may see the recent multilingual shift in Syrian revolutionaries' practices in terms of increased transnational integration, a question that may arise is the extent to which the chronotope of the Syrian protest and that of that transnational engagement coexist and feed into each other. Additionally, while this study has focused predominantly on Syrian revolutionaries' Facebook practices, more recent digital applications with different affordances, such as the audio-only discussion platform Clubhouse, have become places of aggregation for several Syrian dissidents in Europe and the United States. Future work can investigate how spatio-temporal dynamics play out in their engagement with more recent, non-visual digital platforms.

References

Agha, A. (2007), 'Recombinant Selves in Mass Mediated Spacetime', *Language & Communication*, 27: 320–35.

Al Achi, A. (2020), 'How Syrian Civil Society Lost Its Independence in a World of Conflicting Agendas', *Malcom H. Kerr Carnegie Middle East Center*. Available online: https://carnegie-mec.org/2020/05/15/how-syrian-civil-society-lost-its-independence-in-war-of-conflicting-agendas-pub-81802 (accessed 23 November 2021).

Al Zidjaly, N. (2019a), 'Society in Digital Contexts. New Modes of Identity and Community Construction', *Multilingua*, 38 (4): 357–75.

Al Zidjaly, N. (2019b), 'Digital Activism as Nexus Analysis: A Sociolinguistic Example from Arabic Twitter', *Tilburg Papers in Culture Studies*. Paper 221.

Androutsopoulos, J. (2008), 'Potentials and Limitations of Discourse-Centred Online Ethnography', *Language@Internet*, 5 (8): 1–20.

Androutsopoulos, J. (2015), 'Networked Multilingualism. Some Language Practices on Facebook and Their Implications', *International Journal of Bilingualism*, 19 (2): 185–205.

Androutsopoulos, J. and A. Staehr (2018), 'Moving Methods Online. Researching Digital Language Practices', in A. Creese and A. Blackledge (eds), *The Routledge Handbook of Language and Superdiversity*, 118–32, London and New York: Routledge.
Bakhtin, M. (1981), *The Dialogic Imagination*, trans. and ed. M. Holquist and C. Emerson, Austin: University of Texas Press.
Bassiouney, R. (2017), 'A New Direction for Arabic Sociolinguistics', in Hamid Ouali (ed.), *Perspectives on Arabic Linguistics XXIX: Papers from the Annual Symposium on Arabic*, 7–30, Amsterdam and Philadelphia: John Benjamins.
Blommaert, J. (2010), *The Sociolinguistics of Globalization*, Cambridge: Cambridge University Press.
Blommaert, J. (2015), 'Chronotopes, Scales and Complexity in the Study of Language and Society', *Annual Review of Anthropology*, 44: 105–16.
Blommaert, J. (2018), *Durkheim and the Internet. On Sociolinguistics and the Sociological Imagination*, London: Bloomsbury.
Blommaert, J. and A. De Fina (2017), 'Chronotopic Identities: On the Timespace Organization of Who We Are', in D. Ikizoglu, J. Wegner, and A. De Fina (eds), *Diversity and Super-Diversity: Sociocultural Linguistic Perspectives*, 1–16, Washington, DC: Georgetown University Press.
Blommaert, J. and B. Rampton (2011), 'Language and Superdiversity', *Diversities*, 13 (2): 1–21.
Brand, L. (1988), 'Palestinians in Syria: The Policy of Integration', *Middle East Journal*, 42 (4): 621–37.
Canagarajah, S. (2017), 'Introduction: The Nexus of Migration and Language. The Emergence of a Disciplinary Space', in S. Canagarajah (ed.), *The Routledge Handbook of Migration and Language*, 1–28, London and New York: Routledge.
De Fina, A., G. Paternostro, and M. Amoruso (2019), 'Odysseus the Traveler: Appropriation of a Chronotope in a Community of Practice', *Language & Communication*, 70: 71–81.
Esposito, E. and F. L. Sinatora (2021), 'Social Media Discourses of Feminist Protest in the Arab Levant: Digital Mirroring and Transnational Dialogue', *Critical Discourse Studies*. Available online: https://doi.org/10.1080/17405904.2021.1999291.
Eltantawy, N. and J. B. Wiest (2011), 'Social Media in the Egyptian Revolution: Reconsidering Resource Mobilization Theory', *International Journal of Communication*, 5: 1207–24.
Hinnebusch, R. (2016), 'Syria's Alawis and the Ba'ath Party', in M. Kerr and C. Larkin (eds), *The Alawites of Syria. War, Faith and Politics in the Levant*, 107–24, New York: Oxford University Press.
Karimzad, F. and L. Catedral (2018), 'Mobile (Dis)connection. New Technology and Rechronotopized Images of the Homeland', *Journal of Linguistic Anthropology*, 28 (3): 293–312.
Khalaf, R. (2015), 'Governance without Government in Syria: Civil Society and State Building during Conflict', *Syria Studies*, 7 (3): 37–72.
Khoury, R. B. (2017), 'Trajectories of Activism among Syrian Refugees', *Project on Middle East Political Science, POMEPS Studies*, 25: 32–41.
Koven, M. and I. Simões Marques (2015), 'Performing and Evaluating (Non)modernities of Portuguese Migrant Figures on Youtube: The Case of Antonio De Carglouch', *Language in Society*, 44 (2): 213–42.
Kress, G. and T. Van Leeuwen (2006), *Reading Images: The Grammar of Visual Design*, 2nd edition, New York: Routledge.

Kron, S. and J. Swanenberg, eds (2019), *Chronotopic Identity Work. Sociolinguistic Analyses of Cultural and Linguistic Phenomena in Time and Space*, Bristol: Multilingual Matters.
Lynch, M. and L. Brand (2017), 'Introduction. Refugees and Displacement in the Middle East', *Project on Middle East Political Science, POMEPS Studies*, 25: 3–7.
Lyons, A. and C. Tagg (2019), 'The Discursive Construction of Mobile Chronotopes in Mobile-Phone Messaging', *Language in Society* (48): 657–83.
Miller, C. (2003), 'Linguistic Policies and the Issue of Ethno-Linguistic Minorities in the Middle East', in A. Usuki and H. Kato (eds), *Islam in the Middle Eastern Studies: Muslims and Minorities*, JCAS Symposium Series 7, 149–74, Osaka, Japan.
Muasher, M. (2019), 'Is This the Arab Spring 2.0?' *Carnegie Endowment for International Peace*. Available online: https://carnegieendowment.org/2019/10/30/is-this-arab-spring-2.0-pub-80220 (accessed 23 November 2021).
Perrino, S. (2015), 'Chronotopes: Time and Space in Oral Narrative', in A. De Fina and A. Georgakopoulou (eds), *The Handbook of Narrative Analysis*, 140–59, Chichester, West Sussex, UK: Wiley Blackwell.
Pierret, T. (2014), 'The Syrian Baath Party and Sunni Islam: Conflicts and Connivance', *Middle East Brief* 77. Available online: https://www.brandeis.edu/crown/publications/middle-east-briefs/pdfs/1-100/meb77.pdf (accessed 24 November 2021).
Salamandra, C. (2004), *A New Old Damascus: Authenticity and Distinction in Urban Syria*, Bloomington: Indiana University Press.
Sinatora, F. L. (2019), 'Chronotopes, Entextualization and Syrian Political Activism on Facebook', *Multilingua*, 38 (4): 427–58.
Sinatora, F. L. (2020), *Language, Identity, and Syrian Political Activism on Social Media*, London and New York: Routledge.
Sinatora, F. L. (2021), 'Digital Media as Chronotopic Enablers in Syrian Migrants' Political Activism' [paper presentation], in *Sociolinguistics Symposium 22*, Hong Kong: The University of Hong Kong.
Stephan, R. and M. M. Charrad (2020), 'Advancing Women's Rights in the Arab World', in R. Stephan and M. M. Charrad (eds), *Women Rising. In and beyond the Arab Spring*, 1–12, New York: New York University Press.
Taylor-Leech, K. (2020), 'Timorese Talking Back: The Semiotic Construction of Chronotopes in the Timor Sea Protests', *Linguistic Landscape*, 6 (1): 29–51.
Tazi, M. and K. Oumlil (2020), 'The Rise of Fourth-Wave Feminism in the Arab Region? Cyberfeminism and Women's Activism at the Crossroads of the Arab Spring', *CyberOrient*, 14 (1): 44–71.
Tufekci, Z. and C. Wilson (2012), 'Social Media and the Decision to Participate in Political Protest: Observations from Tahrir Square', *Journal of Communication*, 62 (2): 363–79.
Wedeen, L. (2013), 'Ideology and Humor in Dark Times: Notes from Syria', *Critical Inquiry*, 39 (4): 841–73.
Woolard, K. A. (2013), 'Is the Personal Political? Chronotopes and Changing Stances toward Catalan Language and Identity', *International Journal of Bilingual Education and Bilingualism*, 16 (2): 210–24.

Discussion questions

1. How can the notion of chronotope be used in the analysis of digital narratives produced by immigrants/migrants?
2. Using the chronotope approach, what is the role various language registers (and languages) can play in these narratives?
3. How does the background to the Syrian conflict (2011–present) condition the dissidents' linguistic choices?
4. How do the affordances of digital media (e.g. the circulation of multimodal posts) impact discourses of protest?
5. How does digital communication affect the way in which politically engaged migrants position themselves toward their host countries?
6. What type of primary and secondary resources has the author utilized to reconstruct the discourse of Syrian dissidents' digital activism in the diaspora?

Contributors' Notes

Adil Moustaoui Srhir is Associate Professor at the Department of Linguistics and Oriental Studies in the Complutense University of Madrid. He has published on a variety of topics related to Moroccan Arabic, heritage Moroccan Arabic, linguistic landscapes and identity construction in Moroccan immigrant population in Spain. His latest publication is 'The Discourses of Heritage Languages: Development and Maintenance within Transnational Moroccan Families in Spain. From Language Ideologies to Resistance' (*ELIA: Studies in Applied English Linguistics*, 21 (2), 15–51).

Cati Coe is Professor at Carleton University, in Ottawa, Canada. Her research interests centre on transnational migration from West Africa, with a focus on intergenerational relationships, care and ageing. Her most recent book is *Changes in Care: Aging, Migration, and Social Class in West Africa* (Rutgers University Press, 2021).

Fabienne Le Houérou is Director of Research at CNRS-IREMAM at Aix-Marseille University and a fellow at the Institut Convergences Migrations. She is an expert in migration studies, a filmmaker and an image theoretician. Her current research focuses on gender and diaspora, and she is particularly interested in using film as a methodological tool. Her latest published work is *Ethnographie filmée des musiciens du désert du Thar en Inde. Princes et Vagabonds, Poussière d'exils* (L'Harmattan, 2021).

Francesco L. Sinatora is Assistant Professor of Arabic at The George Washington University. His research focuses on the intersection of language, identity and digital discourses of political protest and social activism in the Arab Levant. He is the author of the book *Language, Identity, and Syrian Political Activism on Social Media* (Routledge, 2020).

Ildikó Schmidt is Senior Lecturer at the Károli Gáspár University of the Reformed Church in Hungary, in the Department of Hungarian Linguistics. Her main research fields are bilingualism and multilingualism, in particular the linguistic aspects of the institutional integration of language learners. Her interests focus on the interrelations between language acquisition and language learning, as well as on the dynamics of language dominance changes in bilingual and multilingual speakers' language use. She is the author of *A magyar írás és olvasás tanítása - az alfabetizálás folyamata* [Reading and Writing in Hungarian – the Process of Alphabetisation] (L'Harmattan, 2019).

Jan Jaap de Ruiter is an Arabist at Tilburg University with a focus on Arabic language and Islam in Europe and the Islamic world. He has authored numerous studies, including monographs and edited volumes on Arabic and Islam, mostly with l'Harmattan (France). He was the guest editor of a special issue of *Sociolinguistic Studies* (2018) on contemporary Arabic sociolinguistics, and is now editing the special issue on 'Sexuality in the Arab Islamic World' for the journal *Religions* (2022).

Mike Baynham is Emeritus Professor of TESOL at the University of Leeds, a fellow of the Academy of Social Sciences and former Chair of the British Association for Applied Linguistics (BAAL). He is a Visiting Professor at York St John University. His recent publications include 'Narrative Analysis in Migrant and Transnational Contexts', with Anna De Fina, in *Researching Multilingualism. Critical and Ethnographic Perspectives* (Martin-Jones, M. & D. Martin, eds., Routledge, 2017) and *Translation and Translanguaging* (with T. K. Lee, Routledge, 2019).

Odile Heynders is Professor of Comparative Literature at the Department of Culture Studies at Tilburg University. She has published books and numerous articles on European literature and authorship. Her book *Writers as Public Intellectuals, Literature, Celebrity, Democracy* (2016) appeared at Palgrave McMillan. Her current (book) project is on *Fictions of Migration* (Cambridge Publishers). She is also working on a research project on silence and the ethics of listening.

Ruslan Zaripov (University of Navarra) is an expert in African languages and cultures. He obtained a master's degree in African Studies from Moscow State University and a NOHA Master's Degree in International Humanitarian Assistance from the Université Catholique de Louvain/Universidad de Deusto. After working on UN missions in Africa for several years, he has returned to his academic career in order to complete a PhD on migrant narratives, tracking African migrants from their places of origin to their destinations, and recording their narratives in a variety of African languages. In addition, Ruslan is combining his PhD research with work for Doctors Without Borders, and is currently on a mission in the Republic of South Sudan.

Ruth Breeze is Full Professor of English at the University of Navarra, Spain, and Principal Investigator of the Public Discourse Research Group in the Institute for Culture and Society. She has published widely on political discourse, media discourse, legal discourse and specialized communication. Her most recent books are *Imagining the Peoples of Europe: Populist Discourses across the Political Spectrum* (with Jan Zienkowski, John Benjamins, 2019), and *Pandemic and Crisis Discourse: Communicating COVID-19 and Public Health Strategy* (with Andreas Musolff, Sara Vilar-Lluch and Kayo Kondo, Bloomsbury, 2022).

Sarali Gintsburg is a researcher at the Institute for Culture and Society (University of Navarra) and a former Marie Skłodowska-Curie fellow (2017–19). Sarali is an Arabic philologist with a focus on Arabic sociolinguistics, identity studies and the literary canon. Her scholarly publications include 'Arabic Language in Zanzibar: Past, Present, and Future' (*Journal of World Languages*, 2019) and 'The Asymmetric Linguistic Identities of African Soqotris: A Triadic Interaction', with Eleonora Esposito, in *Language and Identity in the Arab World* (Rushdi, F. & S. Mehta, eds., Routledge, 2022).

Silvia Melo-Pfeifer is Full Professor at the Faculty of Education, University of Hamburg. Her research interests include foreign and heritage language education, pluralistic approaches to teaching and learning, and multilingual interaction. She has published on these themes in journals such as *Language Awareness* and *International Journal of Multilingualism*.

Index

Concepts

African time (also see *sasa* and *zamani*) 5, 9
Amazigh 104, 108, 110, 112, 116, 125, 132, 162, 168, 170
Arabic language 5, 6, 11 (note), 104, 109–13, 115–16, 124–6, 132–3, 138, 140 (note), 162, 165–6, 172 (notes), 185, 192, 194, 196, 197
Arabic literature 4, 12 (note), 158–9, 170, 178, 179, 197

Bakhtin, Mikhail 2–4, 87, 88, 122, 139, 160, 172 (note), 191
Ballet 7, 175–89
Bantu languages 5, 29–49
Bergson, Henri 51–3, 56, 58, 63, 65
Biography 73, 83, 104
Borders 2, 7–8, 10, 21, 29, 33, 36, 41, 46, 67–86, 104, 107, 143, 145
Bourdieu, Pierre 22, 103, 105, 131

Calendar 1–2, 11, 53, 61
Children 67–86, 87–101, 103–20
Christianity 6, 31, 32, 36, 56, 65, 70, 114, 197
Chronotope 3–4, 7, 9, 10, 11, 34, 47, 88–9, 95, 98, 122, 139, 142, 159, 160, 169, 173 (note), 174, 191–212
Colonialism 5, 6, 108, 124, 143, 166
Community 5, 8–9, 18, 34, 43, 46, 57, 59–63, 90, 92–3, 107–8, 110, 123, 126, 130, 134, 138, 146, 176, 179, 184, 194, 197
Cultural activities 157–74, 204

Deleuze, Gilles 11, 51–2, 59, 60, 62–3, 65, 154
Digital spaces 10, 36, 157–74, 191–212

Discourse 3, 69, 70, 72, 73, 87, 97, 122, 130, 138, 150, 191, 192–5, 199, 205–6, 208, 212
Documentary 51–65, 145, 180–1, 183–4, 187 (note)
Domestic service 15–28
Drawing 9, 17, 67–86, 143
Durkheim, Émile 6, 122

Education 1, 67–86, 87–101, 103–20, 121, 125, 132, 137, 138, 144, 151, 167, 170, 196, 202
Employment 15–28
Epstein, Mikhail 7, 122, 139, 160
Exile 11, 51–65, 89, 132, 192–3, 195

Family 15–28, 103–20
Fiction 143–56
Food 19, 23, 25, 57, 61, 150, 154, 165
Frontiers 7, 8, 62, 150

Gender 2, 6, 36, 51–65, 71, 83, 84 (note), 121–42, 196
Gesture 29–49, 123, 172
Guattari, Félix 11, 51–2, 59, 60, 62–3, 65

Habitus 103–5, 115, 124, 126, 133
Health 15, 17, 21, 23, 24, 25, 56, 62, 112
Heritage language 103–20
History 32, 56, 63 (note), 76, 98, 149, 158, 166, 170 189 (note)

Interview 2, 19–20, 37, 38–9, 41, 42, 44, 57, 87–8, 90–8, 108–13, 114, 121, 124–5, 128, 138 178, 182
Islam 4–7, 8, 12 (note), 32, 36–8, 40, 53, 54, 65 (note), 70, 104, 108, 116, 121,

123–4, 130–5, 136–7, 139, 146, 175–80, 185–7, 189, 194, 195, 198, 201
Isolation 8, 10, 57, 130

Kagame, Alexis 6, 34

Language learning 103–20
Lefevbre, Henri 68, 73, 122
Literacy 103–20

Mbiti, John 5, 9, 34, 35, 40
Moroccan literature 157–74
Multimodality 29–49, 157–74, 192–212

Oral Narrative 157–74

Parallel time and space 10, 129, 136
Parents 87–101, 90–3, 103–20, 133, 151, 180
People trafficking 146–7, 149, 151–2
Physical appearance 55, 58, 131, 151, 152, 153, 168
Politics 7, 9, 15, 16, 29, 31, 51, 54, 55, 68, 69, 84 (note), 103, 108, 139, 145, 162, 192–212
Property ownership 15–28, 109
Protest 192–212

Qur'an 114, 133, 178, 179

Recreation of home 15–28, 121–42
Refugees 1, 7–8, 29–49, 51–65
Religion 11, 33, 36, 84 (note), 108, 109, 133, 176, 178–9
Rhizome 11, 51–65

Ricoeur, Paul 2, 32
Rural 2, 6, 7, 33, 61, 92, 121–142

Schooling 67–86, 87–101, 103–20
Sasa (also see African time) 5, 35, 37, 40, 46
Separation 67–86, 198
Sex workers 146, 150, 152
Social exclusion 92, 121–42
Social media 2, 6, 19, 63 (notes), 171–3, 192–212, 159–60, 182
Swahili 29–49

Television 157–74, 180
Time and space in Islam 4–6, 137–9, 178–9
Timelessness 9, 12 (note), 61, 112, 137, 178, 185
Topochrone 7, 10, 122, 131–2, 136, 139, 142, 160–1, 174
Trauma 8, 9, 11, 17, 33, 34, 40, 46, 56–8, 61, 62, 69, 72, 90, 96–9

Unemployment 22, 57, 125, 144
Urban 2, 6, 22, 26, 60, 62, 123, 124, 138, 194, 195

Walls 7, 8, 67–86, 128, 186, 203, 204
War 7, 29–32, 41, 51, 72, 74, 76–8, 80, 82, 83, 144, 148, 175–7, 180–2, 184–6, 195, 198, 202
Western time and space 2, 6, 34, 46, 137

Zamani (also see African time) 5, 35, 40, 46

Places

Afghanistan 7, 70, 71, 91, 92, 203
Africa 1, 7, 8, 11, 22, 23, 29–34, 41, 49, 51, 53, 61, 121, 126, 143–6, 149, 153, 159, 175
Algeria 30, 145, 170
Aristotle 2, 3, 4, 160, 172 (note), 177, 185
Asia 6, 61

Bahrain 176

Cameroon 30
Congo (DRC) 7, 29–49

Egypt 51–65, 176, 199, 200
Eritrea 51–65, 70
Ethiopia 7, 51–65, 131
Europe 1, 2, 7, 32, 67, 121, 123, 143–56, 166, 176, 183, 189, 191, 193, 196, 209

France 70, 90, 123, 143, 146, 149, 154 (note), 162, 163, 165–7, 170, 173 (note), 176, 192, 197, 208, 214

Germany 7, 36, 67–86, 90, 181
Ghana 7, 8, 15–28, 143, 149
Greece 92, 148

Hungary 7, 80, 87–101

Iran 70, 91, 92, 94, 176, 195
Iraq 70, 71, 75–7, 176, 203
Israel 180, 181
Italy 6, 20, 33, 90, 138, 143, 162, 163, 164, 168, 170, 171

Jordan 176, 192, 195–7

Kenya 30, 32

Lebanon 176, 195, 199, 202, 203
Libya 143, 144, 145, 176

Macedonia 94
Middle East 1, 11, 30, 53, 61, 67–86, 87–101, 121, 137, 175, 189
Morocco 6, 103–20, 121–42, 143, 144, 145, 150, 157–74

Netherlands 7, 9, 123, 175–89
Niger 145
Nigeria 143

Pakistan 203
Palestine 180, 205, 207, 208, 209

Russia 176, 195
Rwanda 6, 30, 31, 32, 34

Senegal 143, 144, 149, 154 (notes)
Serbia 94
South Africa 23, 32
Spain 7, 9, 103–20, 121–42, 143, 144, 145, 165
Sudan 7, 51–65, 131, 199, 201
Syria 7, 70, 71, 81, 175–89, 191–212

Tanzania 36
Tunisia 176
Turkey 1, 76–80, 91, 92, 94, 148, 176, 195

Uganda 7, 9, 29–49
United States of America 7, 8, 15–28, 36, 123, 149, 170, 176, 195, 203, 209

Yemen 176

Zaire 31
Zanzibar 30